Adam Ferguson · An Essay on the History of Civil Society

Anglistica & Americana

A Series of Reprints Selected by
Bernhard Fabian, Edgar Mertner,
Karl Schneider and Marvin Spevack

184

2000
Georg Olms Verlag
Hildesheim · Zürich · New York

Adam Ferguson

An Essay on the History of Civil Society

(1767)

2000
Georg Olms Verlag
Hildesheim · Zürich · New York

Note

The present slightly reduced facsimile of the first edition is reproduced from a copy in the possession of Staatsbibliothek Berlin – Preußischer Kulturbesitz, Signatur Fa 1500.
The *Essay* was subsequently published in Dublin (1767), London (1768, revised; 1773, 1793, 1814) and Basle (1789).
It was edited by Duncan Forbes (Edinburgh, 1966).

B.F.

Die Deutsche Bibliothek – CIP-Einheitsaufnahme
Ein Titeldatensatz für diese Publikation ist bei
Der Deutschen Bibliothek erhältlich

ISO 9706
Nachdruck der Ausgabe Edinburgh 1767
Printed in Germany
Gedruckt auf säurefreiem, alterungsbeständigem Papier
Herstellung: Verlagsdienstleistungen, Berlin-Charlottenburg
ISBN 3-487-11210-8

AN ESSAY ON THE HISTORY OF CIVIL SOCIETY.

By ADAM FERGUSON, LL. D.
Professor of Moral Philosophy in the University of Edinburgh.

EDINBURGH:
Printed for A. MILLAR & T. CADDEL in the Strand, *London*,
and A. KINCAID & J. BELL, *Edinburgh*.
MDCCLXVII.

C O N T E N T S.

P A R T I.

Of the General Characteristics of Human Nature.

SECT.

SECT. II.

SECT. III.

SECT. IV.

PART V.

Of the Decline of Nations.

SECTION I.

SECT. II.

SECT. III.

SECT IV.

SECT V.

PART VI.

Of Corruption and Political Slavery.

ER-

ERRATA.

Pag. 311. lin. 4. for *a model* read *as a model.*

Pag. 313. lin. ult. for *genteel* read *gentil.*

AN

ESSAY

ON THE HISTORY OF

CIVIL SOCIETY.

PART FIRST.

Of the General Characteristics of Human Nature.

SECTION I.

Of the question relating to the State of Nature.

NATURAL productions are generally formed by degrees. Vegetables grow from a tender shoot, and animals from an infant state. The latter being destined to act, extend their operations as their powers increase: they exhibit a progress in what they perform, as well as in the faculties they acquire. This progress in the case of man is continued to a greater extent than in that of any other animal. Not only the individual advances from infancy to manhood, but the ſpecies itſelf from rudeneſs to civilization. Hence the ſuppoſed departure of mankind from the ſtate of their nature; hence our conjectures and different opinions of what man muſt have been in the firſt age of his being. The poet, the hiſtorian, and the moraliſt, frequently allude to this ancient time; and under the emblems of gold, or of iron, repreſent a condition, and a manner of life, from which mankind have either degenerated, or on which they have greatly improved. On either ſuppoſition, the firſt ſtate of our nature muſt have borne no reſemblance to what men have exhibited in any ſubſequent period; hiſtorical monuments, even of the earlieſt date, are to be conſidered as novelties; and the moſt common eſtabliſhments of human ſociety are to be claſſed among the incroachments which fraud, oppreſſion, or a buſy invention, have made upon the reign of nature, by which the chief of our grievances or bleſſings were equally with-held.

Among the writers who have attempted to diſtinguiſh, in the human character, its original qualities, and to point out the limits between nature and art, ſome have repreſented mankind in their firſt condition, as poſſeſſed of mere animal ſenſibility, without any exercise of the faculties that render them ſuperior to the brutes, without any political union, without any means of explaining their ſentiments, and even without poſſeſſing any of the apprehenſions and paſſions which the voice

voice and the gesture are so well fitted to express. Others have made the state of nature to consist in perpetual wars, kindled by competition for dominion and interest, where every individual had a separate quarrel with his kind, and where the presence of a fellow-creature was the signal of battle.

The desire of laying the foundation of a favourite system, or a fond expectation, perhaps, that we may be able to penetrate the secrets of nature, to the very source of existence, have, on this subject, led to many fruitless inquiries, and given rise to many wild suppositions. Among the various qualities which mankind possess, we select one or a few particulars on which to establish a theory, and in framing our account of what man was in some imaginary state of nature, we overlook what he has always appeared within the reach of our own observation, and in the records of history.

In every other instance, however, the natural historian thinks himself obliged to collect facts, not to offer conjectures. When he treats of any particular species of animals, he supposes, that their present dispositions and instincts are the same they originally had, and that their present manner of life is a continuance of their first destination. He admits, that his knowledge of the material system of the world consists in a collection of facts, or at most, in general tenets derived from particular observations and experiments. It is only in what relates to himself, and in matters the most important, and the moſt eaſily known, that he ſubſtitutes hypotheſis inſtead of reality, and confounds the provinces of imagination and reaſon, of poetry and ſcience.

But without entering any farther on queſtions either in moral or phyſical ſubjects, relating to the manner or to the origin of our knowledge; without any diſparagement to that ſubtilty which would analyze every ſentiment, and trace every mode of being to its ſource; it may be ſafely affirmed, That the character of man, as he now exiſts, that the laws of this animal and intellectual ſyſtem, on which his happineſs now depends, deſerve our principal ſtudy; and that general principles relating to this, or any other ſubject, are uſeful only ſo far as they are founded on juſt obſervation, and lead to the knowledge of important conſequences, or ſo far as they enable us to act with ſucceſs when we would apply either the intellectual or the phyſical powers of nature, to the great purpoſes of human life.

If both the earlieſt and the lateſt accounts collected from every quarter of the earth, repreſent mankind as aſſembled in troops and companies; and the individual always joined by affection to one party, while he is poſſibly oppoſed to another; employed in the exerciſe of recollection and foreſight; inclined to communicate his own ſentiments, and to be made acquainted with thoſe of others; theſe facts muſt be admitted as the foundation of all our reaſoning relative to man. His mixed diſpoſition to friendſhip or enmity, his reaſon, his uſe of lan-

guage

guage and articulate ſounds, like the ſhape and the erect poſition of his body, are to be conſidered as ſo many attributes of his nature: they are to be retained in his deſcription, as the wing and the paw are in that of the eagle and the lion, and as different degrees of fierceneſs, vigilance, timidity, or ſpeed, are made to occupy a place in the natural hiſtory of different animals.

If the queſtion be put, What the mind of man could perform, when left to itſelf, and without the aid of any foreign direction? we are to look for our anſwer in the hiſtory of mankind. Particular experiments which have been found ſo uſeful in eſtabliſhing the principles of other ſciences, could probably, on this ſubject, teach us nothing important, or new: we are to take the hiſtory of every active being from his conduct in the ſituation to which he is formed, not from his appearance in any forced or uncommon condition; a wild man therefore, caught in the woods, where he had always lived apart from his ſpecies, is a ſingular inſtance, not a ſpecimen of any general character. As the anatomy of an eye which had never received the impreſſions of light, or that of an ear which had never felt the impulſe of ſounds, would probably exhibit defects in the very ſtructure of the organs themſelves, ariſing from their not being applied to their proper functions; ſo any particular caſe of this ſort would only ſhew in what degree the powers of apprehenſion and ſentiment could exiſt where they had not been employed, and what would be the defects and imbecilities of a heart in which the emotions that pertain to ſociety had never been felt.

MANKIND are to be taken in groupes, as they have always ſubſiſted. The hiſtory of the individual is but a detail of the ſentiments and thoughts he has entertained in the view of his ſpecies: and every experiment relative to this ſubject ſhould be made with entire ſocieties, not with ſingle men. We have every reaſon, however, to believe, that in the caſe of ſuch an experiment made, we ſhall ſuppoſe, with a colony of children tranſplanted from the nurſery, and left to form a ſociety apart, untaught, and undiſciplined, we ſhould only have the ſame things repeated, which, in ſo many different parts of the earth, have been tranſacted already. The members of our little ſociety would feed and ſleep, would herd together and play, would have a language of their own, would quarrel and divide, would be to one another the moſt important objects of the ſcene, and, in the ardour of their friendſhips and competitions, would overlook their perſonal danger, and ſuſpend the care of their ſelf-preſervation. Has not the human race been planted like the colony in queſtion? Who has directed their courſe? whoſe inſtruction have they heard? or whoſe example have they followed?

NATURE, therefore, we ſhall preſume, having given to every animal its mode of exiſtence, its diſpoſitions and manner of life, has dealt equally with thoſe of the human race; and the natural hiſtorian who would collect the properties of this ſpecies, may fill up every article now, as well as he could have done in any former age. Yet one property by which man is diſtinguiſhed,

has

has been ſometimes overlooked in the account of his nature, or has only ſerved to miſlead our attention. In other claſſes of animals, the individual advances from infancy to age or maturity; and he attains, in the compaſs of a ſingle life, to all the perfection his nature can reach: but, in the human kind, the ſpecies has a progreſs as well as the individual; they build in every ſubſequent age on foundations formerly laid; and, in a ſucceſſion of years, tend to a perfection in the application of their faculties, to which the aid of long experience is required, and to which many generations muſt have combined their endeavours. We obſerve the progreſs they have made; we diſtinctly enumerate many of its ſteps; we can trace them back to a diſtant antiquity; of which no record remains, nor any monument is preſerved, to inform us what were the openings of this wonderful ſcene. The conſequence is, that inſtead of attending to the character of our ſpecies, where the particulars are vouched by the ſureſt authority, we endeavour to trace it through ages and ſcenes unknown; and, inſtead of ſuppoſing that the beginning of our ſtory was nearly of a piece with the ſequel, we think ourſelves warranted to reject every circumſtance of our preſent condition and frame, as adventitious, and foreign to our nature. The progreſs of mankind from a ſuppoſed ſtate of animal ſenſibility, to the attainment of reaſon, to the uſe of language, and to the habit of ſociety, has been accordingly painted with a force of imagination, and its ſteps have been marked with a boldneſs of invention, that would tempt us to admit, among the materials of hiſtory, the ſuggeſtions of fancy, and to receive, perhaps, as the model of our nature in its original ſtate, ſome of the animals whoſe ſhape has the greateſt reſemblance to ours *.

It would be ridiculous to affirm, as a diſcovery, that the ſpecies of the horſe was probably never the ſame with that of the lion; yet, in oppoſition to what has dropped from the pens of eminent writers, we are obliged to obſerve, that men have always appeared among animals a diſtinct and a ſuperior race; that neither the poſſeſſion of ſimilar organs, nor the approximation of ſhape, nor the uſe of the hand †, nor the continued intercourſe with this ſovereign artiſt, has enabled any other ſpecies to blend their nature or their inventions with his; that in his rudeſt ſtate, he is found to be above them; and in his greateſt degeneracy, never deſcends to their level. He is, in ſhort, a man in every condition; and we can learn nothing of his nature from the analogy of other animals. If we would know him, we muſt attend to himſelf, to the courſe of his life, and the tenor of his conduct. With him the ſociety appears to be as old as the individual, and the uſe of the tongue as univerſal as that of the hand or the foot. If there was a time in which he had his acquaintance with his own ſpecies to make, and his faculties to acquire, it is a time of which we have no

* *Rouſſeau* ſur l'origine de l'inegalité parmi les hommes.
† Traité de l'eſprit.

record,

record, and in relation to which our opinions can serve no purpose, and are supported by no evidence.

We are often tempted into these boundless regions of ignorance or conjecture, by a fancy which delights in creating rather than in merely retaining the forms which are presented before it: we are the dupes of a subtilty, which promises to supply every defect of our knowledge, and, by filling up a few blanks in the story of nature, pretends to conduct our apprehension nearer to the source of existence. On the credit of a few observations, we are apt to presume, that the secret may soon be laid open, and that what is termed *wisdom* in nature, may be referred to the operation of physical powers. We forget that physical powers, employed in succession, and combined to a salutary purpose, constitute those very proofs of design from which we infer the existence of God; and that this truth being once admitted, we are no longer to search for the source of existence; we can only collect the laws which the author of nature has established; and in our latest as well as our earliest discoveries, only come to perceive a mode of creation or providence before unknown.

We speak of art as distinguished from nature; but art itself is natural to man. He is in some measure the artificer of his own frame, as well as his fortune, and is destined, from the first age of his being, to invent and contrive. He applies the same talents to a variety of purposes, and acts nearly the same part in very different ſcenes. He would be always improving on his ſubject, and he carries this intention where-ever he moves, through the ſtreets of the populous city, or the wilds of the foreſt. While he appears equally fitted to every condition, he is upon this account unable to ſettle in any. At once obſtinate and fickle, he complains of innovations, and is never ſated with novelty. He is perpetually buſied in reformations, and is continually wedded to his errors. If he dwell in a cave, he would improve it into a cottage; if he has already built, he would ſtill build to a greater extent. But he does not propoſe to make rapid and haſty tranſitions; his ſteps are progreſſive and ſlow; and his force, like the power of a ſpring, ſilently preſſes on every reſiſtance; an effect is ſometimes produced before the cauſe is perceived; and with all his talent for projects, his work is often accompliſhed before the plan is deviſed. It appears, perhaps, equally difficult to retard or to quicken his pace; if the projector complain he is tardy, the moraliſt thinks him unſtable; and whether his motions be rapid or ſlow, the ſcenes of human affairs perpetually change in his management: his emblem is a paſſing ſtream, not a ſtagnating pool. We may deſire to direct his love of improvement to its proper object, we may wiſh for ſtability of conduct; but we miſtake human nature, if we wiſh for a termination of labour, or a ſcene of repoſe.

THE occupations of men, in every condition, beſpeak their freedom of choice, their various opinions, and the multiplicity of wants by which they are urged: but they enjoy,

enjoy, or endure, with a ſenſibility, or a phlegm, which are nearly the ſame in every ſituation. They poſſeſs the ſhores of the Caſpian, or the Atlantic, by a different tenure, but with equal eaſe. On the one they are fixed to the ſoil, and ſeem to be formed for ſettlement, and the accommodation of cities: The names they beſtow on a nation, and on its territory, are the ſame. On the other they are mere animals of paſſage, prepared to roam on the face of the earth, and with their herds, in ſearch of new paſture and favourable ſeaſons, to follow the ſun in his annual courſe.

MAN finds his lodgment alike in the cave, the cottage, and the palace; and his ſubſiſtence equally in the woods, in the dairy, or the farm. He aſſumes the diſtinction of titles, equipage, and dreſs; he deviſes regular ſyſtems of government, and a complicated body of laws: or, naked in the woods, has no badge of ſuperiority but the ſtrength of his limbs and the ſagacity of his mind; no rule of conduct but choice; no tie with his fellow-creatures but affection, the love of company, and the deſire of ſafety. Capable of a great variety of arts, yet dependent on none in particular for the preſervation of his being; to whatever length he has carried his artifice, there he ſeems to enjoy the conveniencies that ſuit his nature, and to have found the condition to which he is deſtined. The tree which an American, on the banks of the Oroonoko *, has choſen to climb for the retreat, and the lodgement of his family, is to him a convenient dwelling. The

* Lafitau mœurs des ſauvages.

ſopha, the vaulted dome, and the colonade, do not more effectually content their native inhabitant.

If we are aſked therefore, Where the ſtate of nature is to be found? we may anſwer, It is here; and it matters not whether we are underſtood to ſpeak in the iſland of Great Britain, at the Cape of Good Hope, or the Straits of Magellan. While this active being is in the train of employing his talents, and of operating on the ſubjects around him, all ſituations are equally natural. If we are told, That vice, at leaſt, is contrary to nature; we may anſwer, It is worſe; it is folly and wretchedneſs. But if nature is only oppoſed to art, in what ſituation of the human race are the footſteps of art unknown? In the condition of the ſavage, as well as in that of the citizen, are many proofs of human invention; and in either is not any permanent ſtation, but a mere ſtage through which this travelling being is deſtined to paſs. If the palace be unnatural, the cottage is ſo no leſs; and the higheſt refinements of political and moral apprehenſion, are not more artificial in their kind, than the firſt operations of ſentiment and reaſon.

If we admit that man is ſuſceptible of improvement, and has in himſelf a principle of progreſſion, and a deſire of perfection, it appears improper to ſay, that he has quitted the ſtate of his nature, when he has begun to proceed; or that he finds a ſtation for which he was not intended, while, like other animals, he only follows the

diſpoſition,

disposition, and employs the powers that nature has given.

The latest efforts of human invention are but a continuation of certain devices which were practised in the earliest ages of the world, and in the rudest state of mankind. What the savage projects, or observes, in the forest, are the steps which led nations, more advanced, from the architecture of the cottage to that of the palace, and conducted the human mind from the perceptions of sense, to the general conclusions of science.

Acknowledged defects are to man in every condition matter of dislike. Ignorance and imbecility are objects of contempt: penetration and conduct give eminence, and procure esteem. Whither should his feelings and apprehensions on these subjects lead him? To a progress, no doubt, in which the savage, as well as the philosopher, is engaged; in which they have made different advances, but in which their ends are the same. The admiration Cicero entertained for literature, eloquence, and civil accomplishments, was not more real than that of a Scythian for such a measure of similar endowments as his own apprehension could reach. "Were I to "boast," says a Tartar prince *, "it would be of that "wisdom I have received from God. For as, on the one "hand, I yield to none in the conduct of war, in the "disposition of armies, whether of horse or of foot, and

* Abulgaze Bahadur Chan.; History of the Tartars.

" in directing the movements of great or ſmall bodies ;
" ſo, on the other, I have my talent in writing, in-
" ferior perhaps only to thoſe who inhabit the great ci-
" ties of Perſia or India. Of other nations, unknown to
" me, I do not ſpeak."

MAN may miſtake the objects of his purſuit ; he may miſapply his induſtry, and miſplace his improvements. If under a ſenſe of ſuch poſſible errors, he would find a ſtandard by which to judge of his own proceedings, and arrive at the beſt ſtate of his nature, he cannot find it perhaps in the practice of any individual, or of any nation whatever ; not even in the ſenſe of the majority, or the prevailing opinion of his kind. He muſt look for it in the beſt conceptions of his underſtanding, in the beſt movements of his heart ; he muſt thence diſcover what is the perfection and the happineſs of which he is capable. He will find, on the ſcrutiny, that the proper ſtate of his nature, taken in this ſenſe, is not a condition from which mankind are for ever removed, but one to which they may now attain ; not prior to the exerciſe of their faculties, but procured by their juſt application.

OF all the terms that we employ in treating of human affairs, thoſe of *natural* and *unnatural* are the leaſt determinate in their meaning. Oppoſed to affectation, frowardneſs, or any other defect of the temper or character, the natural is an epithet of praiſe ; but employed to ſpecify a conduct which proceeds from the nature of man, can ſerve to diſtinguiſh nothing: for all the ac-

tions

tions of men are equally the result of their nature. At most, this language can only refer to the general and prevailing sense or practice of mankind; and the purpose of every important inquiry on this subject may be served by the use of a language equally familiar and more precise. What is just, or unjust? What is happy, or wretched, in the manners of men? What, in their various situations, is favourable or adverse to their amiable qualities? are questions to which we may expect a satisfactory answer; and whatever may have been the original state of our species, it is of more importance to know the condition to which we ourselves should aspire, than that which our ancestors may be supposed to have left.

S E C T. II.

Of the principles of Self-preservation.

IF in human nature there are qualities by which it is distinguished from every other part of the animal creation, men are themselves in different climates and in different ages greatly diversified. So far as we are able to account for this diversity on principles either moral or physical, we perform a task of great curiosity or signal utility. It appears necessary, however, that we attend to the universal qualities of our nature, before we regard its varieties, or attempt to explain differences consisting fifting in the unequal poffeffion or application of difpofitions and powers that are in fome meafure common to all mankind.

MAN, like the other animals, has certain inftinctive propenfities, which, prior to the perception of pleafure or pain, and prior to the experience of what is pernicious or ufeful, lead him to perform many functions of nature relative to himfelf and to his fellow-creatures. He has one fet of difpofitions which refer to his animal prefervation, and to the continuance of his race; another which lead to fociety, and by inlifting him on the fide of one tribe or community, frequently engage him in war and contention with the reft of mankind. His powers of difcernment, or his intellectual faculties, which, under the appellation of *reafon*, are diftinguifhed from the analogous endowments of other animals, refer to the objects around him, either as they are fubjects of mere knowledge, or as they are fubjects of approbation or cenfure. He is formed not only to know, but likewife to admire and to contemn; and thefe proceedings of his mind have a principal reference to his own character, and to that of his fellow-creatures, as being the fubjects on which he is chiefly concerned to diftinguifh what is right from what is wrong. He enjoys his felicity likewife on certain fixed and determinate conditions; and either as an individual apart, or as a member of civil fociety, muft take a particular courfe in order to reap the advantages of his nature. He is, withal, in a very high degree fufceptible of habits; and can, by forbearance or exer-

cife,

cise, so far weaken, confirm, or even diversify his talents, and his dispositions, as to appear, in a great measure, the arbiter of his own rank in nature, and the author of all the varieties which are exhibited in the actual history of his species. The universal characteristics, in the mean time, to which we have now referred, must, when we would treat of any part of this history, constitute the first subject of our attention; and they require not only to be enumerated, but to be distinctly considered.

The dispositions which refer to the preservation of the individual, while they continue to operate in the manner of instinctive desires, are nearly the same in man that they are in the other animals: but in him they are sooner or later combined with reflection and foresight; they give rise to his apprehensions on the subject of property, and make him acquainted with that object of care which he calls his interest. Without the instincts which teach the beaver and the squirrel, the ant and the bee, to make up their little hoards for winter, at first improvident, and, where no immediate object of passion is near, addicted to sloth, he becomes, in process of time, the great storemaster among animals. He finds in a provision of wealth, which he is probably never to employ, an object of his greatest solicitude, and the principal idol of his mind. He apprehends a relation between his person and his property, which renders what he calls his own in a manner a part of himself, a constituent of his rank, his condition, and his character, in which, independent of any real enjoyment, he may be fortunate or unhappy; and, independent of any personal merit, he may be an object of consideration or neglect; and in which he may be wounded and injured, while his person is safe, and every want of his nature completely supplied.

In these apprehensions, while other passions only operate occasionally, the interested find the object of their ordinary cares; their motive to the practice of mechanic and commercial arts; their temptation to trespass on the laws of justice; and, when extremely corrupted, the price of their prostitutions, and the standard of their opinions on the subject of good and of evil. Under this influence, they would enter, if not restrained by the laws of civil society, on a scene of violence or meanness, which would exhibit our species, by turns, under an aspect more terrible and odious, or more vile and contemptible, than that of any animal which inherits the earth.

Although the consideration of interest is founded on the experience of animal wants and desires, its object is not to gratify any particular appetite, but to secure the means of gratifying all; and it imposes frequently a restraint on the very desires from which it arose, more powerful and more severe than those of religion or duty. It arises from the principles of self-preservation in the human frame; but is a corruption, or at least a partial result, of those principles. and is upon many accounts very improperly termed *self-love*.

Love

Love is an affection which carries the attention of the mind beyond itſelf, and has a quality, which we call *tenderneſs*, that never can accompany the conſiderations of intereſt. This affection being a complacency and a continued ſatisfaction in its object, independent of any external event, it has, in the midſt of diſappointment and ſorrow, pleaſures and triumphs unknown to thoſe who act without any regard to their fellow-creatures; and in every change of condition, it continues entirely diſtinct from the ſentiments which we feel on the ſubject of perſonal ſucceſs or adverſity. But as the care a man entertains for his own intereſt, and the attention his affection makes him pay to that of another, may have ſimilar effects, the one on his own fortune, the other on that of his friend, we confound the principles from which he acts; we ſuppoſe that they are the ſame in kind, only referred to different objects; and we not only miſapply the name of love, in conjunction with ſelf, but, in a manner tending to degrade our nature, we limit the aim of this ſuppoſed ſelfiſh affection to the ſecuring or accumulating the conſtituents of intereſt, or the means of mere animal life.

It is ſomewhat remarkable, that notwithſtanding men value themſelves ſo much on qualities of the mind, on parts, learning and wit, on courage, generoſity, and honour, thoſe men are ſtill ſuppoſed to be in the higheſt degree ſelfiſh or attentive to themſelves, who are moſt careful of animal life, and who are leaſt mindful of rendering that life an object worthy of care. It will be difficult, however, to tell why a good underſtanding, a reſolute and generous mind, ſhould not, by every man in his ſenſes, be reckoned as much parts of himſelf, as either his ſtomach or his palate, and much more than his eſtate or his dreſs. The epicure, who conſults his phyſician, how he may reſtore his reliſh for food, and by creating an appetite, may increaſe the means of enjoyment, might at leaſt with an equal regard to himſelf, conſult how he might ſtrengthen his affection to a parent or a child, to his country or to mankind; and it is probable that an appetite of this ſort would prove a ſource of enjoyment not leſs than the former.

By our ſuppoſed ſelfiſh maxims, notwithſtanding, we generally exclude from among the objects of our perſonal cares, many of the happier and more reſpectable qualities of human nature. We conſider affection and courage as mere follies, that lead us to neglect or expoſe ourſelves; we make wiſdom conſiſt in a regard to our intereſt; and without explaining what intereſt means, we would have it underſtood as the only reaſonable motive of action with mankind. There is even a ſyſtem of philoſophy founded upon tenets of this ſort, and ſuch is our opinion of what men are likely to do upon ſelfiſh principles, that we think it muſt have a tendency very dangerous to virtue. But the errors of this ſyſtem do not conſiſt ſo much in general principles, as in their particular applications; not ſo much in teaching men to regard themſelves, as in leading them to forget that their happieſt affections, their candour, and their independence

dence of mind, are in reality parts of themselves. And the adversaries of this supposed selfish philosophy, where it makes self-love the ruling passion with mankind, have had reason to find fault, not so much with its general representations of human nature, as with the obtrusion of a mere innovation in language for a discovery in science.

When the vulgar speak of their different motives, they are satisfied with ordinary names, which refer to known and obvious distinctions. Of this kind are the terms *benevolence* and *selfishness*, by which they express their desire of the welfare of others, or the care of their own. The speculative are not always satisfied with this proceeding; they would analyze, as well as enumerate the principles of nature; and the chance is, that, merely to gain the appearance of something new, without any prospect of real advantage, they will disturb the order of vulgar apprehension. In the case before us, they have actually found, that benevolence is no more than a species of self-love; and would oblige us, if possible, to look out for a new set of words, by which we may distinguish the selfishness of the parent when he takes care of his child, from his selfishness when he only takes care of himself. For according to this philosophy, as in both cases he only means to gratify a desire of his own, he is in both cases equally selfish. The term *benevolent*, in the mean time, is not employed to characterise persons who have no desires of their own, but persons whose own desires prompt them to procure the welfare of others. The fact is, that we should need only a fresh supply of lan-

guage,

guage, inſtead of that which by this ſeeming diſcovery we ſhould have loſt, in order to make the reaſonings of men proceed as they formerly did. But it is certainly impoſſible to live and to act with men, without employing different names to diſtinguiſh the humane from the cruel, and the benevolent from the ſelfiſh.

THESE terms have their equivalents in every tongue; they were invented by men of no refinement, who only meant to expreſs what they diſtinctly perceived or ſtrongly felt. And if a man of ſpeculation ſhould prove that we are ſelfiſh in a ſenſe of his own, it does not follow that we are ſo in the ſenſe of the vulgar; or, as ordinary men would underſtand his concluſion, that we are condemned in every inſtance to act on motives of intereſt, covetouſneſs, puſillanimity, and cowardice; for ſuch is conceived to be the ordinary import of ſelfiſhneſs in the character of man.

AN affection or paſſion of any kind is ſometimes ſaid to give us an intereſt in its object; and humanity itſelf gives an intereſt in the welfare of mankind. This term *intereſt*, which commonly implies little more than our regard to property, is ſometimes put for utility in general, and this for happineſs; inſomuch that, under theſe ambiguities, it is not ſurpriſing we are ſtill unable to determine, whether intereſt is the only motive of human action, and the ſtandard by which to diſtinguiſh our good from our ill.

So

So much is said in this place, not from any desire to have a share in any controversy of this sort, but merely to confine the meaning of the term *interest* to its most common acceptation, and to intimate our intention of employing it in expressing those objects of care which refer to our external condition, and the preservation of our animal nature. When taken in this sense, it will not surely be thought to comprehend at once all the motives of human conduct. If men be not allowed to have disinterested benevolence, they will not be denied to have disinterested passions of another kind. Hatred, indignation, and rage, frequently urge them to act in opposition to their known interest, and even to hazard their lives, without any hopes of compensation in any future returns of preferment or profit.

SECT. III.

Of the principles of Union among Mankind.

MANKIND have always wandered or settled, agreed or quarrelled, in troops and companies. The cause of their assembling, whatever it be, is the principle of their alliance or union.

IN collecting the materials of history, we are seldom willing to put up with our subject merely as we find it. We are loth to be embarrassed with a multiplicity of particulars,

ticulars, and apparent inconsistencies. In theory we profess the investigation of general principles; and in order to bring the matter of our inquiries within the reach of our comprehension, are disposed to adopt any system. Thus, in treating of human affairs, we would draw every consequence from a principle of union, or a principle of dissension. The state of nature is a state of war or of amity, and men are made to unite from a principle of affection, or from a principle of fear, as is most suitable to the system of different writers. The history of our species indeed abundantly shews, that they are to one another mutual objects both of fear and of love; and they who would prove them to have been originally either in a state of alliance, or of war, have arguments in store to maintain their assertions. Our attachment to one division, or to one sect, seems often to derive much of its force from an animosity conceived to an opposite one: and this animosity in its turn, as often arises from a zeal in behalf of the side we espouse, and from a desire to vindicate the rights of our party.

" MAN is born in society," says Montesquieu, " and " there he remains." The charms that detain him are known to be manifold. We may reckon the parental affection, which, instead of deserting the adult, as among the brutes, embraces more close, as it becomes mixed with esteem, and the memory of its early effects; together with a propensity common to man and other animals, to mix with the herd, and, without reflection, to follow the croud of his species. What this propensity was in the

the firſt moment of its operation, we know not; but with men accuſtomed to company, its enjoyments and diſappointments are reckoned among the principal pleaſures or pains of human life. Sadneſs and melancholy are connected with ſolitude; gladneſs and pleaſure with the concourſe of men. The track of a Laplander on the ſnowy ſhore, gives joy to the lonely mariner; and the mute ſigns of cordiality and kindneſs which are made to him, awaken the memory of pleaſures which he felt in ſociety. In fine, ſays the writer of a voyage to the north, after deſcribing a mute ſcene of this ſort, "We were extremely pleaſed to converſe with men, ſince in thirteen "months we had ſeen no human creature *." But we need no remote obſervation to confirm this poſition: The wailings of the infant, and the languors of the adult, when alone; the lively joys of the one, and the chearfulneſs of the other, upon the return of company, are a ſufficient proof of its ſolid foundations in the frame of our nature.

In accounting for actions we often forget that we ourſelves have acted; and inſtead of the ſentiments which ſtimulate the mind in the preſence of its object, we aſſign as the motives of conduct with men, thoſe conſiderations which occur in the hours of retirement and cold reflection. In this mood frequently we can find nothing important, beſides the deliberate proſpects of intereſt; and a great work, like that of forming ſociety, muſt in

* Collection of Dutch voyages.

our apprehenſion ariſe from deep reflections, and be car-ried on with a view to the advantages which mankind derive from commerce and mutual ſupport. But neither a propenſity to mix with the herd, nor the ſenſe of advantages enjoyed in that condition, comprehend all the principles by which men are united together. Thoſe bands are even of a feeble texture, when compared to the reſolute ardour with which a man adheres to his friend, or to his tribe, after they have for ſome time run the career of fortune together. Mutual diſcoveries of generoſity, joint trials of fortitude, redouble the ardours of friendſhip, and kindle a flame in the human breaſt, which the conſiderations of perſonal intereſt or ſafety cannot ſuppreſs. The moſt lively tranſports of joy are ſeen, and the loudeſt ſhrieks of deſpair are heard, when the objects of a tender affection are beheld in a ſtate of triumph or of ſuffering. An Indian recovered his friend unexpectedly on the iſland of Juan Fernandes: He proſtrated himſelf on the ground, at his feet: "We "ſtood gazing in ſilence," ſays Dampier, "at this ten-"der ſcene." If we would know what is the religion of a wild American, what it is in his heart that moſt reſembles devotion: it is not his fear of the ſorcerer, nor his hope of protection from the ſpirits of the air or the wood; it is the ardent affection with which he ſelects and embraces his friend; with which he clings to his ſide in every ſeaſon of peril; and with which he invokes his ſpirit from a diſtance, when dangers ſurpriſe him alone *. Whatever proofs we may have of the ſocial diſ-

* Charlevoix; Hiſt. of Canada.

poſition

position of man in familiar and contiguous scenes, it is possibly of importance, to draw our observations from the examples of men who live in the simplest condition, and who have not learned to affect what they do not actually feel.

MERE acquaintance and habitude nourish affection, and the experience of society brings every passion of the human mind upon its side. Its triumphs and prosperities, its calamities and distresses, bring a variety and a force of emotion, which can only have place in the company of our fellow-creatures. It is here that a man is made to forget his weakness, his cares of safety, and his subsistence; and to act from those passions which make him discover his force. It is here he finds that his arrows fly swifter than the eagle, and his weapons wound deeper than the paw of the lion, or the tooth of the boar. It is not alone his sense of a support which is near, nor the love of distinction in the opinion of his tribe, that inspire his courage, or swell his heart with a confidence that exceeds what his natural force should bestow. Vehement passions of animosity or attachment are the first exertions of vigour in his breast; under their influence, every consideration, but that of his object, is forgotten; dangers and difficulties only excite him the more.

THAT condition is surely favourable to the nature of any being, in which his force is increased; and if courage be the gift of society to man, we have reason to consider his union with his species as the noblest part of his fortune.

tune. From this ſource are derived, not only the force, but the very exiſtence of his happieſt emotions; not only the better part, but almoſt the whole of his rational character. Send him to the deſert alone, he is a plant torn from its roots: the form indeed may remain, but every faculty droops and withers; the human perſonage and the human character ceaſe to exiſt.

MEN are ſo far from valuing ſociety on account of its mere external conveniencies, that they are commonly moſt attached where thoſe conveniencies are leaſt frequent; and are there moſt faithful, where the tribute of their allegiance is paid in blood. Affection operates with the greateſt force, where it meets with the greateſt difficulties: In the breaſt of the parent, it is moſt ſolicitous amidſt the dangers and diſtreſſes of the child: In the breaſt of a man, its flame redoubles where the wrongs or ſufferings of his friend, or his country, require his aid. It is, in ſhort, from this principle alone that we can account for the obſtinate attachment of a ſavage to his unſettled and defenceleſs tribe, when temptations on the ſide of eaſe and of ſafety might induce him to fly from famine and danger, to a ſtation more affluent, and more ſecure. Hence the ſanguine affection which every Greek bore to his country, and hence the devoted patriotiſm of an early Roman. Let thoſe examples be compared with the ſpirit which reigns in a commercial ſtate, where men may be ſuppoſed to have experienced, in its full extent, the intereſt which individuals have in the preſervation of their

country.

country. It is here indeed, if ever, that man is sometimes found a detached and a solitary being: he has found an object which sets him in competition with his fellow-creatures, and he deals with them as he does with his cattle and his soil, for the sake of the profits they bring. The mighty engine which we suppose to have formed society, only tends to set its members at variance, or to continue their intercourse after the bands of affection are broken.

SECT. IV.

Of the principles of War and Dissension.

"THERE are some circumstances in the lot of mankind," says Socrates, "that shew them to be destined to friendship and amity: Those are, their mutual need of one another; their mutual compassion; their sense of mutual benefits; and the pleasures arising in company. There are other circumstances which prompt them to war and dissension; the admiration and the desire which they entertain for the same subjects; their opposite pretensions; and the provocations which they mutually offer in the course of their competitions."

WHEN we endeavour to apply the maxims of natural justice to the solution of difficult questions, we find that some cases may be supposed, and actually happen, where oppositions oppofitions take place, and are lawful, prior to any provocation, or act of injuftice; that where the fafety and prefervation of numbers are mutually inconfiftent, one party may employ his right of defence, before the other has begun an attack. And when we join with fuch examples, the inftances of miftake, and mifunderftanding, to which mankind are expofed, we may be fatisfied that war does not always proceed from an intention to injure; and that even the beft qualities of men, their candour, as well as their refolution, may operate in the midft of their quarrels.

THERE is ftill more to be obferved on this fubject. Mankind not only find in their condition the fources of variance and diffenfion; they appear to have in their minds the feeds of animofity, and to embrace the occafions of mutual oppofition, with alacrity and pleafure. In the moft pacific fituation there are few who have not their enemies, as well as their friends; and who are not pleafed with oppofing the proceedings of one, as much as with favouring the defigns of another. Small and fimple tribes, who in their domeftic fociety have the firmeft union, are in their ftate of oppofition as feparate nations, frequently animated with the moft implacable hatred. Among the citizens of Rome, in the early ages of that republic, the name of a foreigner, and that of an enemy, were the fame. Among the Greeks, the name of Barbarian, under which that people comprehended every nation that was of a race, and fpoke a language, different from their own, became a term of indifcriminate contempt

and

and aversion. Even where no particular claim to superiority is formed, the repugnance to union, the frequent wars, or rather the perpetual hostilities, which take place among rude nations and separate clans, discover how much our species is disposed to opposition, as well as to concert.

LATE discoveries have brought us to the knowledge of almost every situation in which mankind are placed. We have found them spread over large and extensive continents, where communications are open, and where national confederacy might be easily formed. We have found them in narrower districts, circumscribed by mountains, great rivers, and arms of the sea. They have been found in small and remote islands, where the inhabitants might be easily assembled, and derive an advantage from their union. But in all those situations, alike, they were broke into cantons, and affected a distinction of name and community. The titles of *fellow-citizen* and *countryman*, unopposed to those of *alien* and *foreigner*, to which they refer, would fall into disuse, and lose their meaning. We love individuals on account of personal qualities; but we love our country, as it is a party in the divisions of mankind; and our zeal for its interest, is a predilection in behalf of the side we maintain.

IN the promiscuous concourse of men, it is sufficient that we have an opportunity of selecting our company. We turn away from those who do not engage us, and we fix our resort where the society is more to our mind.

We

We are fond of diſtinctions; we place ourſelves in oppoſition, and quarrel under the denominations of faction and party, without any material ſubject of controverſy. Averſion, like affection, is foſtered by a continued direction to its particular object. Separation and eſtrangement, as well as oppoſition, widen a breach which did not owe its beginnings to any offence. And it would ſeem, that till we have reduced mankind to the ſtate of a family, or found ſome external conſideration to maintain their connection in greater numbers, they will be for ever ſeparated into bands, and form a plurality of nations.

THE ſenſe of a common danger, and the aſſaults of an enemy, have been frequently uſeful to nations, by uniting their members more firmly together, and by preventing the ſeceſſions and actual ſeparations in which their civil diſcord might otherwiſe terminate. And this motive to union which is offered from abroad, may be neceſſary, not only in the caſe of large and extenſive nations, where coalitions are weakened by diſtance, and the diſtinction of provincial names; but even in the narrow ſociety of the ſmalleſt ſtates. Rome itſelf was founded by a ſmall party, which took its flight from Alba; her citizens were often in danger of ſeparating; and if the villages and cantons of the Volſci had been further removed from the ſcene of their diſſenſions, the Mons Sacer might have received a new colony before the mother-country was ripe for ſuch a diſcharge. She continued long to feel the quarrels of her nobles and her people; and

and the gates of Janus were frequently opened, to remind her inhabitants of the duties they owed to their country.

If societies, as well as individuals, be charged with the care of their own preservation, and if in both we apprehend a separation of interest, which may give rise to jealousies and competitions, we cannot be surprised to find hostilities arise from this source. But were there no angry passions of a different sort, the animosities which attend an opposition of interest, should bear a proportion to the supposed value of the subject. "The Hotten-
"tot nations," says Kolben, "trespass on one another
"by thefts of cattle and of women; but such injuries
"are seldom committed, except with a view to exaspe-
"rate their neighbours, and bring them to a war."
Such depredations then are not the foundation of a war, but the effects of a hostile intention already conceived. The nations of North America, who have no herds to preserve, nor settlements to defend, are yet engaged in almost perpetual wars, for which they can assign no reason, but the point of honour, and a desire to continue the struggle their fathers maintained. They do not regard the spoils of an enemy; and the warrior who has seized any booty, easily parts with it to the first person who comes in his way *.

* See Charlevoix's history of Canada.

BUT we need not crofs the Atlantic to find proofs of animofity, and to obferve, in the collifion of feparate focieties, the influence of angry paffions, that do not arife from an oppofition of intereft. Human nature has no part of its character, of which more flagrant examples are given on this fide of the globe. What is it that ftirs in the breafts of ordinary men when the enemies of their country are named? Whence are the prejudices that fubfift between different provinces, cantons, and villages, of the fame empire and territory? What is it that excites one half of the nations of Europe againft the other? The ftatefman may explain his conduct on motives of national jealoufy and caution, but the people have diflikes and antipathies, for which they cannot account. Their mutual reproaches of perfidy and injuftice, like the Hottentot depredations, are but fymptoms of an animofity, and the language of a hoftile difpofition, already conceived. The charge of cowardice and pufillanimity, qualities which the interefted and cautious enemy fhould, of all others, like beft to find in his rival, is urged with averfion, and made the ground of diflike. Hear the peafants on different fides of the Alps, and the Pyrenees, the Rhine, or the Britifh channel, give vent to their prejudices and national paffions; it is among them that we find the materials of war and diffenfion laid without the direction of government, and fparks ready to kindle into a flame, which the ftatefman is frequently difpofed to extinguifh. The fire will not always catch where his reafons of ftate would direct, nor ftop where the concurrence of intereft has produced an alliance.

ance. " My Father," said a Spanish peasant, " would " rise from his grave, if he could foresee a war with " France." What interest had he, or the bones of his father, in the quarrels of princes?

THESE observations seem to arraign our species, and to give an unfavourable picture of mankind; and yet the particulars we have mentioned are consistent with the most amiable qualities of our nature, and often furnish a scene for the exercise of our greatest abilities. They are sentiments of generosity and self-denial that animate the warrior in defence of his country; and they are dispositions most favourable to mankind, that become the principles of apparent hostility to men. Every animal is made to delight in the exercise of his natural talents and forces: The lion and the tyger sport with the paw; the horse delights to commit his mane to the wind, and forgets his pasture to try his speed in the field; the bull even before his brow is armed, and the lamb while yet an emblem of innocence, have a disposition to strike with the forehead, and anticipate, in play, the conflicts they are doomed to sustain. Man too is disposed to opposition, and to employ the forces of his nature against an equal antagonist; he loves to bring his reason, his eloquence, his courage, even his bodily strength, to the proof. His sports are frequently an image of war; sweat and blood are freely expended in play; and fractures or death are often made to terminate the pastimes of idleness and festivity. He was not made to live for ever, and even his love of amuſement has opened a path that leads to the grave.

WITHOUT the rivalſhip of nations, and the practice of war, civil ſociety itſelf could ſcarcely have found an object, or a form. Mankind might have traded without any formal convention, but they cannot be ſafe without a national concert. The neceſſity of a public defence, has given riſe to many departments of ſtate, and the intellectual talents of men have found their buſieſt ſcene in wielding their national forces. To overawe, or intimidate, or, when we cannot perſuade with reaſon, to reſiſt with fortitude, are the occupations which give its moſt animating exerciſe, and its greateſt triumphs, to a vigorous mind; and he who has never ſtruggled with his fellow-creatures, is a ſtranger to half the ſentiments of mankind.

THE quarrels of individuals, indeed, are frequently the operations of unhappy and deteſtable paſſions; malice, hatred, and rage. If ſuch paſſions alone poſſeſs the breaſt, the ſcene of diſſenſion becomes an object of horror; but a common oppoſition maintained by numbers, is always allayed by paſſions of another ſort. Sentiments of affection and friendſhip mix with animoſity; the active and ſtrenuous become the guardians of their ſociety; and violence itſelf is, in their caſe, an exertion of generoſity as well as of courage. We applaud, as proceeding from a national or party ſpirit, what we could not endure as the effect of a private diſlike; and amidſt the

competitions

competitions of rival states, think we have found, for the patriot and the warrior, in the practice of violence and stratagem, the most illustrious career of human virtue. Even personal opposition here does not divide our judgement on the merits of men. The rival names of Agesilaus and Epaminondas, of Scipio and Hannibal, are repeated with equal praise; and war itself, which in one view appears so fatal, in another is the exercise of a liberal spirit; and in the very effects which we regret, is but one distemper more by which the author of nature has appointed our exit from human life.

THESE reflections may open our view into the state of mankind; but they tend to reconcile us to the conduct of Providence, rather than to make us change our own: where, from a regard to the welfare of our fellow-creatures, we endeavour to pacify their animosities, and unite them by the ties of affection. In the pursuit of this amiable intention, we may hope, in some instances, to disarm the angry passions of jealousy and envy; we may hope to instil into the breasts of private men sentiments of candour toward their fellow-creatures, and a disposition to humanity and justice. But it is vain to expect that we can give to the multitude of a people a sense of union among themselves, without admitting hostility to those who oppose them. Could we at once, in the case of any nation, extinguish the emulation which is excited from abroad, we should probably break or weaken the bands of society at home, and close the busiest scenes of national occupations and virtues.

SECT.

SECT. V.

Of Intellectual Powers.

MANY attempts have been made to analyze the dispositions which we have now enumerated; but one purpose of science, perhaps the most important, is served, when the existence of a disposition is established. We are more concerned in its reality, and in its consequences, than we are in its origin, or manner of formation.

THE same observation may be applied to the other powers and faculties of our nature. Their existence and use are the principal objects of our study. Thinking and reasoning, we say, are the operations of some faculty; but in what manner the faculties of thought or reason remain, when they are not exerted, or by what difference in the frame they are unequal in different persons, are questions which we cannot resolve. Their operations alone discover them: when unapplied, they lie hid even from the person to whom they pertain; and their action is so much a part of their nature, that the faculty itself, in many cases, is scarcely to be distinguished from a habit acquired in its frequent exertion.

PERSONS who are occupied with different subjects, who act in different scenes, generally appear to have different

ferent talents, or at leaſt to have the ſame faculties variouſly formed, and ſuited to different purpoſes. The peculiar genius of nations, as well as of individuals, may in this manner ariſe from the ſtate of their fortunes. And it is proper that we endeavour to find ſome rule, by which to judge of what is admirable in the capacities of men, or fortunate in the application of their faculties, before we venture to paſs a judgement on this branch of their merits, or pretend to meaſure the degree of reſpect they may claim by their different attainments.

To receive the informations of ſenſe, is perhaps the earlieſt function of an animal combined with an intellectual nature; and one great accompliſhment of the living agent conſiſts in the force and ſenſibility of his animal organs. The pleaſures or pains to which he is expoſed from this quarter, conſtitute to him an important difference between the objects which are thus brought to his knowledge; and it concerns him to diſtinguiſh well, before he commits himſelf to the direction of appetite. He muſt ſcrutinize the objects of one ſenſe by the perceptions of another; examine with the eye, before he ventures to touch; and employ every means of obſervation, before he gratifies the appetites of thirſt and of hunger. A diſcernment acquired by experience, becomes a faculty of his mind; and the inferences of thought are ſometimes not to be diſtinguiſhed from the perceptions of ſenſe.

THE

The objects around us, beside their separate appearances, have their relations to one another. They suggest, when compared, what would not occur when they are considered apart; they have their effects, and mutual influences; they exhibit, in like circumstances, similar operations, and uniform consequences. When we have found and expressed the points in which the uniformity of their operations consists, we have ascertained a physical law. Many such laws, and even the most important, are known to the vulgar, and occur upon the smallest degrees of reflection: but others are hid under a seeming confusion, which ordinary talents cannot remove; and are therefore the objects of study, long observation, and superior capacity. The faculties of penetration and judgement, are, by men of business, as well as of science, employed to unravel intricacies of this sort; and the degree of sagacity with which either is endowed, is to be measured by the success with which they are able to find general rules, applicable to a variety of cases that seemed to have nothing in common, and to discover important distinctions between subjects which the vulgar are apt to confound.

To collect a multiplicity of particulars under general heads, and to refer a variety of operations to their common principle, is the object of science. To do the same thing, at least within the range of his active engagements, pertains to the man of pleasure, or business: and it would seem, that the studious and the active are

so

so far employed in the same task, from observation and experience, to find the general views under which their objects may be considered, and the rules which may be usefully applied in the detail of their conduct. They do not always apply their talents to different subjects; and they seem to be distinguished chiefly by the unequal reach and variety of their remarks, or by the intentions which they severally have in collecting them.

WHILST men continue to act from appetites and passions, leading to the attainment of external ends, they seldom quit the view of their objects in detail, to go far in the road of general inquiries. They measure the extent of their own abilities, by the promptitude with which they apprehend what is important in every subject, and the facility with which they extricate themselves on every trying occasion. And these, it must be confessed, to a being who is destined to act in the midst of difficulties, are the proper test of capacity and force. The parade of words, and general reasonings, which sometimes carry an appearance of so much learning and knowledge, are of little avail in the conduct of life. The talents from which they proceed, terminate in mere ostentation, and are seldom connected with that superior discernment which the active apply in times of perplexity; much less with that intrepidity and force of mind which are required in passing through difficult scenes.

THE abilities of active men, however, have a variety corresponding to that of the subjects on which they are occupied. A ſagacity applied to external and inanimate nature, forms one ſpecies of capacity; that which is turned to ſociety and human affairs, another. Reputation for parts in any ſcene is equivocal, till we know by what kind of exertion that reputation is gained. That they underſtand well the ſubjects to which they apply, is all that can be ſaid, in commending men of the greateſt abilities: and every department, every profeſſion, would have its great men, if there were not a choice of objects for the underſtanding, and of talents for the mind, as well as of ſentiments for the heart, and of habits for the active character.

THE meaneſt profeſſions, indeed, ſo far ſometimes forget themſelves, or the reſt of mankind, as to arrogate, in commending what is diſtinguiſhed in their own way, every epithet the moſt reſpectable claim as the right of ſuperior abilities. Every mechanic is a great man with the learner, and the humble admirer, in his particular calling; and we can, perhaps, with more aſſurance pronounce what it is that ſhould make a man happy and amiable, than what ſhould make his abilities reſpected, and his genius admired. This, upon a view of the talents themſelves, may perhaps be impoſſible. The effect, however, will point out the rule and the ſtandard of our judgement. To be admired and reſpected, is to have an aſcendant among men. The talents which moſt directly procure that aſcendant, are thoſe which operate on mankind, penetrate their views, prevent their wiſhes, or fruſtrate their deſigns. The ſuperior capacity leads with

a

a ſuperior energy, where every individual would go, and ſhews the heſitating and the irreſolute a clear paſſage to the attainment of their ends.

THIS deſcription does not pertain to any particular craft or profeſſion; or perhaps it implies a kind of ability, which the ſeparate application of men to particular callings, only tends to ſuppreſs or to weaken. Where ſhall we find the talents which are fit to act with men in a collective body, if we break that body into parts, and confine the obſervation of each to a ſeparate track?

To act in the view of his fellow-creatures, to produce his mind in public, to give it all the exerciſe of ſentiment and thought, which pertain to man as a member of ſociety, as a friend, or an enemy, ſeems to be the principal calling and occupation of his nature. If he muſt labour, that he may ſubſiſt, he can ſubſiſt for no better purpoſe than the good of mankind; nor can he have better talents than thoſe which qualify him to act with men. Here, indeed, the underſtanding appears to borrow very much from the paſſions; and there is a felicity of conduct in human affairs, in which it is difficult to diſtinguiſh the promptitude of the head from the ardour and ſenſibility of the heart. Where both are united, they conſtitute that ſuperiority of mind, the frequency of which among men, in particular ages and nations, much more than the progreſs they have made in ſpeculation, or in the practice of mechanic and liberal arts, ſhould determine the rate of their genius, and aſſign the palm of diſtinction and honour.

WHEN nations ſucceed one another in the career of diſcoveries and inquiries, the laſt is always the moſt knowing. Syſtems of ſcience are gradually formed. The globe itſelf is traverſed by degrees, and the hiſtory of every age, when paſt, is an acceſſion of knowledge to thoſe who ſucceed. The Romans were more knowing than the Greeks; and every ſcholar of modern Europe is, in this ſenſe, more learned than the moſt accompliſhed perſon that ever bore either of thoſe celebrated names. But is he on that account their ſuperior?

MEN are to be eſtimated, not from what they know, but from what they are able to perform; from their ſkill in adapting materials to the ſeveral purpoſes of life; from their vigour and conduct in purſuing the objects of policy, and in finding the expedients of war and national defence. Even in literature, they are to be eſtimated from the works of their genius, not from the extent of their knowledge. The ſcene of mere obſervation was extremely limited in a Grecian republic; and the buſtle of an active life appeared inconſiſtent with ſtudy: but there the human mind, notwithſtanding, collected its greateſt abilities, and received its beſt informations, in the midſt of ſweat and of duſt.

IT is peculiar to modern Europe, to reſt ſo much of the human character on what may be learned in retirement,

tirement, and from the information of books. A juſt admiration of ancient literature, an opinion that human ſentiment, and human reaſon, without this aid, were to have vaniſhed from the ſocieties of men, have led us into the ſhade, where we endeavour to derive from imagination and thought, what is in reality matter of experience and ſentiment: and we endeavour, through the grammar of dead languages, and the channel of commentators, to arrive at the beauties of thought and elocution, which ſprang from the animated ſpirit of ſociety, and were taken from the living impreſſions of an active life. Our attainments are frequently limited to the elements of every ſcience, and ſeldom reach to that enlargement of ability and power which uſeful knowledge ſhould give. Like mathematicians, who ſtudy the Elements of Euclid, but never think of menſuration, we read of ſocieties, but do not propoſe to act with men: we repeat the language of politics, but feel not the ſpirit of nations: we attend to the formalities of a military diſcipline, but know not how to employ numbers of men to obtain any purpoſe by ſtratagem or force.

But for what end, it may ſaid, point out a miſfortune that cannot be remedied? If national affairs called for exertion, the genius of men would awake; but in the receſs of better employment, the time which is beſtowed on ſtudy, if even attended with no other advantage, ſerves to occupy with innocence the hours of leiſure, and ſet bounds to the purſuit of ruinous and frivolous amuſements. From no better reaſon than this,

we

we employ ſo many of our early years, under the rod, to acquire what it is not expected we ſhould retain beyond the threſhold of the ſchool; and whilſt we carry the ſame frivolous character in our ſtudies that we do in our amuſements, the human mind could not ſuffer more from a contempt of letters, than it does from the falſe importance which is given to literature, as a buſineſs for life, not as a help to our conduct, and the means of forming a character that may be happy in itſelf, and uſeful to mankind.

If that time which is paſſed in relaxing the powers of the mind, and in with-holding every object but what tends to weaken and to corrupt, were employed in fortifying thoſe powers, and in teaching the mind to recogniſe its objects, and its ſtrength, we ſhould not, at the years of maturity, be ſo much at a loſs for occupation; nor, in attending the chances of a gaming-table, miſemploy our talents, or waſte the fire which remains in the breaſt. They, at leaſt, who by their ſtations have a ſhare in the government of their country, might believe themſelves capable of buſineſs; and while the ſtate had its armies and councils, might find objects enough to amuſe, without throwing a perſonal fortune into hazard, merely to cure the yawnings of a liſtleſs and inſignificant life. It is impoſſible for ever to maintain the tone of ſpeculation; it is impoſſible not ſometimes to feel that we live among men.

SECT. VI.

Of Moral Sentiment.

UPON a ſlight obſervation of what paſſes in human life, we ſhould be apt to conclude, that the care of ſubſiſtence is the principal ſpring of human actions. This conſideration leads to the invention and practice of mechanical arts; it ſerves to diſtinguiſh amuſement from buſineſs; and, with many, ſcarcely admits into competition any other ſubject of purſuit or attention. The mighty advantages of property and fortune, when ſtript of the recommendations they derive from vanity, or the more ſerious regards to independence and power, only mean a proviſion that is made for animal enjoyment; and if our ſolicitude on this ſubject were removed, not only the toils of the mechanic, but the ſtudies of the learned, would ceaſe; every department of public buſineſs would become unneceſſary; every ſenate-houſe would be ſhut up, and every palace deſerted.

Is man therefore, in reſpect to his object, to be claſſed with the mere brutes, and only to be diſtinguiſhed by faculties that qualify him to multiply contrivances for the ſupport and convenience of animal life, and by the extent of a fancy that renders the care of animal preſervation to him more burdenſome than it is to the herd with which he ſhares in the bounty of nature? If this

were

were his caſe, the joy which attends on ſucceſs, or the griefs which ariſe from diſappointment, would make the ſum of his paſſions. The torrent that waſted, or the inundation that enriched his poſſeſſions, would give him all the emotion with which he is ſeized, on the occaſion of a wrong by which his fortunes are impaired, or of a benefit by which they are preſerved and enlarged. His fellow-creatures would be conſidered merely as they affected his intereſt. Profit or loſs would ſerve to mark the event of every tranſaction; and the epithets *uſeful* or *detrimental* would ſerve to diſtinguiſh his mates in ſociety, as they do the tree which bears plenty of fruit, from that which ſerves only to cumber the ground, or intercept his view.

This, however, is not the hiſtory of our ſpecies. What comes from a fellow-creature is received with peculiar attention; and every language abounds with terms that expreſs ſomewhat in the tranſactions of men, different from ſucceſs and diſappointment. The boſom kindles in company, while the point of intereſt in view has nothing to inflame; and a matter frivolous in itſelf, becomes important, when it ſerves to bring to light the intentions and characters of men. The foreigner, who believed that Othello, on the ſtage, was enraged for the loſs of his handkerchief, was not more miſtaken, than the reaſoner who imputes any of the more vehement paſſions of men to the impreſſions of mere profit or loſs.

MEN assemble to deliberate on business; they separate from jealousies of interest; but in their several collisions, whether as friends or as enemies, a fire is struck out which the regards to interest or safety cannot confine. The value of a favour is not measured when sentiments of kindness are perceived; and the term *misfortune* has but a feeble meaning, when compared to that of *insult* and *wrong*.

As actors or spectators, we are perpetually made to feel the difference of human conduct, and from a bare recital of transactions which have passed in ages and countries remote from our own, are moved with admiration and pity, or transported with indignation and rage. Our sensibility on this subject gives their charm, in retirement, to the relations of history, and to the fictions of poetry; sends forth the tear of compassion, gives to the blood its briskest movement, and to the eye its liveliest glances of displeasure or joy. It turns human life into an interesting spectacle, and perpetually solicits even the indolent to mix, as opponents or friends, in the scenes which are acted before them. Joined to the powers of deliberation and reason, it constitutes the basis of a moral nature; and whilst it dictates the terms of praise and of blame, serves to class our fellow-creatures by the most admirable and engaging, or the most odious and contemptible, denominations.

IT is pleasant to find men, who, in their speculations, deny the reality of moral distinctions, forget in detail the general poſitions they maintain, and give looſe to ridicule, indignation, and ſcorn, as if any of theſe ſentiments could have place, were the actions of men indifferent; and with acrimony pretend to detect the fraud by which moral reſtraints have been impoſed, as if to cenſure a fraud were not already to take a part on the ſide of morality *.

CAN we explain the principles upon which mankind adjudge the preference of characters, and upon which they indulge ſuch vehement emotions of admiration or contempt? If it be admitted that we cannot, are the facts leſs true? or muſt we ſuſpend the movements of the heart until they who are employed in framing ſyſtems of ſcience have diſcovered the principle from which thoſe movements proceed? If a finger burn, we care not for information on the properties of fire: if the heart be torn, or the mind overjoyed, we have not leiſure for ſpeculations on the ſubject of moral ſenſibility.

IT is fortunate in this, as in other articles to which ſpeculation and theory are applied, that nature proceeds in her courſe, whilſt the curious are buſied in the ſearch of her principles. The peaſant, or the child, can reaſon, and judge, and ſpeak his language, with a diſcernment, a conſiſtency, and a regard to analogy, which perplex the logician, the moraliſt, and the grammarian, when they would find the principle upon which the proceeding

* Mandeville.

is founded, or when they would bring to general rules, what is so familiar, and so well sustained in particular cases. The felicity of our conduct is more owing to the talent we possess for detail, and to the suggestion of particular occasions, than it is to any direction we can find in theory and general speculations.

We must, in the result of every inquiry, encounter with facts which we cannot explain; and to bear with this mortification would save us frequently a great deal of fruitless trouble. Together with the sense of our existence, we must admit many circumstances which come to our knowledge at the same time, and in the same manner; and which do, in reality, constitute the mode of our being. Every peasant will tell us, that a man hath his rights; and that to trespass on those rights is injustice. If we ask him farther, what he means by the term *right?* we probably force him to substitute a less significant, or less proper term, in the place of this; or require him to account for what is an original mode of his mind, and a sentiment to which he ultimately refers, when he would explain himself upon any particular application of his language.

The rights of individuals may relate to a variety of subjects, and be comprehended under different heads. Prior to the establishment of property, and the distinction of ranks, men have a right to defend their persons, and to act with freedom; they have a right to maintain the apprehensions of reason, and the feelings of the heart; and they cannot for a moment converſe with one another, without feeling that the part they maintain may be juſt or unjuſt. It is not, however, our buſineſs here to carry the notion of a right into its ſeveral applications, but to reaſon on the ſentiment of favour with which that notion is entertained in the mind.

If it be true, that men are united by inſtinct, that they act in ſociety from affections of kindneſs and friendſhip; if it be true, that even prior to acquaintance and habitude, men, as ſuch, are commonly to one another objects of attention, and ſome degree of regard; that while their proſperity is beheld with indifference, their afflictions are conſidered with commiſeration; if calamities be meaſured by the numbers and the qualities of men they involve; and if every ſuffering of a fellow-creature draws a croud of attentive ſpectators; if even in the caſe of thoſe to whom we do not habitually wiſh any poſitive good, we are ſtill averſe to be the inſtruments of harm; it ſhould ſeem, that in theſe various appearances of an amicable diſpoſition, the foundations of a moral apprehenſion are ſufficiently laid, and the ſenſe of a right which we maintain for ourſelves, is by a movement of humanity and candour extended to our fellow-creatures.

What is it that prompts the tongue when we cenſure an act of cruelty or oppreſſion? What is it that conſtitutes our reſtraint from offences that tend to diſtreſs our fellow-creatures? It is probably, in both caſes, a particular

particular application of that principle, which, in presence of the sorrowful, sends forth the tear of compassion; and a combination of all those sentiments, which constitute a benevolent disposition; and if not a resolution to do good, at least an aversion to be the instrument of harm *.

It may be difficult, however, to enumerate the motives of all the censures and commendations which are applied to the actions of men. Even while we moralize, every disposition of the human mind may have its share in forming the judgement, and in prompting the tongue. As jealousy is often the most watchful guardian of chastity, so malice is often the quickest to spy the failings of our neighbour. Envy, affectation, and vanity, may

* Mankind, we are told, are devoted to interest; and this, in all commercial nations, is undoubtedly true: but it does not follow, that they are, by their natural dispositions, averse to society and mutual affection: proofs of the contrary remain, even where interest triumphs most. What must we think of the force of that disposition to compassion, to candour, and good-will, which, notwithstanding the prevailing opinion that the happiness of a man consists in possessing the greatest possible share of riches, preferments, and honours, still keeps the parties who are in competition for those objects, on a tolerable footing of amity, and leads them to abstain even from their own supposed good, when their seizing it appears in the light of a detriment to others? What might we not expect from the human heart in circumstances which prevented this apprehension on the subject of fortune, or under the influence of an opinion as steady and general as the former, that human felicity does not consist in the indulgences of animal appetite, but in those of a benevolent heart; not in fortune or interest, but in the contempt of this very object, in the courage and freedom which arise from this contempt, joined to a resolute choice of conduct, directed to the good of mankind, or to the good of that particular society to which the party belongs?

dictate the verdicts we give, and the worst principles of our nature may be at the bottom of our pretended zeal for morality; but if we only mean to inquire, why they who are well disposed to mankind, apprehend, in every instance, certain rights pertaining to their fellow-creatures, and why they applaud the consideration that is paid to those rights, we cannot perhaps assign a better reason, than that the person who applauds, is well disposed to the welfare of the parties to whom his applauses refer.

When we consider, that the reality of any amicable propensity in the human mind has been frequently contested; when we recollect the prevalence of interested competitions, with their attendant passions of jealousy, envy, and malice; it may seem strange to alledge, that love and compassion are the most powerful principles in the human breast: but they are destined, on many occasions, to urge with the most irresistible vehemence; and if the desire of self-preservation be more constant, and more uniform, these are a more plentiful source of enthusiasm, satisfaction, and joy. With a power, not inferior to that of resentment and rage, they hurry the mind into every sacrifice of interest, and bear it undismayed through every hardship and danger.

The disposition on which friendship is grafted, glows with satisfaction in the hours of tranquillity, and is pleasant, not only in its triumphs, but even in its sorrows. It throws a grace on the external air, and, by its expresſion on the countenance, compenſates for the want of beauty, or gives a charm which no complexion or features can equal. From this ſource the ſcenes of human life derive their principal felicity; and their imitations in poetry, their principal ornament. Deſcriptions of nature, even repreſentations of a vigorous conduct, and a manly courage, do not engage the heart, if they be not mixed with the exhibition of generous ſentiments, and the pathetic, which is found to ariſe in the ſtruggles, the triumphs, or the misfortunes of a tender affection. The death of Polites, in the Æneid, is not more affecting than that of many others who periſhed in the ruins of Troy; but the aged Priam was preſent when this laſt of his ſons was ſlain; and the agonies of grief and ſorrow force the parent from his retreat, to fall by the hand that ſhed the blood of his child. The pathetic of Homer conſiſts in exhibiting the force of affections, not in exciting mere terror and pity; paſſions he has never perhaps, in any inſtance, attempted to raiſe.

WITH this tendency to kindle into enthuſiaſm, with this command over the heart, with the pleaſure that attends its emotions, and with all its effects in meriting confidence, and procuring eſteem, it is not ſurpriſing, that a principle of humanity ſhould give the tone to our commendations and our cenſures, and even where it is hindered from directing our conduct, ſhould ſtill give to the mind, on reflection, its knowledge of what is deſirable in the human character. *What haſt thou done with thy brother Abel?* was the firſt expoſtulation in behalf of morality;

rality; and if the firſt anſwer has been often repeated, mankind have notwithſtanding, in one ſenſe, ſufficiently acknowledged the charge of their nature. They have felt, they have talked, and even acted, as the keepers of their fellow-creatures: They have made the indications of candour and mutual affection the teſt of what is meritorious and amiable in the characters of men: They have made cruelty and oppreſſion the principal objects of their indignation and rage: Even while the head is occupied with projects of intereſt, the heart is often ſeduced into friendſhip; and while buſineſs proceeds on the maxims of ſelf-preſervation, the careleſs hour is employed in generoſity and kindneſs.

HENCE the rule by which men commonly judge of external actions, is taken from the ſuppoſed influence of ſuch actions on the general good. To abſtain from harm, is the great law of natural juſtice; to diffuſe happineſs is the law of morality; and when we cenſure the conferring a favour on one or a few at the expence of many, we refer to public utility, as the great object at which the actions of men ſhould be aimed.

AFTER all, it muſt be confeſſed, that if a principle of affection to mankind, be the baſis of our moral approbation and diſlike, we ſometimes proceed in diſtributing applauſe or cenſure, without preciſely attending to the degree in which our fellow-creatures are hurt or obliged; and that, beſides the virtues of candour, friendſhip, generoſity, and public ſpirit, which bear an immediate reference

reference to this principle, there are others which may ſeem to derive their commendation from a different ſource. Temperance, prudence, fortitude, are thoſe qualities likewiſe admired from a principle of regard to our fellow-creatures? Why not, ſince they render men happy in themſelves, and uſeful to others? He who is qualified to promote the welfare of mankind, is neither a ſot, a fool, nor a coward. Can it be more clearly expreſſed, that temperance, prudence, and fortitude, are neceſſary to the character we love and admire? I know well why I ſhould wiſh for them in myſelf; and why likewiſe I ſhould wiſh for them in my friend, and in every perſon who is an object of my affection. But to what purpoſe ſeek for reaſons of approbation, where qualities are ſo neceſſary to our happineſs, and ſo great a part in the perfection of our nature? We muſt ceaſe to eſteem ourſelves, and to diſtinguiſh what is excellent, when ſuch qualifications incur our neglect.

A perſon of an affectionate mind, poſſeſſed of a maxim, That he himſelf, as an individual, is no more than a part of the whole that demands his regard, has found, in that principle, a ſufficient foundation for all the virtues; for a contempt of animal pleaſures, that would ſupplant his principal enjoyment; for an equal contempt of danger or pain, that come to ſtop his purſuits of public good. "A vehement and ſteady affection "magnifies its object, and leſſens every difficulty or "danger that ſtands in the way." "Aſk thoſe who have "been in love," ſays Epictetus, "they will know that I "ſpeak truth."

"I have before me," ſays another eminent moraliſt *, "an idea of juſtice, which, if I could follow in every "inſtance, I ſhould think myſelf the moſt happy of "men." And it is, perhaps, of conſequence to their happineſs, as well as to their conduct, if thoſe can be disjoined, that men ſhould have this idea properly formed: It is perhaps but another name for that good of mankind, which the virtuous are engaged to promote. If virtue be the ſupreme good, its beſt and moſt ſignal effect is, to communicate and diffuſe itſelf.

To love, and even to hate, on the apprehenſion of moral qualities, to eſpouſe one party from a ſenſe of juſtice, to oppoſe another with indignation excited by iniquity, are the common indications of probity, and the operations of an animated, upright, and generous ſpirit. To guard againſt unjuſt partialities, and ill-grounded antipathies; to maintain that compoſure of mind, which, without impairing its ſenſibility or ardour, proceeds in every inſtance with diſcernment and penetration, are the marks of a vigorous and cultivated ſpirit. To be able to follow the dictates of ſuch a ſpirit through all the varieties of human life, and with a mind always maſter of itſelf, in proſperity or adverſity, and poſſeſſed of all its abilities, when the ſubjects in hazard are life, or freedom, as much

* Perſian Letters.

as in treating ſimple queſtions of intereſt, are the triumphs of magnanimity, and true elevation of mind. "The event of the day is decided. Draw this javelin "from my body now," ſaid Epaminondas, "and let me "bleed."

In what ſituation, or by what inſtruction, is this wonderful character to be formed? Is it found, in the nurſeries of affectation, pertneſs, and vanity, from which faſhion is propagated, and the genteel is announced? in great and opulent cities, where men vie with one another in equipage, dreſs, and the reputation of fortune? Is it within the admired precincts of a court, where we may learn to ſmile without being pleaſed, to careſs without affection, to wound with the ſecret weapons of envy and jealouſy, and to reſt our perſonal importance on circumſtances which we cannot always with honour command? No: but in a ſituation where the great ſentiments of the heart are awakened; where the characters of men, not their ſituations and fortunes, are the principal diſtinction; where the anxieties of intereſt, or vanity, periſh in the blaze of more vigorous emotions; and where the human ſoul, having felt and recogniſed its objects, like an animal who has taſted the blood of his prey, cannot deſcend to purſuits that leave its talents and its force unemployed.

Proper occaſions alone operating on a raiſed and a happy diſpoſition, may produce this admirable effect, whilſt mere inſtruction may always find mankind at a loſs to comprehend its meaning, or inſenſible to its dictates. The caſe, however, is not deſperate, till we have formed our ſyſtem of politics, as well as manners; till we have ſold our freedom for titles, equipage, and diſtinctions; till we ſee no merit but proſperity and power, no diſgrace but poverty and neglect. What charm of inſtruction can cure the mind that is tainted with this diſorder? What ſyren voice can awaken a deſire of freedom, that is held to be meanneſs, and a want of ambition? or what perſuaſion can turn the grimace of politeneſs into real ſentiments of humanity and candour?

SECT. VII.

Of Happineſs.

HAVING had under our conſideration the active powers and the moral qualities which diſtinguiſh the nature of man, is it ſtill neceſſary that we ſhould treat of his happineſs apart? This ſignificant term, the moſt frequent, and the moſt familiar, in our converſation, is, perhaps, on reflection, the leaſt underſtood. It ſerves to expreſs our ſatisfaction, when any deſire is gratified: It is pronounced with a ſigh, when our object is diſtant: It means what we wiſh to obtain, and what we ſeldom ſtay to examine. We eſtimate the value of every ſubject by its utility, and its influence on happineſs; but

we

we think that utility itself, and happiness, require no explanation.

Those men are commonly esteemed the happiest, whose desires are most frequently gratified. But if, in reality, the possession of what we desire, and a continued fruition, were requisite to happiness, mankind for the most part would have reason to complain of their lot. What they call their enjoyments, are generally momentary; and the object of sanguine expectation, when obtained, no longer continues to occupy the mind: A new passion succeeds, and the imagination, as before, is intent on a distant felicity.

How many reflections of this sort are suggested by melancholy, or by the effects of that very languor and inoccupation into which we would willingly sink, under the notion of freedom from care and trouble?

When we enter on a formal computation of the enjoyments or sufferings which are prepared for mankind, it is a chance but we find that pain, by its intenseness, its duration, or frequency, is greatly predominant. The activity and eagerness with which we press from one stage of life to another, our unwillingness to return on the paths we have trod, our aversion in age to renew the frolics of youth, or to repeat in manhood the amusements of children, have been accordingly stated as proofs, that

our

our memory of the paſt, and our feeling of the preſent, are equal ſubjects of diſlike and diſpleaſure *.

THIS concluſion, however, like many others, drawn from our ſuppoſed knowledge of cauſes, does not correſpond with experience. In every ſtreet, in every village, in every field, the greater number of perſons we meet, carry an aſpect that is chearful or thoughleſs, indifferent, compoſed, buſy, or animated. The labourer whiſtles to his team, and the mechanic is at eaſe in his calling; the frolicſome and the gay feel a ſeries of pleaſures, of which we know not the ſource; even they who demonſtrate the miſeries of human life, when intent on their argument, eſcape from their ſorrows, and find a tolerable paſtime in proving that men are unhappy.

THE very terms *pleaſure* and *pain*, perhaps, are equivocal; but if they are confined, as they appear to be in many of our reaſonings, to the mere ſenſations which have a reference to external objects, either in the memory of the paſt, the feeling of the preſent, or the apprehenſion of the future, it is a great error to ſuppoſe, that they comprehend all the conſtituents of happineſs or miſery; or that the good humour of an ordinary life is maintained by the prevalence of thoſe pleaſures which have their ſeparate names, and are, on reflection, diſtinctly remembered.

* Maupertuis; Eſſai de Morale.

THE

The mind, during the greater part of its exiſtence, is employed in active exertions, not in merely attending to its own feelings of pleaſure or pain; and the liſt of its faculties, underſtanding, memory, foreſight, ſentiment, will, and intention, only contains the names of its different operations.

If, in the abſence of every ſenſation to which we commonly give the names either of *enjoyment* or *ſuffering*, our very exiſtence may have its oppoſite qualities of *happineſs* or *miſery*; and if what we call *pleaſure* or *pain*, occupies but a ſmall part of human life, compared to what paſſes in contrivance and execution, in purſuits and expectations, in conduct, reflection, and ſocial engagements; it muſt appear, that our active purſuits, at leaſt on account of their duration, deſerve the greater part of our attention. When their occaſions have failed, the demand is not for pleaſure, but for ſomething to do; and the very complaints of a ſufferer are not ſo ſure a mark of diſtreſs, as the ſtare of the languid.

We ſeldom, however, reckon any taſk which we are bound to perform, among the bleſſings of life. We always aim at a period of pure enjoyment, or a termination of trouble; and overlook the ſource from which moſt of our preſent ſatisfactions are really drawn. Aſk the buſy, Where is the happineſs to which they aſpire? they will anſwer, perhaps, That it is to be found in the object of ſome preſent purſuit. If we aſk, Why they are not miſerable in the abſence of that happineſs? they will ſay, That they hope to attain it. But is it hope alone that ſupports the mind in the midſt of precarious and uncertain proſpects? and would aſſurance of ſucceſs fill the intervals of expectation with more pleaſing emotions? Give the huntſman his prey, give the gameſter the gold which is ſtaked on the game, that the one may not need to fatigue his perſon, nor the other to perplex his mind, and both will probably laugh at our folly: the one will ſtake his money anew, that he may be perplexed; the other will turn his ſtag to the field, that he may hear the cry of the dogs, and follow through danger and hardſhip. Withdraw the occupations of men, terminate their deſires, exiſtence is a burden, and the iteration of memory is a torment.

THE men of this country, ſays one lady, ſhould learn to ſow and to knit; it would hinder their time from being a burden to themſelves, and to other people. That is true, ſays another; for my part, though I never look abroad, I tremble at the proſpect of bad weather; for then the gentlemen come mopping to us for entertainment; and the ſight of a huſband in diſtreſs, is but a melancholy ſpectacle.

IN deviſing, or in executing a plan, in being carried on the tide of emotion and ſentiment, the mind ſeems to unfold its being, and to enjoy itſelf. Even where the end and the object are known to be of little avail, the talents and the fancy are often intenſely applied, and buſineſs or play may amuſe them alike. We only deſire repoſe

to

to recruit our limited and our wasting force: when business fatigues, amusement is often but a change of occupation. We are not always unhappy, even when we complain. There is a kind of affliction which makes an agreeable state of the mind; and lamentation itself is sometimes an expression of pleasure. The painter and the poet have laid hold of this handle, and find, among the means of entertainment, a favourable reception for works that are composed to awaken our sorrows.

To a being of this description, therefore, it is a blessing to meet with incentives to action, whether in the desire of pleasure, or the aversion to pain. His activity is of more importance than the very pleasure he seeks, and langour a greater evil than the suffering he shuns.

The gratifications of animal appetite are of short duration; and sensuality is but a distemper of the mind, which ought to be cured by remembrance, if it were not perpetually inflamed by hope. The chace is not more surely terminated by the death of the game, than the joys of the voluptuary by the means of completing his debauch. As a bond of society, as a matter of distant pursuit, the objects of sense make an important part in the system of human life. They lead us to fulfil the purpose of nature, in preserving the individual, and in perpetuating the species: but to rely on their use as a principal constituent of human felicity, were an error in speculation, and would be still more an error in practice. Even the master of the seraglio, for whom all the treaſures of empire are extorted from the hoards of its frighted inhabitants, for whom alone the choiceſt emerald and the diamond are drawn from the mine, for whom every breeze is enriched with perfumes, for whom beauty is aſſembled from every quarter, and, animated by paſſions that ripen under the vertical ſun, is confined to the grate for his uſe, is ſtill, perhaps, more wretched than the very herd of the people, whoſe labours and properties are devoted to relieve him of trouble, and to procure him enjoyment.

SENSUALITY is eaſily overcome by any of the habits of purſuit which uſually engage an active mind. When curioſity is awake, or when paſſion is excited, even in the midſt of the feaſt when converſation grows warm, grows jovial, or ſerious, the pleaſures of the table we know are forgotten. The boy contemns them for play, and the man of age declines them for buſineſs.

WHEN we reckon the circumſtances that correſpond to the nature of any animal, or to that of man in particular, ſuch as ſafety, ſhelter, food, and the other means of enjoyment or preſervation, we ſometimes think that we have found a ſenſible and a ſolid foundation on which to reſt his felicity. But thoſe who are leaſt diſpoſed to moralize, obſerve, that happineſs is not connected with fortune, although fortune includes at once all the means of ſubſiſtence, and the means of ſenſual indulgence. The circumſtances that require abſtinence, cou-

rage,

rage, and conduct, expose us to hazard, and are in description of the painful kind; yet the able, the brave, and the ardent, seem most to enjoy themselves when placed in the midst of difficulties, and obliged to employ the powers they possess.

SPINOLA being told, that Sir Francis Vere died of having nothing to do, said, "That was enough "to kill a general.*" How many are there to whom war itself is a pastime, who chuse the life of a soldier, exposed to dangers and continued fatigues; of a mariner, in conflict with every hardship, and bereft of every conveniency; of a politician, whose sport is the conduct of parties and factions; and who, rather than be idle, will do the business of men and of nations for whom he has not the smallest regard. Such men do not chuse pain as preferable to pleasure, but they are incited by a restless disposition to make continued exertions of capacity and resolution; they triumph in the midst of their struggles; they droop, and they languish, when the occasion of their labour has ceased.

WHAT was enjoyment, in the sense of that youth, who, according to Tacitus, loved danger itself, not the rewards of courage? What is the prospect of pleasure, when the sound of the horn or the trumpet, the cry of the dogs, or the shout of war, awaken the ardour of the sportsman and the soldier? The most animating occa-

* Life of Lord Herbert.

ſions of human life, are calls to danger and hardſhip, not invitations to ſafety and eaſe: and man himſelf, in his excellence, is not an animal of pleaſure, nor deſtined merely to enjoy what the elements bring to his uſe; but, like his aſſociates, the dog and the horſe, to follow the exerciſes of his nature, in preference to what are called its enjoyments; to pine in the lap of eaſe and of affluence, and to exult in the midſt of alarms that ſeem to threaten his being. In all which, his diſpoſition to action only keeps pace with the variety of powers with which he is furniſhed; and the moſt reſpectable attributes of his nature, magnanimity, fortitude, and wiſdom, carry a manifeſt reference to the difficulties with which he is deſtined to ſtruggle.

If animal pleaſure becomes inſipid when the ſpirit is rouſed by a different object, it is well known likewiſe, that the ſenſe of pain is prevented by any vehement affection of the ſoul. Wounds received in a heat of paſſion, in the hurry, the ardour, or conſternation of battle, are never felt till the ferment of the mind ſubſides. Even torment, deliberately applied, and induſtriouſly prolonged, are borne with firmneſs, and with an appearance of eaſe, when the mind is poſſeſſed with ſome vigorous ſentiment, whether of religion, enthuſiaſm, or love to mankind. The continued mortifications of ſuperſtitious devotees in ſeveral ages of the Chriſtian church; the wild penances, ſtill voluntarily borne, during many years, by the religioniſts of the eaſt; the contempt in which famine and torture are held by moſt ſavage nations; the chearful

ful or obſtinate patience of the ſoldier in the field; the hardſhips endured by the ſportſman in his paſtime, ſhow how much we may err in computing the miſeries of men, from the meaſures of trouble and of ſuffering they ſeem to incur. And if there be a refinement in affirming, that their happineſs is not to be meaſured by the contrary enjoyments, it is a refinement which was made by Regulus and Cincinnatus before the date of philoſophy; it is a refinement, which every boy knows at his play, and every ſavage confirms, when he looks from his foreſt on the pacific city, and ſcorns the plantation, whoſe maſter he cares not to imitate.

MAN, it muſt be confeſſed, notwithſtanding all this activity of his mind, is an animal in the full extent of that deſignation. When the body ſickens, the mind droops; and when the blood ceaſes to flow, the ſoul takes its departure. Charged with the care of his preſervation, admoniſhed by a ſenſe of pleaſure or pain, and guarded by an inſtinctive fear of death, nature has not intruſted his ſafety to the mere vigilance of his underſtanding, nor to the government of his uncertain reflections.

THE diſtinction betwixt mind and body is followed by conſequences of the greateſt importance; but the facts to which we now refer, are not founded on any tenets whatever. They are equally true, whether we admit or reject the diſtinction in queſtion, or whether we ſuppoſe, that this living agent is formed of one, or is an aſſemblage of ſeparate natures. And the materialiſt, by treating

treating of man as of an engine, cannot make any change in the state of his history. He is a being, who, by a multiplicity of visible organs, performs a variety of functions. His joints are bent, and his muscles relax and contract in our sight; the heart beats in his breast, and the blood flows to every part of his frame. He performs other operations which we cannot refer to any coporeal organ. He perceives, he recollects, and forecasts; he desires, and he shuns; he admires, and contemns. He enjoys his pleasures, or he endures his pain. All these different functions, in some measure, go well or ill together. When the motion of the blood is languid, the muscles relax, the understanding is tardy, and the fancy is dull: when distemper assails him, the physician must attend no less to what he thinks, than to what he eats, and examine the returns of his passion, together with the strokes of his pulse.

WITH all his sagacity, his precautions, and his instincts, which are given to preserve his being, he partakes in the fate of other animals, and seems to be formed only that he may die. Myriads perish before they reach the perfection of their kind; and the individual, with an option to owe the prolongation of his temporary course to resolution and conduct, or to abject fear, frequently chuses the latter, and by a habit of timidity, imbitters the life he is so intent to preserve.

MAN, however, at times, exempted from this mortifying lot, seems to act without any regard to the length of

his

his period. When he thinks intenſely, or deſires with ardour, pleaſures and pains from any other quarter aſſail him in vain. Even in his dying hour, the muſcles acquire a tone from his ſpirit, and the mind ſeems to depart in its vigour, and in the midſt of a ſtruggle to obtain the recent aim of its toils. Muley Moluck, borne on his litter, and ſpent with diſeaſe, ſtill fought the battle, in the midſt of which he expired; and the laſt effort he made, with a finger on his lips, was a ſignal to conceal his death: the precaution, perhaps, of all which he had hitherto taken, the moſt neceſſary to prevent a defeat.

CAN no reflections aid us in acquiring this habit of the ſoul, ſo uſeful in carrying us through many of the ordinary ſcenes of life? If we ſay, that they cannot, the reality of its happineſs is not the leſs evident. The Greeks and the Romans conſidered contempt of pleaſure, endurance of pain, and neglect of life, as eminent qualities of a man, and a principal ſubject of diſcipline. They truſted, that the vigorous ſpirit would find worthy objects on which to employ its force; and that the firſt ſtep towards a reſolute choice of ſuch objects was to ſhake off the meanneſs of a ſolicitous and timorous mind.

MANKIND, in general, have courted occaſions to diſplay their courage, and frequently, in ſearch of admiration, have preſented a ſpectacle, which to thoſe who have ceaſed to regard fortitude on its own account, becomes a ſubject of horror. Scevola held his arm in the fire,

fire, to ſhake the ſoul of Porſenna. The ſavage inures his body to the torture, that in the hour of trial he may exult over his enemy. Even the Muſſulman tears his fleſh to win the heart of his miſtreſs, and comes in gaiety, ſtreaming with blood, to ſhew that he deſerves her eſteem *.

SOME nations carry the practice of inflicting, or of ſporting with pain, to a degree that is either cruel or abſurd; others regard every proſpect of bodily ſuffering as the greateſt of evils; and in the midſt of their troubles, imbitter every real affliction, with the terrors of a feeble and dejected imagination. We are not bound to anſwer for the follies of either, nor, in treating a queſtion which relates to the nature of man, make an eſtimate of its ſtrength, or its weakneſs, from the habits or apprehenſions peculiar to any nation or age.

SECT. VIII.

The ſame ſubject continued.

WHOEVER has compared together the different conditions and manners of men, under varieties of education or fortune, will be ſatisfied, that mere ſituation does not conſtitute their happineſs or

* Letters of the Right Honourable Lady M—y W——y M——e.

miſery; nor a diverſity of external obſervances imply any oppoſition of ſentiments on the ſubject of morality. They expreſs their kindneſs and their enmity in different actions; but kindneſs or enmity is ſtill the principal article of conſideration in human life. They engage in different purſuits, or acquieſce in different conditions; but act from paſſions nearly the ſame. There is no preciſe meaſure of accommodation required to ſuit their conveniency, nor any degree of danger or ſafety under which they are peculiarly fitted to act. Courage and generoſity, fear and envy, are not peculiar to any ſtation or order of men; nor is there any condition in which ſome of the human race have not ſhewn, that it is poſſible to employ, with propriety, the talents and virtues of their ſpecies.

WHAT, then, is that myſterious thing called *Happineſs*, which may have place in ſuch a variety of ſtations, and to which circumſtances in one age or nation thought neceſſary, are in another held to be deſtructive, or of no effect? It is not the ſucceſſion of mere animal pleaſures, which, apart from the occupation or the company in which they ſerve to engage the mind, can fill up but a few moments in the duration of life. On too frequent a repetition, thoſe pleaſures turn to ſatiety and diſguſt; they tear the conſtitution to which they are applied in exceſs, and, like the lightning of night, only ſerve to darken the gloom through which they occaſionally break. Happineſs is not that ſtate of repoſe, or that imaginary freedom from care, which at a diſtance is ſo frequent an object of deſire, but with its approach brings a tedium, or a languor, more unſupportable than pain itſelf. If the preceding obſervations on this ſubject be juſt, it ariſes more from the purſuit, than from the attainment of any end whatever; and in every new ſituation to which we arrive, even in the courſe of a proſperous life, it depends more on the degree in which our minds are properly employed, than it does on the circumſtances in which we are deſtined to act, on the materials which are placed in our hands, or the tools with which we are furniſhed.

If this be confeſſed in reſpect to that claſs of purſuits which are diſtinguiſhed by the name of *amuſement*, and which, in the caſe of men who are commonly deemed the moſt happy, occupy the greater part of human life, we may apprehend, that it holds, much more than is commonly ſuſpected, in many caſes of buſineſs, where the end to be gained, and not the occupation, is ſuppoſed to have the principal value.

The miſer himſelf, we are told, can ſometimes conſider the care of his wealth as a paſtime, and has challenged his heir, to have more pleaſure in ſpending, than he in amaſſing his fortune. With this degree of indifference to what may be the conduct of others; with this confinement of his care to what he has choſen as his own province, more eſpecially if he has conquered in himſelf the paſſions of jealouſy and envy, which tear the covetous mind; why may not the man whoſe object is money, be underſtood to lead a life of amuſement and

pleaſure,

pleasure, not only more entire than that of the spendthrift, but even as much as the virtuoso, the scholar, the man of taste, or any of that class of persons who have found out a method of passing their leisure without offence, and to whom the acquisitions made, or the works produced, in their several ways, perhaps, are as useless as the bag to the miser, or the counter to those who play from mere dissipation at any game of skill or of chance?

WE are soon tired of diversions that do not approach to the nature of business, that is, that do not engage some passion, or give an exercise proportioned to our talents, and our faculties. The chace and the gaming-table have each their dangers and difficulties, to excite and employ the mind. All games of contention animate our emulation, and give a species of party-zeal. The mathematician is only to be amused with intricate problems, the lawyer and the casuist with cases that try their subtilty, and occupy their judgement.

THE desire of active engagements, like every other natural appetite, may be carried to excess; and men may debauch in amusements, as well as in the use of wine, or other intoxicating liquors. At first, a trifling stake, and the occupation of a moderate passion, may have served to amuse the gamester; but when the drug becomes familiar, it fails to produce its effect: The play is made deep, and the interest increased, to awaken his attention; he is carried on by degrees, and in the end comes to seek for amusement, and to find it only in those passions of anxiety, hope, and deſpair, which are rouſed by the hazard into which he has thrown the whole of his fortunes.

If men can thus turn their amuſements into a ſcene more ſerious and intereſting than that of buſineſs itſelf, it will be difficult to aſſign a reaſon, why buſineſs, and many of the occupations of human life, independent of any diſtant conſequences, or future events, may not be choſen as an amuſement, and adopted on account of the paſtime they bring. This is, perhaps, the foundation on which, without the aid of reflection, the contented and the chearful have reſted the gaiety of their tempers. It is perhaps the moſt ſolid baſis of fortitude which any reflection can lay; and happineſs itſelf is ſecured, by making a certain ſpecies of conduct our amuſement; and, by conſidering life, in the general eſtimate of its value, as well as on every particular occaſion, as a mere ſcene for the exerciſe of the mind, and the engagements of the heart. "I will try and attempt every thing," ſays Brutus, "I will never ceaſe to recal my country from "this ſtate of ſervility. If the event be favourable, it will "prove matter of joy to us all; if not, yet I, notwith-"ſtanding, ſhall rejoice." Why rejoice in a diſappointment? Why not be dejected, when his country was overwhelmed? Becauſe ſorrow, perhaps, and dejection, can do no good Nay, but they muſt be endured when they come. And whence ſhould they come to me? might the Roman ſay; I have followed my mind, and can follow it ſtill. Events may have changed the ſituation in which I am deſtined to act; but can they hinder my act-

ing

ing the part of a man? Shew me a ſituation in which a man can neither act nor die, and I will own he is wretched.

WHOEVER has the force of mind ſteadily to view human life under this aſpect, has only to chuſe well his occupations, in order to command that ſtate of enjoyment, and freedom of ſoul, which probably conſtitute the peculiar felicity to which his active nature is deſtined.

THE diſpoſitions of men, and conſequently their occupations, are commonly divided into two principal claſſes; the ſelfiſh, and the ſocial. The firſt are indulged in ſolitude; and if they carry a reference to mankind, it is that of emulation, competition, and enmity. The ſecond incline us to live with our fellow-creatures, and to do them good; they tend to unite the members of ſociety together; they terminate in a mutual participation of their cares and enjoyments, and render the preſence of men an occaſion of joy. Under this claſs may be enumerated the paſſions of the ſexes, the affections of parents and children, general humanity, or ſingular attachments; above all, that habit of the ſoul by which we conſider ourſelves as but a part of ſome beloved community, and as but individual members of ſome ſociety, whoſe general welfare is to us the ſupreme object of zeal, and the great rule of our conduct. This affection is a principle of candour, which knows no partial diſtinctions, and is confined to no bounds: it may extend its effects beyond our perſonal acquaintance; it may, in the

mind,

mind, and in thought, at leaſt, make us feel a relation to the univerſe, and to the whole creation of God. " Shall any one," ſays Antoninus, " love the city of " Cecrops, and you not love the city of God?"

No emotion of the heart is indifferent. It is either an act of vivacity and joy, or a feeling of ſadneſs; a tranſport of pleaſure, or a convulſion of anguiſh: and the exerciſes of our different diſpoſitions, as well as their gratifications, are likely to prove matter of the greateſt importance to our happineſs or miſery.

THE individual is charged with the care of his animal preſervation. He may exiſt in ſolitude, and, far removed from ſociety, perform many functions of ſenſe, imagination, and reaſon. He is even rewarded for the proper diſcharge of thoſe functions; and all the natural exerciſes which relate to himſelf, as well as to his fellow-creatures, not only occupy without diſtreſſing him, but in many inſtances are attended with poſitive pleaſures, and fill up the hours of life with agreeable occupation.

THERE is a degree, however, in which we ſuppoſe that the care of ourſelves becomes a ſource of painful anxiety and cruel paſſions; in which it degenerates into avarice, vanity, or pride; and in which, by foſtering habits of jealouſy and envy, of fear and malice, it becomes as deſtructive of our own enjoyments, as it is hoſtile to the welfare of mankind. This evil, however, is not to be charged

charged upon any exceſs in the care of ourſelves, but upon a mere miſtake in the choice of our objects. We look abroad for a happineſs which is to be found only in the qualities of the heart: we think ourſelves dependent on accidents; and are therefore kept in ſuſpenſe and ſolicitude: we think ourſelves dependent on the will of other men; and are therefore ſervile and timid: we think our felicity is placed in ſubjects for which our fellow-creatures are rivals and competitors; and in purſuit of happineſs, we engage in thoſe ſcenes of emulation, envy, hatred, animoſity, and revenge, that lead to the higheſt pitch of diſtreſs. We act, in ſhort, as if to preſerve ourſelves were to retain our weakneſs, and perpetuate our ſufferings. We charge the ills of a diſtempered imagination, and a corrupt heart, to the account of our fellow-creatures, to whom we refer the pangs of our diſappointment or malice; and while we foſter our miſery, are ſurpriſed that the care of ourſelves is attended with no better effects. But he who remembers that he is by nature a rational being, and a member of ſociety; that to preſerve himſelf, is to preſerve his reaſon, and to preſerve the beſt feelings of his heart; will encounter with none of theſe inconveniencies; and in the care of himſelf, will find ſubjects only of ſatisfaction and triumph.

THE diviſion of our appetites into benevolent and ſelfiſh, has probably, in ſome degree, helped to miſlead our apprehenſion on the ſubject of perſonal enjoyment and private good; and our zeal to prove that virtue is diſintereſted, has not greatly promoted its cauſe. The

gratification

gratification of a ſelfiſh deſire, it is thought, brings advantage or pleaſure to ourſelves; that of benevolence terminates in the pleaſure or advantage of others: whereas, in reality, the gratification of every deſire is a perſonal enjoyment, and its value being proportioned to the particular quality or force of the ſentiment, it may happen that the ſame perſon may reap a greater advantage from the good fortune he has procured to another, than from that he has obtained for himſelf.

WHILE the gratifications of benevolence, therefore, are as much our own as thoſe of any other deſire whatever, the mere exerciſes of this diſpoſition are, on many accounts, to be conſidered as the firſt and the principal conſtituent of human happineſs. Every act of kindneſs, or of care, in the parent to his child; every emotion of the heart, in friendſhip or in love, in public zeal, or general humanity, are ſo many acts of enjoyment and ſatisfaction. Pity itſelf, and compaſſion, even grief and melancholy, when grafted on ſome tender affection, partake of the nature of the ſtock; and if they are not poſitive pleaſures, are at leaſt pains of a peculiar nature, which we do not even wiſh to exchange but for a very real enjoyment, obtained in relieving our object. Even extremes, in this claſs of our diſpoſitions, as they are the reverſe of hatred, envy, and malice, ſo they are never attended with thoſe excruciating anxieties, jealouſies, and fears, which tear the intereſted mind; or if, in reality, any ill paſſion ariſe from a pretended attachment to our fellow-creatures, that attachment may be ſafely

ſafely condemned, as not genuine. If we be diſtruſtful or jealous, our pretended affection is probably no more than a deſire of attention and perſonal conſideration, a motive which frequently inclines us to be connected with our fellow-creatures; but to which we are as frequently willing to ſacrifice their happineſs. We conſider them as the tools of our vanity, pleaſure, or intereſt; not as the parties on whom we may beſtow the effects of our good-will, and our love.

A mind devoted to this claſs of its affections, being occupied with an object that may engage it habitually, is not reduced to court the amuſements or pleaſures with which perſons of an ill temper are obliged to repair their diſguſts: and temperance becomes an eaſy taſk when gratifications of ſenſe are ſupplanted by thoſe of the heart. Courage too is moſt eaſily aſſumed, or is rather inſeparable from that ardour of the mind, in ſociety, friendſhip, or in public action, which makes us forget ſubjects of perſonal anxiety or fear, and attend chiefly to the object of our zeal or affection, not to the trifling inconveniencies, dangers, or hardſhips, which we ourſelves may encounter in ſtriving to maintain it.

It ſhould ſeem, therefore, to be the happineſs of man, to make his ſocial diſpoſitions the ruling ſpring of his occupations; to ſtate himſelf as the member of a community, for whoſe general good his heart may glow with an ardent zeal, to the ſuppreſſion of thoſe perſonal cares which are the foundation of painful anxieties, fear, jealouſy, and envy; or, as Mr Pope expreſſes the ſame ſentiment,

" Man, like the generous vine, ſupported lives;
" The ſtrength he gains, is from th'embrace he gives *."

If this be the good of the individual, it is likewiſe that of mankind; and virtue no longer impoſes a taſk by which we are obliged to beſtow upon others that good from which we ourſelves refrain; but ſuppoſes, in the higheſt degree, as poſſeſſed by ourſelves, that ſtate of felicity which we are required to promote in the world.

We commonly apprehend, that it is our duty to do kindneſſes, and our happineſs to receive them: but if, in reality, courage, and a heart devoted to the good of mankind, are the conſtituents of human felicity, the kindneſs which is done infers a happineſs in the perſon from whom it proceeds, not in him on whom it is beſtowed; and the greateſt good which men poſſeſſed of fortitude and generoſity can procure to their fellow-creatures, is a participation of this happy character. " You " will confer the greateſt benefit on your city," ſays Epictetus, " not by raiſing the roofs, but by exalting the " ſouls of your fellow-citizens; for it is better that great " ſouls ſhould live in ſmall habitations, than that abject " ſlaves ſhould burrow in great houſes †."

* The ſame maxim will apply throughout every part of nature. *To love, is to enjoy pleaſure: To hate, is to be in pain.*

† Mrs Carter's tranſlation of the works of Epictetus.

To

To the benevolent, the satisfaction of others is a ground of enjoyment; and existence itself, in a world that is governed by the wisdom of God, is a blessing. The mind, freed from cares that lead to pusillanimity and meanness, becomes calm, active, fearless, and bold; capable of every enterprise, and vigorous in the exercise of every talent, by which the nature of man is adorned. On this foundation was raised the admirable character, which, during a certain period of their story, distinguished the celebrated nations of antiquity, and rendered familiar and ordinary in their manners, examples of magnanimity, which, under governments less favourable to the public affections, rarely occur; or which, without being much practised, or even understood, are made subjects of admiration and swelling panegyric. "Thus," says Xenophon, "died Thrasybulus; who indeed appears to have been a good man." What valuable praise, and how significant to those who know the story of this admirable person! The members of those illustrious states, from the habit of considering themselves as part of a community, or at least as deeply involved with some order of men in the state, were regardless of personal considerations: they had a perpetual view to objects which excite a great ardour in the soul; which led them to act perpetually in the view of their fellow-citizens, and to practise those arts of deliberation, elocution, policy, and war, on which the fortunes of nations, or of men, in their collective body, depend. To the force of mind collected in this career, and to the improvements of wit which were made in purſuing it, theſe nations owed, not only their magnanimity, and the ſuperiority of their political and military conduct, but even the arts of poetry and literature, which among them were only the inferior appendages of a genius otherwiſe excited, cultivated, and refined.

To the ancient Greek, or the Roman, the individual was nothing, and the public every thing. To the modern, in too many nations of Europe, the individual is every thing, and the public nothing. The ſtate is merely a combination of departments, in which conſideration, wealth, eminence, or power, are offered as the reward of ſervice. It was the nature of modern government, even in its firſt inſtitution, to beſtow on every individual a fixed ſtation and dignity, which he was to maintain for himſelf. Our anceſtors, in rude ages, during the receſs of wars from abroad, fought for their perſonal claims at home, and by their competitions, and the balance of their powers, maintained a kind of political freedom in the ſtate, while private parties were ſubject to continual wrongs and oppreſſions. Their poſterity, in times more poliſhed, have repreſſed the civil diſorders in which the activity of earlier ages chiefly conſiſted; but they employ the calm they have gained, not in foſtering a zeal for thoſe laws, and that conſtitution of government, to which they owe their protection, but in practiſing apart, and each for himſelf, the ſeveral arts of perſonal advancement, or profit, which their political eſtabliſhments may enable them to purſue with ſucceſs. Commerce,

which

which may be ſuppoſed to comprehend every lucrative art, is accordingly conſidered as the great object of nations, and the principal ſtudy of mankind.

So much are we accuſtomed to conſider perſonal fortune as the ſole object of care, that even under popular eſtabliſhments, and in ſtates where different orders of men are ſummoned to partake in the government of their country, and where the liberties they enjoy cannot be long preſerved, without vigilance and activity on the part of the ſubject; ſtill they, who, in the vulgar phraſe, have not their fortunes to make, are ſuppoſed to be at a loſs for occupation, and betake themſelves to ſolitary paſtimes, or cultivate what they are pleaſed to call a taſte for gardening, building, drawing, or muſic. With this aid, they endeavour to fill up the blanks of a liſtleſs life, and avoid the neceſſity of curing their languors by any poſitive ſervice to their country, or to mankind.

The weak or the malicious are well employed in any thing that is innocent, and are fortunate in finding any occupation which prevents the effects of a temper that would prey upon themſelves, or upon their fellow-creatures. But they who are bleſſed with a happy diſpoſition, with capacity and vigour, incur a real debauchery, by having any amuſement that occupies an improper ſhare of their time; and are really cheated of their happineſs, in being made to believe, that any occupation or paſtime is better fitted to amuſe themſelves,

ſelves, than that which at the ſame time produces ſome real good to their fellow-creatures.

THIS ſort of entertainment, indeed, cannot be the choice of the mercenary, the envious, or the malignant. Its value is known only to perſons of an oppoſite temper; and to their experience alone we appeal. Guided by mere diſpoſition, and without the aid of reflection, in buſineſs, in friendſhip, and in public life, they often acquit themſelves well; and borne with ſatisfaction on the tide of their emotions and ſentiments, enjoy the preſent hour, without recollection of the paſt, or hopes of the future. It is in ſpeculation, not in practice, they are made to diſcover, that virtue is a taſk of ſeverity and ſelf-denial.

SECT. IX.

Of National Felicity.

MAN is, by nature, the member of a community; and when conſidered in this capacity, the individual appears to be no longer made for himſelf. He muſt forego his happineſs and his freedom, where theſe interfere with the good of ſociety. He is only part of a whole; and the praiſe we think due to his virtue, is but a branch of that more general commendation we beſtow on the member of a body, on the part of a fabric or engine, for

for being well fitted to occupy its place, and to produce its effect.

If this follow from the relation of a part to its whole, and if the public good be the principal object with individuals, it is likewise true, that the happiness of individuals is the great end of civil society: for in what sense can a public enjoy any good, if its members, considered apart, be unhappy?

The interests of society, however, and of its members, are easily reconciled. If the individual owe every degree of consideration to the public, he receives, in paying that very consideration, the greatest happiness of which his nature is capable; and the greatest blessing that the public can bestow on its members, is to keep them attached to itself. That is the most happy state, which is most beloved by its subjects; and they are the most happy men, whose hearts are engaged to a community, in which they find every object of generosity and zeal, and a scope to the exercise of every talent, and of every virtuous disposition.

After we have thus found general maxims, the greater part of our trouble remains, their just application to particular cases. Nations are different in respect to their extent, numbers of people, and wealth; in respect to the arts they practise, and the accommodations they have procured. These circumstances may not only affect the manners of men; they even, in our esteem, come into competition

competition with the article of manners itſelf; are ſuppoſed to conſtitute a national felicity, independent of virtue; and give a title, upon which we indulge our own vanity, and that of other nations, as we do that of private men, on the ſcore of their fortunes and honours.

But if this way of meaſuring happineſs, when applied to private men, be ruinous and falſe, it is ſo no leſs when applied to nations. Wealth, commerce, extent of territory, and the knowledge of arts, are, when properly employed, the means of preſervation, and the foundations of power. If they fail in part, the nation is weakened; if they were entirely with-held, the race would periſh: their tendency is to maintain numbers of men, but not to conſtitute happineſs. They will accordingly maintain the wretched, as well as the happy. They anſwer one purpoſe, but are not therefore ſufficient for all; and are of little ſignificance, when only employed to maintain a timid, dejected, and ſervile people.

Great and powerful ſtates are able to overcome and ſubdue the weak; poliſhed and commercial nations have more wealth, and practiſe a greater variety of arts, than the rude: but the happineſs of men, in all caſes alike, conſiſts in the bleſſings of a candid, an active, and ſtrenuous mind. And if we conſider the ſtate of ſociety merely as that into which mankind are led by their propenſities, as a ſtate to be valued from its effect in preſerving the ſpecies, in ripening their talents, and exciting their virtues, we need not enlarge our communities, in

order

order to enjoy these advantages. We frequently obtain them in the most remarkable degree, where nations remain independent, and are of a small extent.

To increase the numbers of mankind, may be admitted as a great and important object: but to extend the limits of any particular state, is not, perhaps, the way to obtain it; while we desire that our fellow-creatures should multiply, it does not follow, that the whole should, if possible, be united under one head. We are apt to admire the empire of the Romans, as a model of national greatness and splendour: but the greatness we admire in this case, was ruinous to the virtue and the happiness of mankind; it was found to be inconsistent with all the advantages which that conquering people had formerly enjoyed in the articles of government and manners.

THE emulation of nations proceeds from their division. A cluster of states, like a company of men, find the exercise of their reason, and the test of their virtues, in the affairs they transact, upon a foot of equality, and of separate interest. The measures taken for safety, including great part of the national policy, are relative in every state to what is apprehended from abroad. Athens was necessary to Sparta, in the exercise of her virtue, as steel is to flint in the production of fire; and if the cities of Greece had been united under one head, we should never have heard of Epaminondas or Thrasybulus, of Lycurgus or Solon.

When we reaſon in behalf of our ſpecies, therefore, although we may lament the abuſes which ſometimes ariſe from independence, and oppoſition of intereſt; yet, whilſt any degrees of virtue remain with mankind, we cannot wiſh to croud, under one eſtabliſhment, numbers of men who may ſerve to conſtitute ſeveral; or to commit affairs to the conduct of one ſenate, one legiſlative or executive power, which, upon a diſtinct and ſeparate footing, might furniſh an exerciſe of ability, and a theatre of glory, to many.

This may be a ſubject upon which no determinate rule can be given, but the admiration of boundleſs dominion is a ruinous error; and in no inſtance, perhaps, is the real intereſt of mankind more entirely miſtaken.

The meaſure of enlargement to be wiſhed for any particular ſtate, is often to be taken from the condition of its neighbours. Where a number of ſtates are contiguous, they ſhould be near an equality, in order that they may be mutually objects of reſpect and conſideration, and in order that they may poſſeſs that independence in which the political life of a nation conſiſts.

When the kingdoms of Spain were united, when the great fiefs in France were annexed to the crown, it was no longer expedient for the nations of Great Britain to continue disjoined.

The

THE ſmall republics of Greece, indeed, by their ſubdiviſions, and the balance of their power, found almoſt in every village the object of nations. Every little diſtrict was a nurſery of excellent men, and what is now the wretched corner of a great empire, was the field on which mankind have reaped their principal honours. But in modern Europe, republics of a ſimilar extent, are like ſhrubs, under the ſhade of a taller wood, choked by the neighbourhood of more powerful ſtates. In their caſe, a certain diſproportion of force fruſtrates, in a great meaſure, the advantage of ſeparation. They are like the trader in Poland, who is the more deſpicable, and the leſs ſecure, that he is neither maſter nor ſlave.

INDEPENDENT communities, in the mean time, however weak, are averſe to a coalition, not only where it comes with an air of impoſition, or unequal treaty, but even where it implies no more than the admiſſion of new members to an equal ſhare of conſideration with the old. The citizen has no intereſt in the annexation of kingdoms; he muſt find his importance diminiſhed, as the ſtate is enlarged: but ambitious men, under the enlargement of territory, find a more plentiful harveſt of power, and of wealth, while government itſelf is an eaſier taſk. Hence the ruinous progreſs of empire; and hence free nations, under the ſhew of acquiring dominion, ſuffer themſelves, in the end, to be yoked with the ſlaves they had conquered.

Our desire to augment the force of a nation is the only pretext for enlarging its territory; but this measure, when pursued to extremes, seldom fails to frustrate itself.

Notwithstanding the advantage of numbers, and superior resources in war, the strength of a nation is derived from the character, not from the wealth, nor from the multitude of its people. If the treasure of a state can hire numbers of men, erect ramparts, and furnish the implements of war; the possessions of the fearful are easily seized; a timorous multitude falls into rout of itself; ramparts may be scaled where they are not defended by valour; and arms are of consequence only in the hands of the brave. The band to which Agesilaus pointed as the wall of his city, made a defence for their country more permanent, and more effectual, than the rock and the cement with which other cities were fortified.

We should owe little to that statesman who were to contrive a defence that might supersede the external uses of virtue. It is wisely ordered for man, as a rational being, that the employment of reason is necessary to his preservation: it is fortunate for him, in the pursuit of distinction, that his personal consideration depends on his character; and it is fortunate for nations, that, in order to be powerful and safe, they must strive to maintain the courage, and cultivate the virtues, of their people. By the use of such means, they at once gain their external ends, and are happy.

Peace

PEACE and unanimity are commonly considered as the principal foundations of public felicity; yet the rivalship of separate communities, and the agitations of a free people, are the principles of political life, and the school of men. How shall we reconcile these jarring and opposite tenets? It is, perhaps, not necessary to reconcile them. The pacific may do what they can to allay the animosities, and to reconcile the opinions, of men; and it will be happy if they can succeed in repressing their crimes, and in calming the wo st of their passions. Nothing, in the mean time, but corruption or slavery can suppress the debates that subsist among men of integrity, who bear an equal part in the administration of state.

A perfect agreement in matters of opinion is not to be obtained in the most select company; and if it were, what would become of society? "The Spartan legis-"lator," says Plutarch, "appears to have sown the seeds "of variance and dissension among his countrymen: "he meant that good citizens should be led to dispute; "he considered emulation as the brand by which their "virtues were kindled; and seemed to apprehend, that "a complaisance, by which men submit their opinions "without examination, is a principal source of corrup-"tion."

FORMS of government are supposed to decide of the happiness or misery of mankind. But forms of government must be varied, in order to suit the extent,

the

the way of ſubſiſtence, the character, and the manners of different nations. In ſome caſes, the multitude may be ſuffered to govern themſelves; in others, they muſt be ſeverely reſtrained. The inhabitants of a village in ſome primitive age, may have been ſafely intruſted to the conduct of reaſon, and to the ſuggeſtion of their innocent views; but the tenants of Newgate can ſcarcely be truſted, with chains locked to their bodies, and bars of iron fixed to their legs. How is it poſſible, therefore, to find any ſingle form of government that would ſuit mankind in every condition?

We proceed, however, in the following ſection, to point out the diſtinctions, and to explain the language which occurs in this place, on the head of different models for ſubordination and government.

SECT. X.

The ſame ſubject continued.

It is a common obſervation, That mankind were originally equal. They have indeed by nature equal rights to their preſervation, and to the uſe of their talents; but they are fitted for different ſtations; and when they are claſſed by a rule taken from this circumſtance, they ſuffer no injuſtice on the ſide of their natural rights. It is obvious, that ſome mode of ſubordination

dination is as neceſſary to men as ſociety itſelf; and this, not only to attain the ends of government, but to comply with an order eſtabliſhed by nature.

Prior to any political inſtitution whatever, men are qualified by a great diverſity of talents, by a different tone of the ſoul, and ardour of the paſſions, to act a variety of parts. Bring them together, each will find his place. They cenſure or applaud in a body; they conſult and deliberate in more ſelect parties; they take or give an aſcendant as individuals; and numbers are by this means fitted to act in company, and to preſerve their communities, before any formal diſtribution of office is made.

We are formed to act in this manner; and if we have any doubts with relation to the rights of government in general, we owe our perplexity more to the ſubtilties of the ſpeculative, than to any uncertainty in the feelings of the heart. Involved in the reſolutions of our company, we move with the croud before we have determined the rule by which its will is collected. We follow a leader, before we have ſettled the ground of his pretenſions, or adjuſted the form of his election: and it is not till after mankind have committed many errors in the capacities of magiſtrate and ſubject, that they think of making government itſelf a ſubject of rules.

If therefore, in conſidering the variety of forms under which ſocieties ſubſiſt, the caſuiſt is pleaſed to inquire,

quire, What title one man, or any number of men, have to controul his actions? he may be anſwered, None at all, provided that his actions have no effect to the prejudice of his fellow-creatures; but if they have, the rights of defence, and the obligation to repreſs the commiſſion of wrongs, belong to collective bodies, as well as to individuals. Many rude nations, having no formal tribunals for the judgement of crimes, aſſemble, when alarmed by any flagrant offence, and take their meaſures with the criminal as they would with an enemy.

But will this conſideration, which confirms the title to ſovereignty, where it is exerciſed by the ſociety in its collective capacity, or by thoſe to whom the powers of the whole are committed, likewiſe ſupport the claim to dominion, where-ever it is caſually lodged, or even where it is only maintained by force?

This queſtion may be ſufficiently anſwered, by obſerving, that a right to do juſtice, and to do good, is competent to every individual, or order of men; and that the exerciſe of this right has no limits but in the defect of power. But a right to do wrong, and commit injuſtice, is an abuſe of language, and a contradiction in terms. It is no more competent to the collective body of a people, than it is to any ſingle uſurper. When we admit ſuch a prerogative in the caſe of any ſovereign, we can only mean to expreſs the extent of his power, and the force with which he is enabled to execute his pleaſure. Such a prerogative is aſſumed by the leader

of

of banditti at the head of his gang, or by a despotic prince at the head of his troops. When the sword is presented by either, the traveller or the inhabitant may submit from a sense of necessity or fear; but he lies under no obligation from a motive of duty or justice.

THE multiplicity of forms, in the mean time, which different societies offer to our view, is almost infinite. The classes into which they distribute their members, the manner in which they establish the legislative and executive powers, the imperceptible circumstances by which they are led to have different customs, and to confer on their governors unequal measures of power and authority, give rise to perpetual distinctions between constitutions the most nearly resembling one another, and give to human affairs a variety in detail, which, in its full extent, no understanding can comprehend, and no memory retain.

IN order to have a general and comprehensive knowledge of the whole, we must be determined on this, as on every other subject, to overlook many particulars and singularities, distinguishing different governments; to fix our attention on certain points, in which many agree; and thereby establish a few general heads, under which the subject may be distinctly considered. When we have marked the characteristics which form the general points of coincidence; when we have pursued them to their consequences in the several modes of legiſlation, execution, and judicature, in the eſtabliſhments which relate to police, commerce, religion, or domeſtic life; we have made an acquiſition of knowledge, which, though it does not ſuperſede the neceſſity of experience, may ſerve to direct our inquiries, and, in the midſt of affairs, to give an order and a method for the arrangement of particulars that occur to our obſervation.

When I recollect what the Preſident Monteſquieu has written, I am at a loſs to tell, why I ſhould treat of human affairs: but I too am inſtigated by my reflections, and my ſentiments; and I may utter them more to the comprehenſion of ordinary capacities, becauſe I am more on the level of ordinary men. If it be neceſſary to pave the way for what follows on the general hiſtory of nations, by giving ſome account of the heads under which various forms of government may be conveniently ranged, the reader ſhould perhaps be referred to what has been already delivered on the ſubject by this profound politician and amiable moraliſt. In his writings will be found, not only the original of what I am now, for the ſake of order, to copy from him, but likewiſe probably the ſource of many obſervations, which, in different places, I may, under the belief of invention, have repeated, without quoting their author.

The ancient philoſophers treated of government commonly under three heads; the Democratic, the Ariſtocratic, and the Despotic. Their attention was chiefly occupied with the varieties of republican government; and they paid little regard to a very important distinction, which Mr Montesquieu has made, between despotism and monarchy. He too has considered government as reducible to three general forms; and, " to " understand the nature of each," he observes, " it is " sufficient to recal ideas which are familiar with men " of the least reflection, who admit three definitions, " or rather three facts: That a republic is a state in " which the people in a collective body, or a part of the " people, possess the sovereign power: That monarchy " is that in which one man governs, according to fixed " and determinate laws: And a despotism is that in " which one man, without law, or rule of administra- " tion, by the mere impulse of will or caprice, decides, " and carries every thing before him."

Republics admit of a very material distinction, which is pointed out in the general definition; that between democracy and aristocracy. In the first, supreme power remains in the hands of the collective body. Every office of magistracy, at the nomination of this sovereign, is open to every citizen; who, in the discharge of his duty, becomes the minister of the people, and accountable to them for every object of his trust.

In the second, the sovereignty is lodged in a particular class, or order of men; who, being once named, continue for life; or by the hereditary distinctions of birth and fortune, are advanced to a ſtation of permanent ſuperiority. From this order, and by their nomination, all the offices of magiſtracy are filled; and in the different aſſemblies which they conſtitute, whatever relates to the legiſlation, the execution, or juriſdiction, is finally determined.

Mr Monteſquieu has pointed out the ſentiments or maxims from which men muſt be ſuppoſed to act under theſe different governments.

In democracy, they muſt love equality; they muſt reſpect the rights of their fellow-citizens; they muſt unite by the common ties of affection to the ſtate. In forming perſonal pretenſions, they muſt be ſatisfied with that degree of conſideration they can procure by their abilities fairly meaſured with thoſe of an opponent; they muſt labour for the public without hope of profit; they muſt reject every attempt to create a perſonal dependence. Candour, force, and elevation of mind, in ſhort, are the props of democracy; and virtue is the principle of conduct required to its preſervation.

How beautiful a pre-eminence on the ſide of popular government! and how ardently ſhould mankind wiſh for the form, if it tended to eſtabliſh the principle, or were, in every inſtance, a ſure indication of its preſence!

But

But perhaps we must have possessed the principle, in order, with any hopes of advantage, to receive the form; and where the first is entirely extinguished, the other may be fraught with evil, if any additional evil deserves to be shunned where men are already unhappy.

At Constantinople or Algiers, it is a miserable spectacle when men pretend to act on a foot of equality: they only mean to shake off the restraints of government, and to seize as much as they can of that spoil, which, in ordinary times, is ingrossed by the master they serve.

It is one advantage of democracy, that the principal ground of distinction being personal qualities, men are classed according to their abilities, and to the merit of their actions. Though all have equal pretensions to power, yet the state is actually governed by a few. The majority of the people, even in their capacity of sovereign, only pretend to employ their senses; to feel, when pressed by national inconveniencies, or threatened by public dangers; and with the ardour which is apt to arise in crouded assemblies, to urge the pursuits in which they are engaged, or to repel the attacks with which they are menaced.

The most perfect equality of rights can never exclude the ascendant of superior minds, nor the assemblies of a collective body govern without the direction of se-

lect

lect councils. On this account, popular government may be confounded with ariſtocracy. But this alone does not conſtitute the character of ariſtocratical government. Here the members of the ſtate are divided, at leaſt, into two claſſes; of which one is deſtined to command, the other to obey. No merits or defects can raiſe or ſink a perſon from one claſs to the other. The only effect of perſonal character is, to procure the individual a ſuitable degree of conſideration with his own order, not to vary his rank. In one ſituation he is taught to aſſume, in another to yield the pre-eminence. He occupies the ſtation of patron or client, and is either the ſovereign or the ſubject of his country. The whole citizens may unite in executing the plans of ſtate, but never in deliberating on its meaſures, or enacting its laws. What belongs to the whole people under democracy, is here confined to a part. Members of the ſuperior order, are among themſelves, poſſibly, claſſed according to their abilities, but retain a perpetual aſcendant over thoſe of inferior ſtation. They are at once the ſervants and the maſters of the ſtate, and pay with their perſonal attendance and their blood for the civil or military honours they enjoy.

To maintain for himſelf, and to admit in his fellow-citizen, a perfect equality of privilege and ſtation, is no longer the leading maxim of the member of ſuch a community. The rights of men are modified by their condition. One order claims more than it is willing to yield; the

the other muſt be ready to yield what it does not aſſume to itſelf: and it is with good reaſon that Mr Monteſquieu gives to the principle of ſuch governments the name of *moderation*, not of *virtue*.

THE elevation of one claſs is a moderated arrogance; the ſubmiſſion of the other a limited deference. The firſt muſt be careful, by concealing the invidious part of their diſtinction, to palliate what is grievous in the public arrangement, and by their education, their cultivated manners, and improved talents, to appear qualified for the ſtations they occupy. The other muſt be taught to yield, from reſpect and perſonal attachment, what could not otherwiſe be extorted by force. When this moderation fails on either ſide, the conſtitution totters. A populace enraged to mutiny, may claim the right of equality to which they are admitted in democratical ſtates; or a nobility bent on dominion, may chuſe among themſelves, or find already pointed out to them, a ſovereign, who, by advantages of fortune, popularity, or abilities, is ready to ſeize for his own family, that envied power, which has already carried his order beyond the limits of moderation, and infected particular men with a boundleſs ambition.

MONARCHIES have accordingly been found with the recent marks of ariſtocracy. There, however, the monarch is only the firſt among the nobles; he muſt be ſatisfied with a limited power; his ſubjects are ranged into claſſes; he finds on every quarter a pretence to privi-

lege,

lege, that circumſcribes his authority; and he finds a force ſufficient to confine his adminiſtration within certain bounds of equity, and determinate laws.

UNDER ſuch governments, however, the love of equality is prepoſterous, and moderation itſelf is unneceſſary. The object of every rank is precedency, and every order may diſplay its advantages to their full extent. The ſovereign himſelf owes great part of his authority to the ſounding titles and the dazzling equipage which he exhibits in public. The ſubordinate ranks lay claim to importance by a like exhibition, and for that purpoſe carry in every inſtant the enſigns of their birth, or the ornaments of their fortune. What elſe could mark out to the individual the relation in which he ſtands to his fellow-ſubjects, or diſtinguiſh the numberleſs ranks that fill up the interval between the ſtate of the ſovereign and that of the peaſant? Or what elſe could, in ſtates of a great extent, preſerve any appearance of order, among members diſunited by ambition and intereſt, and deſtined to form a community, without the ſenſe of any common concern?

MONARCHIES are generally found, where the ſtate is enlarged in population and in territory, beyond the numbers and dimenſions that are conſiſtent with republican government. Together with theſe circumſtances, great inequalities ariſe in the diſtribution of property; and the deſire of pre-eminence becomes the predominant paſſion. Every rank would exerciſe its prerogative, and the ſovereign

reign is perpetually tempted to enlarge his own; if subjects, who despair of precedence, plead for equality, he is willing to favour their claims, and to aid them in procuring what must weaken a force, with which he himself is, on many occasions, obliged to contend. In the event of such a policy, many invidious distinctions and grievances peculiar to monarchical government, may, in appearance, be removed; but the state of equality to which the subjects approach, is that of slaves, equally dependent on the will of a master, not that of freemen in a condition to maintain their own.

The principle of monarchy, according to Montesquieu, is honour. Men may possess good qualities, elevation of mind, and fortitude; but the sense of equality, that will bear no incroachment on the personal rights of the meanest citizen; the indignant spirit, that will not court a protection, nor accept as a favour, what is due as a right; the public affection, which is founded on the neglect of personal considerations, are neither consistent with the preservation of the constitution, nor agreeable to the habits acquired in any station assigned to its members.

Every condition is possessed of peculiar dignity, and points out a propriety of conduct, which men of station are obliged to maintain. In the commerce of superiors and inferiors, it is the object of ambition, and of vanity, to refine on the advantages of rank; while, to facilitate the intercourſe of polite ſociety, it is the aim of good breeding, to diſguiſe or reject them.

THOUGH the objects of conſideration are rather the dignities of ſtation than perſonal qualities; though friendſhip cannot be formed by mere inclination, nor alliances by the mere choice of the heart; yet men ſo united, and even without changing their order, are highly ſuſceptible of moral excellence, or liable to many different degrees of corruption. They may act a vigorous part as members of the ſtate, an amiable one in the commerce of private ſociety; or they may yield up their dignity as citizens, even while they raiſe their arrogance and preſumption as private parties.

IN monarchy, all orders of men derive their honours from the crown; but they continue to hold them as a right, and they exerciſe a ſubordinate power in the ſtate, founded on the permanent rank they enjoy, and on the attachment of thoſe whom they are appointed to lead and protect. Though they do not force themſelves into national councils, and public aſſemblies, and though the name of ſenate is unknown; yet the ſentiments they adopt muſt have weight with the ſovereign; and every individual, in his ſeparate capacity, in ſome meaſure, deliberates for his country. In whatever does not derogate from his rank, he has an arm ready to ſerve the community; in whatever alarms his ſenſe of honour, he has averſions and diſlikes, which amount to a negative on the will of his prince.

INTANGLED

INTANGLED together by the reciprocal ties of dependence and protection, though not combined by the ſenſe of a common intereſt, the ſubjects of monarchy, like thoſe of republics, find themſelves occupied as the members of an active ſociety, and engaged to treat with their fellow-creatures on a liberal footing. If thoſe principles of honour which ſave the individual from ſervility in his own perſon, or from becoming an engine of oppreſſion in the hands of another, ſhould fail; if they ſhould give way to the maxims of commerce, to the refinements of a ſuppoſed philoſophy, or to the miſplaced ardours of a republican ſpirit; if they are betrayed by the cowardice of ſubjects, or ſubdued by the ambition of princes; what muſt become of the nations of Europe?

DESPOTISM is monarchy corrupted, in which a court and a prince in appearance remain, but in which every ſubordinate rank is deſtroyed; in which the ſubject is told, that he has no rights; that he cannot poſſeſs any property, nor fill any ſtation, independent of the momentary will of his prince. Theſe doctrines are founded on the maxims of conqueſt; they muſt be inculcated with the whip and the ſword; and are beſt received under the terror of chains and impriſonment. Fear, therefore, is the principle which qualifies the ſubject to occupy his ſtation: and the ſovereign, who holds out the enſigns of terror ſo freely to others, has abundant reaſon to give this paſſion a principal place with himſelf. That tenure which he has deviſed for the rights of others, is ſoon applied to his own; and from his eager deſire to ſecure, or to extend, his power, he finds it become, like the fortunes of his people, a creature of mere imagination and unſettled caprice.

WHILST we thus, with ſo much accuracy, can aſſign the ideal limits that may diſtinguiſh conſtitutions of government, we find them, in reality, both in reſpect to the principle and the form, variouſly blended together. In what ſociety are not men claſſed by external diſtinctions, as well as perſonal qualities? In what ſtate are they not actuated by a variety of principles; juſtice, honour, moderation, and fear? It is the purpoſe of ſcience, not to diſguiſe this confuſion in its object, but, in the multiplicity and combination of particulars, to find the principal points which deſerve our attention, and which, being well underſtood, ſave us from the embarraſſment which the varieties of ſingular caſes might otherwiſe create. In the ſame degree in which governments require men to act from principles of virtue, of honour, or of fear, they are more or leſs fully compriſed under the heads of republic, monarchy, or deſpotiſm, and the general theory is more or leſs applicable to their particular caſe.

FORMS of government, in fact, mutually approach or recede by many, and often inſenſible gradations. Democracy, by admitting certain inequalities of rank, approaches to ariſtocracy. In popular, as well as ariſtocratical governments, particular men, by their perſonal authority, and ſometimes by the credit of their fami-ly, ly, have maintained a ſpecies of monarchical power. The monarch is limited in different degrees: even the deſpotic prince is only that monarch whoſe ſubjects claim the feweſt privileges, or who is himſelf beſt prepared to ſubdue them by force. All theſe varieties are but ſteps in the hiſtory of mankind, and mark the fleeting and tranſient ſituations through which they have paſſed, while ſupported by virtue, or depreſſed by vice.

PERFECT democracy and deſpotiſm appear to be the oppoſite extremes to which conſtitutions of government are ſometimes carried. Under the firſt, a perfect virtue is required; under the ſecond, a total corruption is ſuppoſed: yet in point of mere form, there being nothing fixed in the ranks and diſtinctions of men, beyond the caſual and temporary poſſeſſion of power, ſocieties eaſily paſs from a condition in which every individual has an equal title to reign, into one in which they are equally deſtined to ſerve. The ſame qualities in both, courage, popularity, addreſs, and military conduct, raiſe the ambitious to eminence. With theſe qualities, the citizen or the ſlave eaſily paſſes from the ranks to the command of an army, from an obſcure to an illuſtrious ſtation. In either, a ſingle perſon may rule with unlimited ſway; and in both, the populace may break down every barrier of order, and reſtraint of law.

IF we ſuppoſe that the equality eſtabliſhed among the ſubjects of a deſpotic ſtate, has inſpired its members with confidence, intrepidity, and the love of juſtice; the deſpotic

ſpotic prince, having ceaſed to be an object of fear, muſt ſink among the croud. If, on the contrary, the perſonal equality which is enjoyed by the members of a democratical ſtate, ſhould be valued merely as an equal pretenſion to the objects of avarice and ambition, the monarch may ſtart up anew, and be ſupported by thoſe who mean to ſhare in his profits. When the covetous and mercenary aſſemble in parties, it is of no conſequence under what leader they inliſt, whether Cæſar or Pompey; the hopes of rapine or power are the only motives from which they become attached to either.

In the diſorder of corrupted ſocieties, the ſcene has been frequently changed from democracy to deſpotiſm, and from the laſt too, in its turn, to the firſt. From amidſt the democracy of corrupt men, and from a ſcene of lawleſs confuſion, the tyrant aſcends a throne with arms reeking in blood. But his abuſes, or his weakneſſes, in the ſtation which he has gained, in their turn, awaken and give way to the ſpirit of mutiny and revenge. The cries of murder and deſolation, which in the ordinary courſe of military government terrified the ſubject in his private retreat, are carried through the vaults, and made to pierce the grates and iron doors of the ſeraglio. Democracy ſeems to revive in a ſcene of wild diſorder and tumult: but both the extremes are but the tranſient fits of paroxyſm or languor in a diſtempered ſtate.

If men be any where arrived at this meaſure of depravity, there appears no immediate hope of redreſs. Neither the aſcendency of the multitude, nor that of the tyrant, will ſecure the adminiſtration of juſtice: neither the licence of mere tumult, nor the calm of dejection and ſervitude, will teach the citizen that he was born for candour and affection to his fellow creatures. And if the ſpeculative would find that habitual ſtate of war which they are ſometimes pleaſed to honour with the name of *the ſtate of nature*, they will find it in the conteſt that ſubſiſts between the deſpotical prince and his ſubjects, not in the firſt approaches of a rude and ſimple tribe to the condition and the domeſtic arrangement of nations.

PART

PART SECOND.

Of the Hiſtory of Rude Nations.

SECT. I.

Of the Informations on this ſubject which are derived from Antiquity.

THE hiſtory of mankind is confined within a limited period, and from every quarter brings an intimation that human affairs have had a beginning. Nations, diſtinguiſhed by the poſſeſſion of arts, and the felicity of their political eſtabliſhments, have been derived from a feeble original, and ſtill preſerve in their ſtory the indications of a ſlow and gradual progreſs, by which this diſtinction was gained. The antiquities of every people, however diverſified, and however diſguiſed, contain the ſame information on this point.

IN ſacred hiſtory, we find the parents of the ſpecies, as yet a ſingle pair, ſent forth to inherit the earth, and

to

to force a ſubſiſtence for themſelves amidſt the briers and thorns which were made to abound on its ſurface. Their race, which was again reduced to a few, had to ſtruggle with the dangers that await a weak and infant ſpecies; and after many ages elapſed, the moſt reſpectable nations took their riſe from one or a few families that had paſtured their flocks in the deſert.

THE Grecians derive their own origin from unſettled tribes, whoſe frequent migrations are a proof of the rude and infant ſtate of their communities; and whoſe warlike exploits, ſo much celebrated in ſtory, only exhibit the ſtruggles with which they diſputed for the poſſeſſion of a country they afterwards, by their talent for fable, by their arts, and their policy, rendered ſo famous in the hiſtory of mankind.

ITALY muſt have been divided into many rude and feeble cantons, when a band of robbers, as we are taught to conſider them, found a ſecure ſettlement on the banks of the Tiber, and when a people, yet compoſed only of one ſex, ſuſtained the character of a nation. Rome, for many ages, ſaw, from her walls, on every ſide, the territory of her enemies, and found as little to check or to ſtifle the weakneſs of her infant power, as ſhe did afterwards to reſtrain the progreſs of her extended empire. Like a Tartar or a Scythian horde, which had pitched on a ſettlement, this naſcent community was equal, if not ſuperior, to every tribe in its neighbourhood; and the oak which has covered the field with its ſhade, was once a feeble plant in the nurſery, and not to be diſtinguiſhed from the weeds by which its early growth was reſtrained.

THE Gauls and the Germans are come to our knowledge with the marks of a ſimilar condition; and the inhabitants of Britain, at the time of the firſt Roman invaſions, reſembled, in many things, the preſent natives of North America: they were ignorant of agriculture; they painted their bodies; and uſed for cloathing, the ſkins of beaſts.

SUCH therefore appears to have been the commencement of hiſtory with all nations, and in ſuch circumſtances are we to look for the original character of mankind. The inquiry refers to a diſtant period, and every concluſion ſhould build on the facts which are preſerved for our uſe. Our method, notwithſtanding, too frequently, is to reſt the whole on conjecture; to impute every advantage of our nature to thoſe arts which we ourſelves poſſeſs; and to imagine, that a mere negation of all our virtues is a ſufficient deſcription of man in his original ſtate. We are ourſelves the ſuppoſed ſtandards of politeneſs and civilization; and where our own features do not appear, we apprehend, that there is nothing which deſerves to be known. But it is probable that here, as in many other caſes, we are ill qualified, from our ſuppoſed knowledge of cauſes, to prognoſticate effects, or to determine what muſt have been the properties and operations, even of our own nature, in the abſence of

thoſe

those circumstances in which we have seen it engaged. Who would, from mere conjecture, suppose, that the naked savage would be a coxcomb and a gamester? that he would be proud and vain, without the distinctions of title and fortune? and that his principal care would be to adorn his person, and to find an amusement? Even if it could be supposed that he would thus share in our vices, and, in the midst of his forest, vie with the follies which are practised in the town; yet no one would be so bold as to affirm, that he would likewise, in any instance, excel us in talents and virtues; that he would have a penetration, a force of imagination and elocution, an ardour of mind, an affection and courage, which the arts, the discipline, and the policy of few nations would be able to improve. Yet these particulars are a part in the description which is delivered by those who have had opportunities of seeing mankind in their rudest condition: and beyond the reach of such testimony, we can neither safely take, nor pretend to give, information on the subject.

If conjectures and opinions formed at a distance, have not sufficient authority in the history of mankind, the domestic antiquities of every nation must, for this very reason, be received with caution. They are, for most part, the mere conjectures or the fictions of subsequent ages; and even where at first they contained some resemblance of truth, they still vary with the imagination of those by whom they are transmitted, and in every generation receive a different form. They are made to bear the ſtamp of the times through which they have paſſed in the form of tradition, not of the ages to which their pretended deſcriptions relate. The information they bring, is not like the light reflected from a mirrour, which delineates the object from which it originally came; but, like rays that come broken and diſperſed from an opaque or unpoliſhed ſurface, only give the colours and features of the body from which they were laſt reflected.

When traditionary fables are rehearſed by the vulgar, they bear the marks of a national character; and though mixed with abſurdities, often raiſe the imagination, and move the heart: when made the materials of poetry, and adorned by the ſkill and the eloquence of an ardent and ſuperior mind, they inſtruct the underſtanding, as well as engage the paſſions. It is only in the management of mere antiquaries, or ſtript of the ornaments which the laws of hiſtory forbid them to wear, that they become even unfit to amuſe the fancy, or to ſerve any purpoſe whatever.

It were abſurd to quote the fable of the Iliad or the Odyſſey, the legends of Hercules, Theſeus, or OEdipus, as authorities in matter of fact relating to the hiſtory of mankind; but they may, with great juſtice, be cited to aſcertain what were the conceptions and ſentiments of the age in which they were compoſed, or to characteriſe the genius of that people, with whoſe imagina-
tions

tions they were blended, and by whom they were fondly rehearſed and admired.

In this manner fiction may be admitted to vouch for the genius of nations, while hiſtory has nothing to offer that is intitled to credit. The Greek fable accordingly conveying a character of its authors, throws light on an age of which no other record remains. The ſuperiority of this people is indeed in no circumſtance more evident than in the ſtrain of their fictions, and in the ſtory of thoſe fabulous heroes, poets, and ſages, whoſe tales, being invented or embelliſhed by an imagination already filled with the ſubject for which the hero was celebrated, ſerved to inflame that ardent enthuſiaſm with which this people afterwards proceeded in the purſuit of every national object.

It was no doubt of great advantage to thoſe nations, that their ſyſtem of fable was original, and being already received in popular traditions, ſerved to diffuſe thoſe improvements of reaſon, imagination, and ſentiment, which were afterwards, by men of the fineſt talents, made on the fable itſelf, or conveyed in its moral. The paſſions of the poet pervaded the minds of the people, and the conceptions of men of genius being communicated to the vulgar, became the incentives of a national ſpirit.

A mythology borrowed from abroad, a literature founded on references to a ſtrange country, and fraught with

with foreign allusions, are much more confined in their use: they speak to the learned alone; and though intended to inform the understanding, and to mend the heart, may, by being confined to a few, have an opposite effect: they may foster conceit on the ruins of common sense, and render what was, at least innocently, sung by the Athenian mariner at his oar, or rehearsed by the shepherd in attending his flock, an occasion of vice, and the foundation of pedantry and scholastic pride.

OUR very learning, perhaps, where its influence extends, serves, in some measure, to depress our national spirit. Our literature being derived from nations of a different race, who flourished at a time when our ancestors were in a state of barbarity, and consequently when they were despised by those who had attained to the literary arts, has given rise to a humbling opinion, that we ourselves are the offspring of mean and contemptible nations, with whom the human imagination and sentiment had no effect, till the genius was in a manner inspired by examples, and directed by lessons that were brought from abroad. The Romans, from whom our accounts are chiefly derived, have admitted, in the rudeness of their own ancestors, a system of virtues, which all simple nations perhaps equally possess; a contempt of riches, love of their country, patience of hardship, danger, and fatigue. They have, notwithstanding, vilified our ancestors for having perhaps only resembled their own; at least, in the defect of their arts, and in the neglect of conveniencies which those arts are employed to procure.

It is from the Greek and the Roman historians, however, that we have not only the most authentic and instructive, but even the most engaging, representations of the tribes from whom we descend. Those sublime and intelligent writers understood human nature, and could collect its features, and exhibit its characters in every situation. They were ill succeeded in this task by the early historians of modern Europe; who, generally bred to the profession of monks, and confined to the monastic life, applied themselves to record what they were pleased to denominate facts, while they suffered the productions of genius to perish, and were unable, either by the matter they selected, or the style of their compositions, to give any representation of the active spirit of mankind in any condition. With them, a narration was supposed to constitute history, whilst it did not convey any knowledge of men; and history itself was allowed to be complete, while, amidst the events and the succession of princes that are recorded in the order of time, we are left to look in vain for those characteristics of the understanding and the heart, which alone, in every human transaction, render the story either engaging or useful.

We therefore willingly quit the history of our early ancestors, where Cæsar and Tacitus have dropped them; and perhaps, till we come within the reach of what is connected with present affairs, and makes a part in the ſyſtem on which we now proceed, have little reaſon to expect any ſubject to intereſt or inform the mind. We have no reaſon, however, from hence to conclude, that the matter itſelf was more barren, or the ſcene of human affairs leſs intereſting, in modern Europe, than it has been on every ſtage where mankind were engaged to exhibit the movements of the heart, the efforts of generoſity, magnanimity, and courage.

THE trial of what thoſe ages contained, is not even fairly made, when men of genius and diſtinguiſhed abilities, with the accompliſhments of a learned and a poliſhed age, collect the materials they have found, and, with the greateſt ſucceſs, connect the ſtory of illiterate ages with tranſactions of a later date: it is difficult even for them, under the names which are applied in a new ſtate of ſociety, to convey a juſt apprehenſion of what mankind were in ſituations ſo different, and in times ſo remote from their own.

IN deriving from hiſtorians of this character the inſtruction which their writings are fit to beſtow, we are frequently to forget the general terms that are employed, in order to collect the real manners of an age, from the minute circumſtances that are occaſionally preſented. The titles of *Royal* and *Noble* were applicable to the families of Tarquin, Collatinus, and Cincinnatus; but Lucretia was employed in domeſtic induſtry with her maids, and Cincinnatus followed the plough. The dignities, and even the offices, of civil ſociety, were known many

ages

ages ago, in Europe, by their present appellations; but we find in the hiſtory of England, that a king and his court being aſſembled to ſolemnize a feſtival, an outlaw, who had ſubſiſted by robbery, came to ſhare in the feaſt. The king himſelf aroſe to force this unworthy gueſt from the company, a ſcuffle enſued between them, and the king was killed *. A chancellor and prime miniſter, whoſe magnificence and ſumptuous furniture were the ſubject of admiration and envy, had his apartments covered every day in winter with clean ſtraw and hay, and in ſummer with green ruſhes or boughs. Even the ſovereign himſelf, in thoſe ages, was provided with forage for his bed †. Theſe picturesque features and characteriſtical ſtrokes of the times, recal the imagination from the ſuppoſed diſtinction of monarch and ſubject, to that ſtate of rough familiarity in which our anceſtors lived, and under which they acted, with a view to objects, and on principles of conduct, which we ſeldom comprehend, when we are employed to record their tranſactions, or to ſtudy their characters.

THUCYDIDES, notwithſtanding the prejudice of his country againſt the name of *Barbarian*, underſtood that it was in the cuſtoms of barbarous nations he was to ſtudy the more ancient manners of Greece.

THE Romans might have found an image of their own anceſtors, in the repreſentations they have given of ours: and if ever an Arab clan ſhall become a civilized nation, or

* Hume's Hiſtory, ch. 8. p. 278.

† Ibid. p. 73.

any American tribe eſcape the poiſon which is adminiſtered by our traders of Europe, it may be from the relations of the preſent times, and the deſcriptions which are now given by travellers, that ſuch a people, in after ages, may beſt collect the accounts of their origin. It is in their preſent condition, that we are to behold, as in a mirrour, the features of our own progenitors; and from thence we are to draw our concluſions with reſpect to the influence of ſituations, in which, we have reaſon to believe, our fathers were placed.

WHAT ſhould diſtinguiſh a German or a Briton, in the habits of his mind or his body, in his manners or apprehenſions, from an American, who, like him, with his bow and his dart, is left to traverſe the foreſt; and in a like ſevere or variable climate, is obliged to ſubſiſt by the chace?

IF, in advanced years, we would form a juſt notion of our progreſs from the cradle, we muſt have recourſe to the nurſery, and from the example of thoſe who are ſtill in the period of life we mean to deſcribe, take our repreſentation of paſt manners, that cannot, in any other way, be recalled.

SECT. II.

Of Rude Nations prior to the Eſtabliſhment of Property.

FROM one to the other extremity of America; from Kamſchatka weſtward to the river Oby, and from the Northern ſea, over that length of country, to the confines of China, of India, and Perſia; from the Caſpian to the Red ſea, with little exception, and from thence over the inland continent and the weſtern ſhores of Africa; we every where meet with nations on whom we beſtow the appellations of barbarous or ſavage. That extenſive tract of the earth, containing ſo great a variety of ſituation, climate, and ſoil, ſhould, in the manners of its inhabitants, exhibit all the diverſities which ariſe from the unequal influence of the ſun, joined to a different nouriſhment and manner of life. Every queſtion, however, on this ſubject is premature, till we have firſt endeavoured to form ſome general conception of our ſpecies in its rude ſtate, and have learned to diſtinguiſh mere ignorance from dullneſs, and the want of arts from the want of capacity.

OF the nations who dwell in thoſe, or any other of the leſs cultivated parts of the earth, ſome intruſt their ſubſiſtence chiefly to hunting, fiſhing, or the natural produce of the ſoil. They have little attention to property, and ſcarcely any beginnings of ſubordination or government. Others having poſſeſſed themſelves of herds, and depending for their provifion on pafture, know what it is to be poor and rich. They know the relations of patron and client, of fervant and mafter, and fuffer themfelves to be claffed according to their meafures of wealth. This diftinction muft create a material difference of character, and may furnifh two feparate heads, under which to confider the hiftory of mankind in their rudeft ftate; that of the favage, who is not yet acquainted with property; and that of the barbarian, to whom it is, although not afcertained by laws, a principal object of care and defire.

It muft appear very evident, that property is a matter of progrefs. It requires, among other particulars which are the effects of time, fome method of defining poffeffion. The very defire of it proceeds from experience; and the induftry by which it is gained, or improved, requires fuch a habit of acting with a view to diftant objects, as may overcome the prefent difpofition either to floth or to enjoyment. This habit is flowly acquired, and is in reality a principal diftinction of nations in the advanced ftate of mechanic and commercial arts.

In a tribe which fubfifts by hunting and fifhing, the arms, the utenfils, and the fur, which the individual carries, are to him the only fubjects of property. The food of to-morrow is yet wild in the foreft, or hid in the lake; it cannot be appropriated before it is caught; and even then, being the purchafe of numbers, who fifh or hunt in a body, it accrues to the community, and is applied

plied to immediate use, or becomes an accession to the stores of the public.

Where savage nations, as in most parts of America, mix with the practice of hunting some species of rude agriculture, they still follow, with respect to the soil and the fruits of the earth, the analogy of their principal object. As the men hunt, so the women labour together; and, after they have shared the toils of the seed-time, they enjoy the fruits of the harvest in common. The field in which they have planted, like the district over which they are accustomed to hunt, is claimed as a property by the nation, but is not parcelled in lots to its members. They go forth in parties to prepare the ground, to plant, and to reap. The harvest is gathered into the public granary, and from thence, at stated times, is divided into shares for the maintenance of separate families *. Even the returns of the market, when they trade with foreigners, are brought home to the stock of the nation †.

As the fur and the bow pertain to the individual, the cabbin and its utensils are appropriated to the family; and as the domestic cares are committed to the women, so the property of the household seems likewise to be vested in them. The children are considered as pertaining to the mother, with little regard to descent on the father's side. The males, before they are married, remain in the cab-

* History of the Caribbees.

† Charlevoix.

bin

bin in which they are born; but after they have formed a new connection with the other ſex, they change their habitation, and become an acceſſion to the family in which they have found their wives. The hunter and the warrior are numbered by the matron as a part of her treaſure; they are reſerved for perils and trying occaſions; and in the receſs of public councils, in the intervals of hunting or war, are maintained by the cares of the women, and loiter about in mere amuſement or ſloth *.

WHILE one ſex continue to value themſelves chiefly on their courage, their talent for policy, and their warlike atchievments, this ſpecies of property which is beſtowed on the other, is in reality a mark of ſubjection; not, as ſome writers alledge, of their having acquired an aſcendant †. It is the care and trouble of a ſubject with which the warrior does not chuſe to be embarraſſed. It is a ſervitude, and a continual toil, where no honours are won; and they whoſe province it is, are in fact the ſlaves and the helots of their country. If in this deſtination of the ſexes, while the men continue to indulge themſelves in the contempt of ſordid and mercenary arts, the cruel eſtabliſhment of ſlavery is for ſome ages deferred; if in this tender, though unequal alliance, the affections of the heart prevent the ſeverities practiſed on ſlaves; we have in the cuſtom itſelf, as perhaps in many other inſtances, reaſon to prefer the firſt ſuggeſtions of nature, to many of her after refinements.

* Lafitau.

† Ibid.

If mankind, in any instance, continue the article of property on the footing we have now represented, we may easily credit what is farther reported by travellers, that they admit of no distinctions of rank or condition; and that they have in fact no degree of subordination different from the distribution of function, which follows the differences of age, talents, and dispositions. Personal qualities give an ascendant in the midst of occasions which require their exertion; but in times of relaxation, leave no vestige of power or prerogative. A warrior who has led the youth of his nation to the slaughter of their enemies, or who has been foremost in the chace, returns upon a level with the rest of his tribe; and when the only business is to sleep, or to feed, can enjoy no pre-eminence; for he sleeps and he feeds no better than they.

Where no profit attends dominion, one party is as much averse to the trouble of perpetual command, as the other is to the mortification of perpetual submission: "I love victory, I love great actions," says Montesquieu in the character of Sylla; "but have no relish for the languid detail of pacific government, or the pageantry of high station." He has touched perhaps what is a prevailing sentiment in the simplest state of society, when the weakness of motives suggested by interest, and the ignorance of any elevation not founded on merit, supplies the place of disdain.

The

THE character of the mind, however, in this ſtate, is not founded on ignorance alone. Men are conſcious of their equality, and are tenacious of its rights. Even when they follow a leader to the field, they cannot brook the pretenſions to a formal command: they liſten to no orders; and they come under no military engagements, but thoſe of mutual fidelity, and equal ardour in the enterpriſe *.

THIS deſcription, we may believe, is unequally applicable to different nations, who have made unequal advances in the eſtabliſhment of property. Among the Caribbees, and the other natives of the warmer climates in America, the dignity of chieftain is hereditary, or elective, and continued for life: the unequal diſtribution of property creates a viſible ſubordination †. But among the Iroquois, and other nations of the temperate zone, the titles of *magiſtrate* and *ſubject*, of *noble* and *mean*, are as little known as thoſe of *rich* and *poor*. The old men, without being inveſted with any coercive power, employ their natural authority in adviſing or in prompting the reſolutions of their tribe: the military leader is pointed out by the ſuperiority of his manhood and valour: the ſtateſman is diſtinguiſhed only by the attention with which his counſel is heard; the warrior by the confidence with which the youth of his nation follow him to the field: and if their concerts muſt

* Charlevoix.

† Wafer's account of the Iſthmus of Darien.

be

be supposed to constitute a species of political government, it is one to which no language of ours can be applied. Power is no more than the natural ascendency of the mind; the discharge of office no more than a natural exercise of the personal character; and while the community acts with an appearance of order, there is no sense of disparity in the breast of any of its members *.

In these happy, though informal, proceedings, where age alone gives a place in the council; where youth, ardour, and valour in the field, give a title to the station of leader; where the whole community is assembled on any alarming occasion, we may venture to say, that we have found the origin of the senate, the executive power, and the assembly of the people; institutions for which ancient legislators have been so much renowned. The senate among the Greeks, as well as the Latins, appears, from the etymology of its name, to have been originally composed of elderly men. The military leader at Rome, in a manner not unlike to that of the American warrior, proclaimed his levies, and the citizen prepared for the field, in consequence of a voluntary engagement. The suggestions of nature, which directed the policy of nations in the wilds of America, were followed before on the banks of the Eurotas and the Tyber; and Lycurgus and Romulus found the model of their institutions where the members of every rude

* Colden's history of the Five Nations.

nation find the earlieſt mode of uniting their talents, and combining their forces.

AMONG the North-American nations, every individual is independent; but he is engaged by his affections and his habits in the cares of a family. Families, like ſo many ſeparate tribes, are ſubject to no inſpection or government from abroad; whatever paſſes at home, even bloodſhed and murder, are only ſuppoſed to concern themſelves. They are, in the mean time, the parts of a canton; the women aſſemble to plant their maize; the old men go to council; the huntſman and the warrior joins the youth of his village in the field. Many ſuch cantons aſſemble to conſtitute a national council, or to execute a national enterpriſe. When the Europeans made their firſt ſettlements in America, ſix ſuch nations had formed a league, had their amphyctiones or ſtates-general, and, by the firmneſs of their union, and the ability of their councils, had obtained an aſcendant from the mouth of the St Laurence to that of the Miſſiſippi *. They appeared to underſtand the objects of the confederacy, as well as thoſe of the ſeparate nation; they ſtudied a balance of power; the ſtateſman of one country watched the deſigns and proceedings of another; and occaſionally threw the weight of his tribe into a different ſcale. They had their alliances and their treaties, which, like the nations of Europe, they maintained, or they broke, upon reaſons of ſtate; and re-

* Lafitau, Charlevoix, Colden, *&c.*

mained at peace from a sense of necessity or expediency, and went to war upon any emergence of provocation or jealousy.

THUS, without any settled form of government, or any bond of union, but what resembled more the suggestion of instinct, than the invention of reason, they conducted themselves with the concert, and the force, of nations. Foreigners, without being able to discover who is the magistrate, or in what manner the senate is composed, always find a council with whom they may treat, or a band of warriors with whom they may fight. Without police or compulsory laws, their domestic society is conducted with order, and the absence of vicious dispositions, is a better security than any public establishment for the suppression of crimes.

DISORDERS, however, sometimes occur, especially in times of debauch, when the immoderate use of intoxicating liquors, to which they are extremely addicted, suspends the ordinary caution of their demeanour, and inflaming their violent passions, engages them in quarrels and bloodshed. When a person is slain, his murderer is seldom called to an immediate account: but he has a quarrel to sustain with the family and the friends; or, if a stranger, with the countrymen of the deceased; sometimes even with his own nation at home, if the injury committed be of a kind to alarm the society. The nation, the canton, or the family, endeavour, by presents, to atone for the offence of any of their members;

 and,

and, by pacifying the parties aggrieved, endeavour to prevent what alarms the community more than the firſt diſorder, the ſubſequent effects of revenge and animoſity *. The ſhedding of blood, however, if the guilty perſon remain where he has committed the crime, ſeldom eſcapes unpuniſhed: the friend of the deceaſed knows how to diſguiſe, though not to ſuppreſs, his reſentment; and even after many years have elapſed, is ſure to repay the injury that was done to his kindred or his houſe.

These conſiderations render them cautious and circumſpect, put them on their guard againſt their paſſions, and give to their ordinary deportment an air of phlegm and compoſure ſuperior to what is poſſeſſed among poliſhed nations. They are, in the mean time, affectionate in their carriage, and in their converſations pay a mutual attention and regard, ſays Charlevoix, more tender and more engaging, than what we profeſs in the ceremonial of poliſhed ſocieties.

This writer has obſerved, that the nations among whom he travelled in North America, never mentioned acts of generoſity or kindneſs under the notion of duty. They acted from affection, as they acted from appetite, without regard to its conſequences. When they had done a kindneſs, they had gratified a deſire; the buſineſs was fi-

* Lafitau.

niſhed,

nished, and it passed from the memory. When they received a favour, it might, or it might not, prove the occasion of friendship: if it did not, the parties appeared to have no apprehensions of gratitude, as a duty by which the one was bound to make a return, or the other intitled to reproach the person who had failed in his part. The spirit with which they give or receive presents, is the same which Tacitus observed among the ancient Germans: They delight in them, but do not consider them as matter of obligation *. Such gifts are of little consequence, except when employed as the seal of a bargain or treaty.

It was their favourite maxim, That no man is naturally indebted to another; that he is not, therefore, obliged to bear with any imposition, or unequal treatment †. Thus, in a principle apparently sullen and inhospitable, they have discovered the foundation of justice, and observe its rules, with a steadiness and candour which no cultivation has been found to improve. The freedom which they give in what relates to the supposed duties of kindness and friendship, serves only to engage the heart more entirely, where it is once possessed with affection. We love to chuse our object without any restraint, and we consider kindness itself as a task, when the duties of friendship are exacted by rule. We therefore, by our demand for attentions, rather corrupt than improve the

* Muneribus gaudent, sed nec data imputant, nec acceptis obligantur.

† Charlevoix.

system

ſyſtem of morality; and by our exactions of gratitude, and our frequent propoſals to inforce its obſervance, we only ſhew, that we have miſtaken its nature; we only give ſymptoms of that growing ſenſibility to intereſt, from which we meaſure the expediency of friendſhip and generoſity itſelf; and by which we would introduce the ſpirit of traffic into the commerce of affection. In conſequence of this proceeding, we are often obliged to decline a favour with the ſame ſpirit that we throw off a ſervile engagement, or reject a bribe. To the unrefining ſavage every favour is welcome, and every preſent received without reſerve or reflection.

THE love of equality, and the love of juſtice, were originally the ſame: and although, by the conſtitution of different ſocieties, unequal privileges are beſtowed on their members; and although juſtice itſelf requires a proper regard to be paid to ſuch privileges; yet he who has forgotten that men were originally equal, eaſily degenerates into a ſlave; or in the capacity of a maſter, is not to be truſted with the rights of his fellow-creatures. This happy principle gives to the mind its ſenſe of independence, renders it indifferent to the favours which are in the power of other men, checks it in the commiſſion of injuries, and leaves the heart open to the affections of generoſity and kindneſs. It gives to the untutored American that air of candour, and of regard to the welfare of others, which, in ſome degree, ſoftens the arrogant pride of his carriage, and in times of confidence and

peace,

peace, without the assistance of government or law, renders the approach and commerce of strangers secure.

AMONG this people, the foundations of honour are eminent abilities and great fortitude; not the distinctions of equipage and fortune: The talents in esteem are such as their situation leads them to employ, the exact knowledge of a country, and stratagem in war. On these qualifications, a captain among the Caribbees underwent an examination. When a new leader was to be chosen, a scout was sent forth to traverse the forests which led to the enemy's country, and, upon his return, the candidate was desired to find the track in which he had travelled. A brook, or a fountain, was named to him on the frontier, and he was desired to find the nearest path to a particular station, and to plant a stake in the place *. They can, accordingly, trace a wild beast, or the human foot, over many leagues of a pathless forest, and find their way across a woody and uninhabited continent, by means of refined observations, which escape the traveller who has been accustomed to different aids. They steer in slender canoes, across stormy seas, with a dexterity equal to that of the most experienced pilot †. They carry a penetrating eye for the thoughts and intentions of those with whom they have to deal; and when they mean to deceive, they cover themselves with arts which the most subtile can seldom elude. They harangue in their public

* Lafitau.

† Charlevoix.

councils with a nervous and figurative elocution; and conduct themſelves in the management of their treaties with a perfect diſcernment of their national intereſts.

THUS being able maſters in the detail of their own affairs, and well qualified to acquit themſelves on particular occaſions, they ſtudy no ſcience, and go in purſuit of no general principles. They even ſeem incapable of attending to any diſtant conſequences, beyond thoſe they have experienced in hunting or war. They intruſt the proviſion of every ſeaſon to itſelf; conſume the fruits of the earth in ſummer; and, in winter, are driven in queſt of their prey, through woods, and over deſerts covered with ſnow. They do not form in one hour thoſe maxims which may prevent the errors of the next; and they fail in thoſe apprehenſions, which, in the intervals of paſſion, produce ingenuous ſhame, compaſſion, remorſe, or a command of appetite. They are ſeldom made to repent of any violence; nor is a perſon, indeed, thought accountable in his ſober mood, for what he did in the heat of a paſſion, or in a time of debauch.

THEIR ſuperſtitions are groveling and mean: and did this happen among rude nations alone, we could not ſufficiently admire the effects of politeneſs; but it is a ſubject on which few nations are intitled to cenſure their neighbours. When we have conſidered the ſuperſtitions of one people, we find little variety in thoſe of another. They are but a repetition of ſimilar weakneſſes and abſurdities, derived from a common ſource, a perplexed ap-

prehenſion

prehension of invisible agents, that are supposed to guide all precarious events to which human foresight cannot extend.

In what depends on the known or the regular course of nature, the mind trusts to itself; but in strange and uncommon situations, it is the dupe of its own perplexity, and, instead of relying on its prudence or courage, has recourse to divination, and a variety of observances, that, for being irrational, are always the more revered. Superstition being founded in doubts and anxiety, is fostered by ignorance and mystery. Its maxims, in the mean time, are not always confounded with those of common life; nor does its weakness or folly always prevent the watchfulness, penetration, and courage, men are accustomed to employ in the management of common affairs. A Roman consulting futurity by the pecking of birds, or a King of Sparta inspecting the intrails of a beast, Mithridates consulting his women on the interpretation of his dreams, are examples sufficient to prove, that a childish imbecility on this subject is consistent with the greatest military and political talents.

Confidence in the effect of superstitious observances is not peculiar to any age or nation. Few, even of the accomplished Greeks and Romans, were able to shake off this weakness. In their case, it was not removed by the highest measures of civilization. It has yielded only to the light of true religion, or to the study of nature, by which we are led to substitute a wise providence operating by phyſical cauſes, in the place of phantoms that terrify or amuſe the ignorant.

THE principal point of honour among the rude nations of America, as indeed in every inſtance where mankind are not greatly corrupted, is fortitude. Yet their way of maintaining this point of honour, is very different from that of the nations of Europe. Their ordinary method of making war is by ambuſcade; and they ſtrive, by over-reaching an enemy, to commit the greateſt ſlaughter, or to make the greateſt number of priſoners, with the leaſt hazard to themſelves. They deem it a folly to expoſe their own perſons in aſſaulting an enemy, and do not rejoice in victories which are ſtained with the blood of their own people. They do not value themſelves, as in Europe, on defying their enemy upon equal terms. They even boaſt, that they approach like foxes, or that they fly like birds, not leſs than that they devour like lions. In Europe, to fall in battle is accounted an honour; among the natives of America, it is reckoned diſgraceful *. They reſerve their fortitude for the trials they abide when attacked by ſurpriſe, or when fallen into their enemies hands; and when they are obliged to maintain their own honour, and that of their nation, in the midſt of torments that require efforts of patience more than of valour.

ON theſe occaſions, they are far from allowing it to be ſuppoſed that they wiſh to decline the conflict. It is held infamous to avoid it, even by a voluntary death; and the greateſt affront which can be offered to a priſoner, is to

* Charlevoix.

refuse him the honours of a man, in the manner of his execution: "With-hold," says an old man, in the midst of his torture, "the stabs of your knife; rather "let me die by fire, that those dogs, your allies, "from beyond the seas, may learn to suffer like men *." With terms of defiance, the victim, in those solemn trials, commonly excites the animosity of his tormentors, as well as his own; and whilst we suffer for human nature, under the effect of its errors, we must admire its force.

THE people with whom this practice prevailed, were commonly desirous of repairing their own losses, by adopting prisoners of war into their families: and even in the last moment, the hand which was raised to torment, frequently gave the sign of adoption, by which the prisoner became the child or the brother of his enemy, and came to share in all the privileges of a citizen. In their treatment of those who suffered, they did not appear to be guided by principles of hatred or revenge: they observed the point of honour in applying as well as in bearing their torments; and, by a strange kind of affection and tenderness, were directed to be most cruel where they intended the highest respect: the coward was put to immediate death by the hands of women: the valiant was supposed to be intitled to all the trials of fortitude that men could invent or employ: "It gave me joy," says an old man to his captive, "that so gallant a youth was allotted to my

* Colden.

" ſhare: I propoſed to have placed you on the couch of " my nephew, who was ſlain by your countrymen; to " have transferred all my tenderneſs to you; and to " have ſolaced my age in your company: but maimed " and mutilated as you now appear, death is better " than life: prepare yourſelf therefore to die like a " man *."

It is perhaps with a view to theſe exhibitions, or rather in admiration of fortitude, the principle from which they proceed, that the Americans are ſo attentive, in their earlieſt years, to harden their nerves †. The children are taught to vie with each other in bearing the ſharpeſt torments; the youth are admitted into the claſs of manhood, after violent proofs of their patience; and leaders are put to the teſt, by famine, burning, and ſuffocation ‡.

It might be apprehended, that among rude nations, where the means of ſubſiſtence are procured with ſo much difficulty, the mind could never raiſe itſelf above the conſideration of this ſubject; and that man would, in this condition, give examples of the meaneſt and moſt mercenary ſpirit. The reverſe, however, is true. Directed in this particular by the deſires of nature, men,

* Charlevoix.

† *Ib.* This writer ſays, that he has ſeen a boy and a girl, having bound their naked arms together, place a burning coal between them, to try who would ſhake it off firſt.

‡ Lafitau.

in their simplest state, attend to the objects of appetite no further than appetite requires; and their desires of fortune extend no further than the meal which gratifies their hunger: they apprehend no superiority of rank in the possession of wealth, such as might inspire any habitual principle of covetousness, vanity, or ambition: they can apply to no task that engages no immediate passion, and take pleasure in no occupation that affords no dangers to be braved, and no honours to be won.

It was not among the ancient Romans alone that commercial arts, or a sordid mind, were held in contempt. A like spirit prevails in every rude and independent society. "I am a warrior, and not a merchant," said an American to the governor of Canada, who proposed to give him goods in exchange for some prisoners he had taken; "your cloaths and utensils do not tempt "me; but my prisoners are now in your power, and "you may seize them: if you do, I must go forth and "take more prisoners, or perish in the attempt; and "if that chance should befal me, I shall die like a man; "but remember, that our nation will charge you as "the cause of my death *." With these apprehensions, they have an elevation, and a stateliness of carriage, which the pride of nobility, where it is most revered by polished nations, seldom bestows.

* Charlevoix.

THEY are attentive to their perſons, and employ much time, as well as endure great pain, in the methods they take to adorn their bodies, to give the permanent ſtains with which they are coloured, or preſerve the paint, which they are perpetually repairing, in order to appear with advantage.

THEIR averſion to every ſort of employment which they hold to be mean, makes them paſs great part of their time in idleneſs or ſleep; and a man who, in purſuit of a wild beaſt, or to ſurpriſe his enemy, will traverſe a hundred leagues on ſnow, will not, to procure his food, ſubmit to any ſpecies of ordinary labour. "Strange," ſays Tacitus, "that the ſame perſon ſhould "be ſo much averſe to repoſe, and ſo much addicted to "ſloth."

GAMES of hazard are not the invention of poliſhed ages; men of curioſity have looked for their origin, in vain, among the monuments of an obſcure antiquity; and it is probable that they belonged to times too remote and too rude even for the conjectures of antiquarians to reach. The very ſavage brings his furs, his utenſils, and his beads, to the hazard-table: he finds here the paſſions and agitations which the applications of a tedious induſtry could not excite: and while the throw is depending, he tears his hair, and beats his breaſt, with a rage which the more accompliſhed gameſter has ſometimes learned to repreſs: he often quits the party naked, and ſtripped of all his poſſeſſions; or where

ſlavery

slavery is in use, stakes his freedom to have one chance more to recover his former loss *.

With all these infirmities, vices, or respectable qualities, belonging to the human species in its rudest state; the love of society, friendship, and public affection, penetration, eloquence, and courage, appear to have been its original properties, not the subsequent effects of device or invention. If mankind are qualified to improve their manners, the subject was furnished by nature; and the effect of cultivation is not to inspire the sentiments of tenderness and generosity, nor to bestow the principal constituents of a respectable character, but to obviate the casual abuses of passion; and to prevent a mind, which feels the best dispositions in their greatest force, from being at times likewise the sport of brutal appetite and ungovernable violence.

Were Lycurgus employed anew to operate on the materials we have described, he would find them, in many important particulars, prepared by nature herself for his use. His equality in matters of property being already established, he would have no faction to apprehend from the opposite interests of the poor and the rich; his senate, his assembly of the people, is constituted; his discipline is in some measure adopted; and the place of his helots is supplied by the task allotted to one of the sexes. With all these advantages, he would still

* Tacitus, Lafitau, Charlevoix.

have had a very important leſſon for civil ſociety to teach, that by which a few learn to command, and the many are taught to obey: he would have all his precautions to take againſt the future intruſion of mercenary arts, the admiration of luxury, and the paſſion for intereſt: he would ſtill perhaps have a more difficult taſk than any of the former, in teaching his citizens the command of appetite, and an indifference to pleaſure, as well as a contempt of pain; in teaching them to maintain, in the field, the formality of uniform precautions, and as much to avoid being themſelves ſurpriſed, as they endeavour to ſurpriſe their enemy.

For want of theſe advantages, rude nations in general, though they are patient of hardſhip and fatigue, though they are addicted to war, and are qualified by their ſtratagem and valour to throw terror into the armies of a more regular enemy; yet, in the courſe of a continued ſtruggle, always yield to the ſuperior arts, and the diſcipline of more civilized nations. Hence the Romans were able to over-run the provinces of Gaul, Germany, and Britain; and hence the Europeans have a growing aſcendency over the nations of Africa and America.

On the credit of a ſuperiority which certain nations poſſeſs, they think that they have a claim to dominion; and even Cæſar appears to have forgotten what were the paſſions, as well as the rights of mankind, when he complained,

complained, that the Britons, after having sent him a submissive message to Gaul, perhaps to prevent his invasion, still pretended to fight for their liberties, and to oppose his descent on their island *.

THERE is not, perhaps, in the whole description of mankind, a circumstance more remarkable than that mutual contempt and aversion which nations, under a different state of commercial arts, bestow on each other. Addicted to their own pursuits, and considering their own condition as the standard of human felicity, all nations pretend to the preference, and in their practice give sufficient proof of sincerity. Even the savage still less than the citizen, can be made to quit that manner of life in which he is trained: he loves that freedom of mind which will not be bound to any task, and which owns no superior: however tempted to mix with polished nations, and to better his fortune, the first moment of liberty brings him back to the woods again; he droops and he pines in the streets of the populous city; he wanders dissatisfied over the open and the cultivated field; he seeks the frontier and the forest, where, with a constitution prepared to undergo the hardships and the difficulties of the situation, he enjoys a delicious freedom from care, and a sedu-

* Cæsar questus, quod quum ultro in continentem legatis missis pacem a se petissent, bellum sine causa intulissent. *Lib.* 4.

cing ſociety, where no rules of behaviour are preſcribed, but the ſimple dictates of the heart.

S E C T. III.

Of Rude Nations under the Impreſſions of Property and Intereſt.

IT was a proverbial imprecation in uſe among the hunting nations on the confines of Siberia, That their enemy might be obliged to live like a Tartar, and be ſeized with the folly of breeding and attending his cattle *. Nature, it ſeems, in their apprehenſion, by ſtoring the woods and the deſert with game, rendered the taſk of the herdſman unneceſſary, and left to man only the trouble of ſelecting and of ſeizing his prey.

THE indolence of mankind, or rather their averſion to any application in which they are not engaged by immediate inſtinct and paſſion, retards their progreſs in extending the notion of property. It has been found, however, even while the means of ſubſiſtence are left in common, and the ſtock of the public is yet undivided, that this notion is already applied to different ſubjects; as the fur and the bow pertain to the in-

* Abulgaze's Genealogical Hiſtory of the Tartars.

dividual;

dividual; the cottage, with its furniture, are appropriated to the family.

When the parent begins to desire a better provision for his children than is found under the promiscuous management of many copartners, when he has applied his labour and his skill apart, he aims at an exclusive possession, and seeks the property of the soil, as well as the use of its fruits.

When the individual no longer finds among his associates the same inclination to commit every subject to public use, he is seized with concern for his personal fortune; and is alarmed by the cares which every person entertains for himself. He is urged as much by emulation and jealousy, as by the sense of necessity. He suffers considerations of interest to rest on his mind, and when every present appetite is sufficiently gratified, he can act with a view to futurity, or rather finds an object of vanity in having amassed what is become a subject of competition, and a matter of universal esteem. Upon this motive, where violence is restrained, he can apply his hand to lucrative arts, confine himself to a tedious task, and wait with patience for the distant returns of his labour.

Thus mankind acquire industry by many and by slow degrees. They are taught to regard their interest; they are taught to abstain from unlawful profits; they are secured in the possession of what they fairly obtain; and by these methods the habits of the labourer, the mechanic, and the trader, are gradually formed. A hoard, collected from the ſimple productions of nature, or a herd of cattle, are, in every rude nation, the firſt ſpecies of wealth. The circumſtances of the ſoil, and the climate, determine whether the inhabitant ſhall apply himſelf chiefly to agriculture or paſture; whether he ſhall fix his reſidence, or be moving continually about with all his poſſeſſions.

In the weſt of Europe; in America, from ſouth to north, with a few exceptions; in the torrid zone, and every where within the warmer climates; mankind have generally applied themſelves to ſome ſpecies of agriculture, and have been diſpoſed to ſettlement. In the eaſt and the north of Aſia, they depended entirely on their herds, and were perpetually ſhifting their ground in ſearch of new paſture. The arts which pertain to ſettlement have been practiſed, and variouſly cultivated, by the inhabitants of Europe. Thoſe which are conſiſtent with perpetual migration, have, from the earlieſt accounts of hiſtory, remained nearly the ſame with the Scythian or Tartar. The tent pitched on a moveable carriage, the horſe applied to every purpoſe of labour, and of war, of the dairy, and of the butcher's ſtall, from the earlieſt to the lateſt accounts, have made up the riches and equipage of this wandering people.

But in whatever way rude nations ſubſiſt, there are certain points in which, under the firſt impreſſions of property, they nearly agree. Homer either lived with a people in this ſtage of their progreſs, or found himſelf engaged to exhibit their character. Tacitus has made them the ſubject of a particular treatiſe; and if this be an a-

ſpect

ſpect under which mankind deſerve to be viewed, it muſt be confeſſed, that we have ſingular advantages in collecting their features. The portrait has already been drawn by the ableſt hands, and gives, at one view, in the writings of theſe celebrated authors, whatever has been ſcattered in the relations of hiſtorians, or whatever we have opportunities to obſerve in the actual manners of men, who ſtill remain in a ſimilar ſtate.

IN paſſing from the condition we have deſcribed, to this we have at preſent in view, mankind ſtill retain many parts of their earlieſt character. They are ſtill averſe to labour, addicted to war, admirers of fortitude, and, in the language of Tacitus, more laviſh of their blood than of their ſweat *. They are fond of fantaſtic ornaments in their dreſs, and endeavour to fill up the liſtleſs intervals of a life addicted to violence, with hazardous ſports, and with games of chance. Every ſervile occupation they commit to women or ſlaves. But we may apprehend, that the individual having now found a ſeparate intereſt, the bands of ſociety muſt become leſs firm, and domeſtic diſorders more frequent. The members of any community, being diſtinguiſhed among themſelves by unequal ſhares in the diſtribution of property, the ground of a permanent and palpable ſubordination is laid.

THESE particulars accordingly take place among mankind, in paſſing from the ſavage to what may be

* Pigrum quin immo et iners videtur, ſudore acquirere quod poſſis ſanguine parare.

called

called the barbarous ſtate. Members of the ſame community enter into quarrels of competition or revenge. They unite in following leaders, who are diſtinguiſhed by their fortunes, and by the luſtre of their birth. They join the deſire of ſpoil with the love of glory; and from an opinion, that what is acquired by force, juſtly pertains to the victor, they become hunters of men, and bring every conteſt to the deciſion of the ſword.

EVERY nation is a band of robbers, who prey without reſtraint, or remorſe, on their neighbours. Cattle, ſays Achilles, may be ſeized in every field; and the coaſts of the Ægean ſea were accordingly pillaged by the heroes of Homer, for no other reaſon, than becauſe thoſe heroes choſe to poſſeſs themſelves of the braſs and iron, the cattle, the ſlaves, and the women, which were found among the nations around them.

A Tartar mounted on his horſe, is an animal of prey, who only inquires where cattle are to be found, and how far he muſt go to poſſeſs them. The monk, who had fallen under the diſpleaſure of Mangu Chan, made his peace, by promiſing, that the Pope, and the Chriſtian princes, ſhould make a ſurrender of all their herds *.

A ſimilar ſpirit reigned, without exception, in all the barbarous nations of Europe, Aſia, and Africa. The

* Rubruquis.

antiquities

antiquities of Greece and Italy, and the fables of every ancient poet, contain examples of its force. It was this spirit that brought our anceſtors firſt into the provinces of the Roman empire; and that afterward, more perhaps than their reverence for the croſs, led them to the Eaſt, to ſhare with the Tartars in the ſpoils of the Saracen empire.

FROM the deſcriptions contained in the laſt ſection, we may incline to believe, that mankind, in their ſimpleſt ſtate, are on the eve of erecting republics. Their love of equality, their habit of aſſembling in public councils, and their zeal for the tribe to which they belong, are qualifications that fit them to act under that ſpecies of government; and they ſeem to have but a few ſteps to make, in order to reach its eſtabliſhment. They have only to define the numbers of which their councils ſhall conſiſt, and to ſettle the forms of their meeting: They have only to beſtow a permanent authority for repreſſing diſorders, and to enact a few rules in favour of that juſtice they have already acknowledged, and from inclination ſo ſtrictly obſerve.

BUT theſe ſteps are far from being ſo eaſily made, as they appear on a ſlight or a tranſient view. The reſolution of chuſing, from among their equals, the magiſtrate to whom they give from thenceforward a right to controul their own actions, is far from the thoughts of ſimple men; and no eloquence, perhaps, could make them

them adopt this meaſure, or give them any ſenſe of its uſe.

Even after nations have choſen a military leader, they do not intruſt him with any ſpecies of civil authority. The captain, among the Caribbees, did not pretend to decide in domeſtic diſputes; the terms *juriſdiction* and *government* were unknown in their tongue *.

Before this important change is admitted, men muſt be accuſtomed to the diſtinction of ranks; and before they are ſenſible that ſubordination is matter of choice, muſt arrive at unequal conditions by chance. In deſiring property, they only mean to ſecure their ſubſiſtence: but the brave who lead in war, have likewiſe the largeſt ſhare in its ſpoils. The eminent are fond of deviſing hereditary honours; and the multitude, who admire the parent, are ready to extend their eſteem to his offspring.

Possessions deſcend, and the luſtre of family grows brighter with age. Hercules, who perhaps was an eminent warrior, became a god with poſterity, and his race was ſet apart for royalty and ſovereign power. When the diſtinctions of fortune and thoſe of birth are conjoined, the chieftain enjoys a pre-eminence, as well at the feaſt as in the field. His followers take their place in ſubordinate ſtations; and inſtead of conſidering them-

* Hiſtory of the Caribbees.

selves as parts of a community, they rank as the followers of a chieftain, and take their designation from the name of their leader. They find a new object of public affection, in defending his person, and in supporting his station; they lend of their substance to form his estate; they are guided by his smiles and his frowns; and court, as the highest distinction, a share in the feast which their own contributions have furnished.

As the former state of mankind seemed to point at democracy, this seems to exhibit the rudiments of monarchical government. But it is yet far short of that establishment which is known in after ages by the name of *monarchy*. The distinction between the leader and the follower, the prince and the subject, is still but imperfectly marked: their pursuits and occupations are not different; their minds are not unequally cultivated; they feed from the same dish; they sleep together on the ground; the children of the king, as well as those of the subject, are employed in tending the flock; and the keeper of the swine was a prime counsellor at the court of Ulysses.

THE chieftain, sufficiently distinguished from his tribe, to excite their admiration, and to flatter their vanity by a supposed affinity to his noble descent, is the object of their veneration, not of their envy: he is considered as the common bond of connection, not as their common master; is foremost in danger, and has a principal share in their troubles: his glory is placed in the number of his attendants, in his ſuperior magnanimity and valour; that of his followers, in being ready to ſhed their blood in his ſervice *.

THE frequent practice of war tends to ſtrengthen the bands of ſociety, and the practice of depredation itſelf engages men in trials of mutual attachment and courage. What threatened to ruin and overſet every good diſpoſition in the human breaſt, what ſeemed to baniſh juſtice from the ſocieties of men, tends to unite the ſpecies in clans and fraternities; formidable, indeed, and hoſtile to one another, but in the domeſtic ſociety of each, faithful, diſintereſted, and generous. Frequent dangers, and the experience of fidelity and valour, awaken the love of thoſe virtues, render them a ſubject of admiration, and endear their poſſeſſors.

ACTUATED by great paſſions, the love of glory, and the deſire of victory; rouſed by the menaces of an enemy, or ſtung with revenge; in ſuſpenſe between the proſpects of ruin or conqueſt, the barbarian ſpends every moment of relaxation in the indulgence of ſloth. He cannot deſcend to the purſuits of induſtry or mechanical labour: the beaſt of prey is a ſluggard; the hunter and the warrior ſleeps, while women or ſlaves are made to toil for his bread. But ſhew him a quarry at a diſtance, he is bold, impetuous, artful, and rapacious: no

* Tacitus de moribus Germanorum.

bar can withstand his violence, and no fatigue can allay his activity.

Even under this description mankind are generous and hospitable to strangers, as well as kind, affectionate, and gentle, in their domestic society *. Friendship and enmity are to them terms of the greatest importance: they mingle not their functions together; they have singled out their enemy, and they have chosen their friend. Even in depredation, the principal object is glory; and spoil is considered as a badge of victory. Nations and tribes are their prey: the solitary traveller, by whom they can acquire only the reputation of generosity, is suffered to pass unhurt, or is treated with splendid munificence.

Though distinguished into small cantons under their several chieftains, and for the most part separated by jealousy and animosity; yet when pressed by wars and formidable enemies, they sometimes unite in greater bodies. Like the Greeks in their expedition to Troy, they follow some remarkable leader, and compose a kingdom of many separate tribes. But such coalitions are merely occasional; and even during their continuance, more resemble republic than monarchy. The inferior chieftains reserve their importance, and intrude, with an air of equality, into the councils of their leader, as the people of

* Jean du Plan Carpen. Rubruquis, Cæsar, Tacit.

their ſeveral clans commonly intrude upon them *. Upon what motive indeed could we ſuppoſe, that men who live together in the greateſt familiarity, and amongſt whom the diſtinctions of rank are ſo obſcurely marked, would reſign their perſonal ſentiments and inclinations, or pay an implicit ſubmiſſion to a leader who can neither overawe nor corrupt?

MILITARY force muſt be employed to extort, or the hire of the venal to buy, that engagement which the Tartar comes under to his prince, when he promiſes, "That he will go where he ſhall be commanded; that "he will come when he ſhall be called; that he will kill "whoever is pointed out to him; and, for the future, that he will conſider the voice of the King as a "ſword †."

THESE are the terms to which even the ſtubborn heart of the barbarian has been reduced, in conſequence of a deſpotiſm he himſelf had eſtabliſhed; and men have, in that low ſtate of the commercial arts, in Europe, as well as in Aſia, taſted of political ſlavery. When intereſt prevails in every breaſt, the ſovereign and his party cannot eſcape the infection: he employs the force with which he is intruſted, to turn his people into a property, and to command their poſſeſſions for his profit or his

* Kolbe; Deſcription of the Cape of Good Hope.

† Simon de St Quintin.

pleaſure.

pleaſure. If riches are by any people made the ſtandard of good and of evil, let them beware of the powers they intruſt to their prince. " With the Suiones," ſays Ta-" citus, riches are in high eſteem; and this people are " accordingly diſarmed, and reduced to ſlavery *."

It is in this woful condition that mankind, being ſlaviſh, intereſted, inſidious, deceitful, and bloody, bear marks, if not of the leaſt curable, ſurely of the moſt lamentable, ſort of corruption †. Among them, war is the mere practice of rapine, to enrich the individual; commerce is turned into a ſyſtem of ſnares and impoſitions; and government by turns oppreſſive or weak.

It were happy for the human race, when guided by intereſt, and not governed by laws, that being ſplit into nations of a moderate extent, they found in every canton ſome natural bar to its further enlargement, and met with occupation enough in maintaining their independence, without being able to extend their dominion.

There is not diſparity of rank, among men in rude ages, ſufficient to give their communities the form of legal monarchy; and in a territory of conſiderable extent, when united under one head, the warlike and turbulent ſpirit of its inhabitants ſeems to require the bridle of deſpotiſm and military force. Where any degree of

* De moribus Germanorum. † Chardin's Travels.

freedom

freedom remains, the powers of the prince are, as they were in moſt of the rude monarchies of Europe, extremely precarious, and depend chiefly on his perſonal character: where, on the contrary, the powers of the prince are above the control of his people, they are likewiſe above the reſtrictions of law. Rapacity and terror become the predominant motives of conduct, and form the character of the only parties into which mankind are divided, that of the oppreſſor, and that of the oppreſſed.

THIS calamity threatened Europe for ages, under the conqueſt and ſettlement of its new inhabitants *. It has actually taken place in Aſia, where ſimilar conqueſts have been made; and even without the ordinary opiates of effeminacy, or a ſervile weakneſs, founded on luxury, it has ſurpriſed the Tartar on his wain, in the rear of his herds. Among this people, in the heart of a great continent, bold and enterpriſing warriors aroſe: they ſubdued, by ſurpriſe, or ſuperior abilities, the contiguous hords; they gained, in their progreſs, acceſſions of numbers and of ſtrength; and, like a torrent increaſing as it deſcends, became too ſtrong for any bar that could be oppoſed to their paſſage. The conquering tribe, during a ſucceſſion of ages, furniſhed the prince with his guards; and while they themſelves were allowed to ſhare

* See Hume's hiſtory of the Tudors. —— There ſeemed to be nothing wanting to eſtabliſh a perfect deſpotiſm in that houſe, but a few regiments of troops under the command of the crown.

in

in its spoils, were the voluntary tools of oppression. In this manner has despotism and corruption made their way into regions so much renowned for the wild freedom of nature: a power which was the terror of every effeminate province is disarmed, and the nursery of nations is itself gone to decay *.

WHERE rude nations escape this calamity, they require the exercise of foreign wars to maintain domestic peace: when no enemy appears from abroad, they have leisure for private feuds, and employ that courage in their dissensions at home, which, in time of war, is employed in defence of their country.

" AMONG the Gauls," says Cæsar, " there are sub-
" divisions, not only in every nation, and in every
" district and village, but almost in every house, every
" one must fly to some patron for protection †." In this distribution of parties, not only the feuds of clans, but the quarrels of families, even the differences and competitions of individuals, are decided by force. The sovereign, when unassisted by superstition, endeavours in vain to employ his jurisdiction, or to procure a submission to the decisions of law. By a people who are accustomed to owe their possessions to violence, and who despise fortune itself without the reputation of courage,

* See the History of the Huns.

† De Bello Gallico, lib. 6.

no umpire is admitted but the ſword. Scipio offered his arbitration to terminate the competition of two Spaniards in a diſputed ſucceſſion: "That," ſaid they, "we have already refuſed to our relations: we do not "ſubmit our difference to the judgement of men; and "even among the gods, we appeal to Mars alone *."

It is well known that the nations of Europe carried this mode of proceeding to a degree of formality unheard of in other parts of the world: the civil and criminal judge could, in moſt caſes, do no more than appoint the liſts, and leave the parties to decide their cauſe by the combat: they apprehended that the victor had a verdict of the gods in his favour: and when they dropped in any inſtance this extraordinary form of proceſs, they ſubſtituted in its place ſome other more capricious appeal to chance; in which they likewiſe thought that the judgement of the gods was declared.

The fierce nations of Europe were even fond of the combat as an exerciſe and a ſport. In the abſence of real quarrels, companions challenged each other to a trial of ſkill, in which one of them frequently periſhed. When Scipio celebrated the funeral of his father and his uncle, the Spaniards came in pairs to fight, and, by a public exhibition of their duels, to increaſe the ſolemnity †.

* Livy.

† Ib. lib. 3.

In this wild and lawless state, where the effects of true religion would have been so desireable, and so salutary, superstition frequently disputes the ascendant even with the admiration of valour; and an order of men, like the Druids among the ancient Gauls and Britons *, or some pretender to divination, as at the Cape of Good Hope, finds, in the credit which is paid to his sorcery, a way to the possession of power: his magic wand comes in competition with the sword itself; and, in the manner of the Druids, gives the first rudiments of civil government to some, or, like the supposed descendent of the sun among the Natchez, and the Lama among the Tartars, to others, an early taste of despotism and absolute slavery.

We are generally at a loss to conceive how mankind can subsist under customs and manners extremely different from our own; and we are apt to exaggerate the misery of barbarous times, by an imagination of what we ourselves should suffer in a situation to which we are not accustomed. But every age hath its consolations, as well as its sufferings †. In the interval of occasional outrages,

* Cæsar.

† Priscus, when employed on an embassy to Attila, was accosted in Greek, by a person who wore the dress of a Scythian. Having expressed surprise, and being desirous to know the cause of his stay in so wild a company, was told, that this Greek had been a captive, and for some time a slave, till he obtained his liberty in reward of some remarkable action. " I live more happily here," says he, " than ever I did under the Roman " government: for they who live with the Scythians, if they can endure " the

rages, the friendly intercourſes of men, even in their rudeſt condition, is affectionate and happy *. In rude ages, the perſons and properties of individuals are ſecure; becauſe each has a friend, as well as an enemy; and, if the one is diſpoſed to moleſt, the other is ready to protect; and the very admiration of valour, which in ſome inſtances tends to ſanctify violence, inſpires likewiſe certain maxims of generoſity and honour, that tend to prevent the commiſſion of wrongs.

MEN bear with the defects of their policy, as they do with hardſhips and inconveniencies in their manner of living. The alarms and the fatigues of war become a neceſſary recreation to thoſe who are accuſtomed to them, and who have the tone of their paſſions raiſed above leſs animating or trying occaſions. Old men, among the courtiers of Attila, wept, when they heard of heroic deeds, which they themſelves could no longer perform †. And among the Celtic nations, when age rendered the

" the fatigues of war, have nothing elſe to moleſt them; they enjoy their " poſſeſſions undiſturbed: whereas you are continually a prey to foreign " enemies, or to bad government; you are forbid to carry arms in your own " defence; you ſuffer from the remiſſneſs and ill conduct of thoſe who are " appointed to protect you; the evils of peace are even worſe than thoſe of " war; no puniſhment is ever inflicted on the powerful or the rich; no " mercy is ſhown to the poor; although your inſtitutions were wiſely deviſed, yet in the management of corrupted men, their effects are pernicious " and cruel." *Excerpta de legationibus*.

* D'Arvieux's Hiſt. of the Wild Arabs.

† Ibid.

warrior

warrior unfit for his former toils, it was the custom, in order to abridge the languors of a listless and inactive life, to sue for death at the hands of his friends *.

WITH all this ferocity of spirit, the rude nations of the West were subdued by the policy and more regular warfare of the Romans. The point of honour, which the barbarians of Europe adopted as individuals, exposed them to a peculiar disadvantage, by rendering them, even in their national wars, averse to assailing their enemy by surprise, or taking the benefit of stratagem; and though separately bold and intrepid, yet, like other rude nations, they were, when assembled in great bodies, addicted to superstition, and subject to panics.

THEY were, from a consciousness of their personal courage and force, sanguine on the eve of battle; they were, beyond the bounds of moderation, elated on success, and dejected in adversity; and being disposed to consider every event as a judgement of the gods, they were never qualified by an uniform application of prudence, to make the most of their forces, to repair their misfortunes, or to improve their advantages.

* Ubi transcendit florentes viribus annos,
Impatiens ævi spernit novisse senectam.

Silius, lib. 1. 225.

RESIGNED to the government of affection and paffion, they were generous and faithful where they had fixed an attachment; implacable, froward, and cruel, where they had conceived a diflike: addicted to debauchery, and the immoderate ufe of intoxicating liquors, they deliberated on the affairs of ftate in the heat of their riot; and in the fame dangerous moments, conceived the defigns of military enterprife, or terminated their domeftic diffenfions by the dagger or the fword.

IN their wars they preferred death to captivity. The victorious armies of the Romans, in entering a town by affault, or inforcing an incampment, have found the mother in the act of deftroying her children, that they might not be taken; and the dagger of the parent, red with the blood of his family, ready to be plunged at laft into his own breaft *.

IN all thefe particulars we perceive that vigour of fpirit, which renders diforder itfelf refpectable, and which qualifies men, if fortunate in their fituation, to lay the bafis of domeftic liberty, as well as to maintain againft foreign enemies their national independence and freedom.

* Liv, lib. xli. 11. Dio Caff.

PART

PART THIRD.

Of the Hiſtory of Policy and Arts.

SECT. I.

Of the Influences of Climate and Situation.

WHAT we have hitherto obſerved on the condition and manners of nations, though chiefly derived from what has paſſed in the temperate climates, may, in ſome meaſure, be applied to the rude ſtate of mankind in every part of the earth: but if we intend to purſue the hiſtory of our ſpecies in its further attainments, we may ſoon enter on ſubjects which will confine our obſervation to more narrow limits. The genius of political wiſdom and civil arts appears to have choſen his ſeats in particular tracts of the earth, and to have ſelected his favourites in particular races of men.

MAN, in his animal capacity, is qualified to ſubſiſt in every climate. He reigns with the lion and the tyger under the equatorial heats of the ſun, or he aſſociates with the

the bear and the rain-deer beyond the polar circle. His verſatile diſpoſition fits him to aſſume the habits of either condition, or his talent for arts enables him to ſupply its defects. The intermediate climates, however, appear moſt to favour his nature; and in whatever manner we account for the fact, it cannot be doubted, that this animal has always attained to the principal honours of his ſpecies within the temperate zone. The arts, which he has on this ſcene repeatedly invented, the extent of his reaſon, the fertility of his fancy, and the force of his genius in literature, commerce, policy, and war, ſufficiently declare either a diſtinguiſhed advantage of ſituation, or a natural ſuperiority of mind.

THE moſt remarkable races of men, it is true, have been rude before they were poliſhed. They have in ſome caſes returned to rudeneſs again: and it is not from the actual poſſeſſion of arts, ſcience, or policy, that we are to pronounce of their genius.

THERE is a vigour, a reach of capacity, and a ſenſibility of mind, which may characteriſe as well the ſavage as the citizen, the ſlave as well as the maſter; and the ſame powers of the mind may be turned to a variety of purpoſes. A modern Greek, perhaps, is miſchievous, ſlaviſh, and cunning, from the ſame animated temperament that made his anceſtor ardent, ingenious, and bold, in the camp, or in the council of his nation. A modern Italian is diſtinguiſhed by ſenſibility, quickneſs, and art, while he employs on trifles the capacity of an ancient Roman; and exhibits now, in the ſcene of amuſement, and in the ſearch of a frivolous applauſe, that fire, and thoſe paſſions, with which Gracchus burned in the forum, and ſhook the aſſemblies of a ſeverer people.

THE commercial and lucrative arts have been, in ſome climates, the principal object of mankind, and have been retained through every diſaſter; in others, even under all the fluctuations of fortune, they have ſtill been neglected; while in the temperate climates of Europe and Aſia, they have had their ages of admiration as well as contempt.

IN one ſtate of ſociety, arts are ſlighted, from that very ardour of mind, and principle of activity, by which, in another, they are practiſed with the greateſt ſucceſs. While men are ingroſſed by their paſſions, heated and rouſed by the ſtruggles and dangers of their country; while the trumpet ſounds, or the alarm of ſocial engagement is rung, and the heart beats high, it were a mark of dullneſs, or of an abject ſpirit, to find leiſure for the ſtudy of eaſe, or the purſuit of improvements, which have mere convenience or eaſe for their object.

THE frequent viciſſitudes and reverſes of fortune, which nations have experienced on that very ground where the arts have proſpered, are probably the effects of a buſy, inventive, and verſatile ſpirit, by which men have carried every national purſuit to extremes. They have raiſed the fabric of deſpotic empire to its greateſt

eſt height, where they had beſt underſtood the foundations of freedom. They periſhed in the flames which they themſelves had kindled; and they only, perhaps, were capable of diſplaying, by turns, the greateſt improvements, or the loweſt corruptions, to which the human mind can be brought.

On this ſcene, mankind have twice, within the compaſs of hiſtory, aſcended from rude beginnings to very high degrees of refinement. In every age, whether deſtined by its temporary diſpoſition to build or to deſtroy, they have left the veſtiges of an active and vehement ſpirit. The pavement and the ruins of Rome are buried in duſt, ſhaken from the feet of barbarians, who trod with contempt on the refinements of luxury, and ſpurned thoſe arts, the uſe of which it was reſerved for the poſterity of the ſame people to diſcover and to admire. The tents of the wild Arab are even now pitched among the ruins of magnificent cities; and the waſte fields which border on Paleſtine and Syria, are perhaps become again the nurſery of infant nations. The chieftain of an Arab tribe, like the founder of Rome, may have already fixed the roots of a plant that is to flouriſh in ſome future period, or laid the foundations of a fabric, that will attain to its grandeur in ſome diſtant age.

Great part of Africa has been always unknown; but the ſilence of fame, on the ſubject of its revolutions, is an argument, where no other proof can be found, of weakneſs in the genius of its people. The torrid zone,

every

every where round the globe, however known to the geographer, has furniſhed few materials for hiſtory; and though in many places ſupplied with the arts of life in no contemptible degree, has no where matured the more important projects of political wiſdom, nor inſpired the virtues which are connected with freedom, and required in the conduct of civil affairs.

IT was indeed in the torrid zone that mere arts of mechaniſm and manufacture were found, among the inhabitants of the new world, to have made the greateſt advance: it is in India, and in the regions of this hemiſphere, which are viſited by the vertical ſun, that the arts of manufacture, and the practice of commerce, are of the greateſt antiquity, and have ſurvived, with the ſmalleſt diminution, the ruins of time, and the revolutions of empire.

THE ſun, it ſeems, which ripens the pine-apple and the tamarind, inſpires a degree of mildneſs that can even aſſuage the rigours of deſpotical government: and ſuch is the effect of a gentle and pacific diſpoſition in the natives of the Eaſt, that no conqueſt, no irruption of barbarians, terminates, as they did among the ſtubborn natives of Europe, by a total deſtruction of what the love of eaſe and of pleaſure had produced.

TRANSFERRED, without any great ſtruggle, from one maſter to another, the natives of India are ready, upon every change, to purſue their induſtry, to acquieſce in the enjoyment of life, and the hopes of animal pleaſure: the wars of conqueſt are not prolonged to exaſperate the parties engaged in them, or to deſolate the land for which thoſe parties contend: even the barbarous invader leaves untouched the commercial ſettlement which has not provoked his rage: though maſter of opulent cities, he only incamps in their neighbourhood, and leaves to his heirs the option of entering, by degrees, on the pleaſures, the vices, and the pageantries his acquiſitions afford: his ſucceſſors, ſtill more than himſelf, are diſpoſed to foſter the hive, in proportion as they taſte more of its ſweets; and they ſpare the inhabitant, together with his dwelling, as they ſpare the herd or the ſtall, of which they are become the proprietors.

The modern deſcription of India is a repetition of the ancient, and the preſent ſtate of China is derived from a diſtant antiquity, to which there is no parallel in the hiſtory of mankind. The ſucceſſion of monarchs has been changed; but no revolutions have affected the ſtate. The African and the Samoiede are not more uniform in their ignorance and barbarity, than the Chineſe and the Indian, if we may credit their own ſtory, have been in the practice of manufacture, and in the obſervance of a certain police, which was calculated only to regulate their traffic, and to protect them in their application to ſervile or lucrative arts.

If we paſs from theſe general repreſentations of what mankind have done, to the more minute deſcription of the

the animal himſelf, as he has occupied different climates, and is diverſified in his temper, complexion, and character, we ſhall find a variety of genius correſponding to the effects of his conduct, and the reſult of his ſtory.

MAN, in the perfection of his natural faculties, is quick and delicate in his ſenſibility; extenſive and various in his imaginations and reflections; attentive, penetrating, and ſubtile, in what relates to his fellow-creatures; firm and ardent in his purpoſes; devoted to friendſhip or to enmity; jealous of his independence and his honour, which he will not relinquiſh for ſafety or for profit: under all his corruptions or improvements, he retains his natural ſenſibility, if not his force; and his commerce is a bleſſing or a curſe, according to the direction his mind has received.

BUT under the extremes of heat or of cold, the active range of the human ſoul appears to be limited; and men are of inferior importance, either as friends, or as enemies. In the one extreme, they are dull and ſlow, moderate in their deſires, regular and pacific in their manner of life; in the other, they are feveriſh in their paſſions, weak in their judgements, and addicted by temperament to animal pleaſure. In both the heart is mercenary, and makes important conceſſions for childiſh bribes: in both the ſpirit is prepared for ſervitude: in the one it is ſubdued by fear of the future; in the other it is not rouſed even by its ſenſe of the preſent.

The nations of Europe who would ſettle or conquer on the ſouth or the north of their own happier climates, find little reſiſtance: they extend their dominion at pleaſure, and find no where a limit but in the ocean, and in the ſatiety of conqueſt. With few of the pangs and the ſtruggles that precede the reduction of nations, mighty provinces have been ſucceſſively annexed to the territory of Ruſſia; and its ſovereign, who accounts within his domain, entire tribes, with whom perhaps none of his emiſſaries have ever converſed, diſpatched a few geometers to extend his empire, and thus to execute a project, in which the Romans were obliged to employ their conſuls and their legions *. Theſe modern conquerors complain of rebellion, where they meet with repugnance; and are ſurpriſed at being treated as enemies, where they come to impoſe their tribute.

It appears, however, that on the ſhores of the Eaſtern ſea, they have met with nations † who have queſtioned their title to reign, and who have conſidered the requiſition of a tax as the demand of effects for nothing. Here perhaps may be found the genius of ancient Europe, and under its name of ferocity, the ſpirit of national independence ‡; that ſpirit which diſputed

* See Ruſſian Atlas.

† The Tchutzi.

‡ Notes to the Genealogical Hiſtory of the Tartars.

its ground in the West with the victorious armies of Rome, and baffled the attempts of the Persian monarchs to comprehend the villages of Greece within the bounds of their extensive dominion.

THE great and striking diversities which obtain betwixt the inhabitants of climates far removed from each other, are, like the varieties of other animals in different regions, easily observed. The horse and the raindeer are just emblems of the Arab and the Laplander: the native of Arabia, like the animal for whose race his country is famed, whether wild in the woods, or tutored by art, is lively, active, and fervent in the exercise on which he is bent. This race of men, in their rude state, fly to the desert for freedom, and in roving bands alarm the frontiers of empire, and strike a terror in the province to which their moving encampments advance *. When roused by the prospect of conquest, or disposed to act on a plan, they spread their dominion, and their system of imagination, over mighty tracts of the earth: when possessed of property and of settlement, they set the example of a lively invention, and superior ingenuity, in the practice of arts, and the study of science. The Laplander, on the contrary, like the associate of his climate, is hardy, indefatigable, and patient of famine; dull rather than tame; serviceable in a particular tract; and incapable of change. Whole nations continue from age to age in the same condition, and, with immoveable

* D'Arvieux.

phlegm,

phlegm, ſubmit to the appellations of *Dane*, of *Swede*, or of *Muſcovite*, according to the land they inhabit; and ſuffer their country to be ſevered like a common, by the line on which thoſe nations have traced their limits of empire.

IT is not in the extremes alone that theſe varieties of genius may be clearly diſtinguiſhed. Their continual change keeps pace with the variations of climate with which we ſuppoſe them connected: and though certain degrees of capacity, penetration, and ardour, are not the lot of entire nations, nor the vulgar properties of any people; yet their unequal frequency, and unequal meaſure, in different countries, are ſufficiently manifeſt from the manners, the tone of converſation, the talent for buſineſs, amuſement, and literary compoſition, which predominate in each.

IT is to the Southern nations of Europe, both ancient and modern, that we owe the invention and the embelliſhment of that mythology, and thoſe early traditions, which continue to furniſh the materials of fancy, and the field of poetic alluſion. To them we owe the romantic tales of chivalry, as well as the ſubſequent models of a more rational ſtyle, by which the heart and the imagination are kindled, and the underſtanding informed.

THE fruits of induſtry have abounded moſt in the North, and the ſtudy of ſcience has here received its moſt ſolid improvements: the efforts of imagination and ſenti-

ment

ment were moſt frequent and moſt ſucceſsful in the South. While the ſhores of the Baltic became famed for the ſtudies of Copernicus, Tycho Brahe, and Kepler, thoſe of the Mediterranean were celebrated for giving birth to men of genius in all its variety, and for having abounded with poets and hiſtorians, as well as with men of ſcience.

ON one ſide, learning took its riſe from the heart and the fancy; on the other, it is ſtill confined to the judgement and the memory. A faithful detail of public tranſactions, with little diſcernment of their comparative importance; the treaties and the claims of nations, the births and genealogies of princes, are, in the literature of Northern nations, amply preſerved; while the lights of the underſtanding, and the feelings of the heart, are ſuffered to periſh. The hiſtory of the human character; the intereſting memoir, founded no leſs on the careleſs proceedings of a private life, than on the formal tranſactions of a public ſtation; the ingenious pleaſantry, the piercing ridicule, the tender, pathetic, or the elevated ſtrain of elocution, have been confined in modern as well as ancient times, with a few exceptions, to the ſame latitudes with the fig and the vine.

THESE diverſities of natural genius, if real, muſt have great part of their foundation in the animal frame: and it has been often obſerved, that the vine flouriſhes, where, to quicken the ferments of the human blood, its aids are the leaſt required. While ſpirituous liquors are, among Southern nations, from a ſenſe of their ruinous effects, prohibited; or from a love of decency, and the possession of a temperament sufficiently warm, not greatly desired; they carry in the North a peculiar charm, while they awaken the mind, and give a taste of that lively fancy and ardour of passion, which the climate is found to deny.

THE melting desires, or the fiery passions, which in one climate take place between the sexes, are in another changed into a sober consideration, or a patience of mutual disgust. This change is remarked in crossing the Mediterranean, in following the course of the Missisippi, in ascending the mountains of Caucasus, and in passing from the Alps and the Pyrenees to the shores of the Baltic.

THE female sex domineers on the frontier of Louisiana, by the double engine of superstition, and of passion. They are slaves among the native inhabitants of Canada, and chiefly valued for the toils they endure, and the domestic service they yield *.

THE burning ardours, and the torturing jealousies, of the seraglio and the haram, which have reigned so long in Asia and Africa, and which, in the Southern parts of Europe, have scarcely given way to the difference of religion and civil establishments, are found, however, with an abatement of heat in the climate, to be more ea-

* Charlevoix.

sily

sily changed, in one latitude, into a temporary passion which ingrosses the mind, without enfeebling it, and which excites to romantic atchievements: by a farther progress to the North, it is changed into a spirit of gallantry, which employs the wit and the fancy more than the heart; which prefers intrigue to enjoyment; and substitutes affectation and vanity, where sentiment and desire have failed. As it departs from the sun, the same passion is farther composed into a habit of domestic connection, or frozen into a state of insensibility, under which the sexes at freedom scarcely chuse to unite their society.

THESE variations of temperament and character, do not indeed correspond with the number of degrees that are measured from the equator to the pole; nor does the temperature of the air itself depend on the latitude. Varieties of soil and position, the distance or neighbourhood of the sea, are known to affect the atmosphere, and may have signal effects in composing the animal frame.

THE climates of America, though taken under the same parallel, are observed to differ from those of Europe. There, extensive marshes, great lakes, aged, decayed, and crouded forests, with the other circumstances that mark an uncultivated country, are supposed to replenish the air with heavy and noxious vapours, that give a double asperity to the winter, and, during many months, by the frequency and continuance of fogs, snow, and frost, carry the inconveniencies of the frigid zone far into the temperate. The Samoiede and the Laplander, however, have their counterpart, though on a lower latitude, on the ſhores of America: the Canadian and the Iroquois bear a reſemblance to the ancient inhabitants of the middling climates of Europe: the Mexican, like the Aſiatic of India, being addicted to pleaſure, was ſunk in effeminacy; and in the neighbourhood of the wild and the free, had ſuffered to be raiſed on his weakneſs, a domineering ſuperſtition, and a permanent fabric of deſpotical government.

GREAT part of Tartary lies under the ſame parallels with Greece, Italy, and Spain; but the climates are found to be different; and while the ſhores, not only of the Mediterranean, but even thoſe of the Atlantic, are favoured with a moderate change and viciſſitude of ſeaſons, the eaſtern parts of Europe, and the northern continent of Aſia, are afflicted with all their extremes. In one ſeaſon, we are told, that the plagues of an ardent ſummer reach almoſt to the frozen ſea; and that the inhabitant is obliged to ſcreen himſelf from noxious vermin in the ſame clouds of ſmoke in which he muſt, at a different time of the year, take ſhelter from the rigours of cold. When winter returns, the tranſition is rapid, and with an aſperity almoſt equal in every latitude, lays waſte the face of the earth, from the northern confines of Siberia, to the deſcents of Mount Caucaſus and the frontier of India.

With this unequal distribution of climate, by which the lot, as well as the national character, of the Northern Asiatic may be deemed inferior to that of Europeans who lie under the same parallels, a similar gradation of temperament and spirit, however, has been observed, in following the meridian on either tract; and the Southern Tartar has over the Tonguses and the Samoiede, the same pre-eminence that certain nations of Europe are known to possess over their Northern neighbours, in situations more advantageous to both.

The Southern hemisphere scarcely offers a subject of like observation. The temperate zone is there still undiscovered, or is only known in two promontories, the Cape of Good Hope, and Cape Horn, which stretch into moderate latitudes on that side of the line. But the savage of South America, notwithstanding the interposition of the nations of Peru and of Mexico, is found to resemble his counterpart on the North; and the Hottentot, in many things, the barbarian of Europe: he is tenacious of freedom, has rudiments of policy, and a national vigour, which serve to distinguish his race from the other African tribes, who are exposed to the more vertical rays of the sun.

While we have, in these observations, only thrown out what must present itself on the most cursory view of the history of mankind, or what may be presumed from the mere obscurity of some nations, who inhabit great tracts of the earth, as well as from the luſtre of others, we are ſtill unable to explain the manner in which climate may affect the temperament, or foſter the genius, of its inhabitant.

THAT the temper of the heart, and the intellectual operations of the mind, are, in ſome meaſure, dependent on the ſtate of the animal organs, is well known from experience. Men differ from themſelves in ſickneſs and in health; under a change of diet, of air, and of exerciſe: but we are, even in theſe familiar inſtances, at a loſs how to connect the cauſe with its ſuppoſed effect: and though climate, by including a variety of ſuch cauſes, may, by ſome regular influence, affect the characters of men, we can never hope to explain the manner of thoſe influences till we have underſtood what probably we ſhall never underſtand, the ſtructure of thoſe finer organs with which the operations of the ſoul are connected.

WHEN we point out, in the ſituation of a people, circumſtances which, by determining their purſuits, regulate their habits, and their manner of life; and when, inſtead of referring to the ſupppoſed phyſical ſource of their diſpoſitions, we aſſign their inducements to a determinate conduct; in this we ſpeak of effects and of cauſes whoſe connection is more familiarly known. We can underſtand, for inſtance, why a race of men like the Samoiede, confined, during great part of the year, to darkneſs, or retired into caverns, ſhould differ, in their manners and apprehenſions, from thoſe who are at liberty in

every

every ſeaſon; or who, inſtead of ſeeking relief from the extremities of cold, are employed in ſearch of precautions againſt the oppreſſions of a burning ſun. Fire and exerciſe are the remedies of cold; repoſe and ſhade the ſecurities from heat. The Hollander is laborious and induſtrious in Europe; he becomes more languid and ſlothful in India *.

GREAT extremities, either of heat or cold, are, perhaps, in a moral view, equally unfavourable to the active genius of mankind, and by preſenting alike inſuperable difficulties to be overcome, or ſtrong inducements to indolence and ſloth, equally prevent the firſt applications of ingenuity, or limit their progreſs. Some intermediate degrees of inconvenience in the ſituation, at once excite the ſpirit, and, with the hopes of ſucceſs, encourage its efforts. "It is in the leaſt favourable ſituations," ſays Mr Rouſſeau, "that arts have flouriſhed the moſt. I could "ſhow them in Egypt, as they ſpread with the overflow-"ing of the Nile; and in Africa, as they mounted up to "the clouds, from a rocky ſoil and from barren ſands; "while on the fertile banks of the Eurotas, they were not "able to faſten their roots."

WHERE mankind from the firſt ſubſiſt by toil, and in the midſt of difficulties, the defects of their ſituation

* The Dutch ſailors who were employed in the ſiege of Malaco, tore or burnt the ſail-cloth which was given them to make tents, that they might not have the trouble of making or pitching them. *Voy. de Matelief.*

are

are ſupplied by induſtry: and while dry, tempting, and healthful lands are left uncultivated *, the peſtilent marſh is drained with great labour, and the ſea is fenced off with mighty barriers, the materials and the coſts of which, the ſoil to be gained can ſcarcely afford, or repay. Harbours are opened, and crouded with ſhipping, where veſſels of burden, if they are not conſtructed with a view to the ſituation, have not water to float. Elegant and magnificent edifices are raiſed on foundations of ſlime; and all the conveniencies of human life are made to abound, where nature does not ſeem to have prepared a reception for men. It is in vain to expect, that the reſidence of arts and commerce ſhould be determined by the poſſeſſion of natural advantages. Men do more when they have certain difficulties to ſurmount, than when they have ſuppoſed bleſſings to enjoy: and the ſhade of the barren oak and the pine are more favourable to the genius of mankind, than that of the palm or the tamarind.

AMONG the advantages which enable nations to run the career of policy, as well as of arts, it may be expected, from the obſervations already made, that we ſhould reckon every circumſtance which enables them to divide and to maintain themſelves in diſtinct and independent communities. The ſociety and concourſe of other men, are not more neceſſary to form the individual, than the rivalſhip and competition of nations are to invigorate the

* Compare the ſtate of Hungary with that of Holland.

principles

principles of political life in a ſtate. Their wars, and their treaties, their mutual jealouſies, and the eſtabliſhments which they deviſe with a view to each other, conſtitute more than half the occupations of mankind, and furniſh materials for their greateſt and moſt improving exertions. For this reaſon, cluſters of iſlands, a continent divided by many natural barriers, great rivers, ridges of mountains, and arms of the ſea, are beſt fitted for becoming the nurſery of independent and reſpectable nations. The diſtinction of ſtates being clearly maintained, a principle of political life is eſtabliſhed in every diviſion, and the capital of every diſtrict, like the heart in an animal body, communicates with eaſe the vital blood and the national ſpirit to its members.

THE moſt reſpectable nations have always been found where at leaſt one part of the frontier has been waſhed by the ſea. This barrier, perhaps the ſtrongeſt of all in the times of barbarity, does not, however, even then ſuperſede the cares of a national defence; and in the advanced ſtate of arts, gives the greateſt ſcope and facility to commerce.

THRIVING and independent nations were accordingly ſcattered on the ſhores of the Pacific and the Atlantic. They ſurrounded the Red ſea, the Mediterranean, and the Baltic; while, a few tribes excepted, who retire among the mountains bordering on India and Perſia, or who have found ſome rude eſtabliſhment among the creeks and the ſhores of the Caſpian and the Euxine, there is ſcarcely a people

people in the vaſt continent of Aſia who deſerves the name of a nation. The unbounded plain is traverſed at large by hordes, who are in perpetual motion, or who are diſplaced and haraſſed by their mutual hoſtilities. Although they are never perhaps actually blended together in the courſe of hunting, or in the ſearch of paſture, they cannot bear one great diſtinction of nations, which is taken from the territory, and which is deeply impreſſed by an affection to the native ſeat. They move in troops, without the arrangement or the concert of nations; they become eaſy acceſſions to every new empire among themſelves, or to the Chineſe and the Muſcovite, with whom they hold a traffic for the means of ſubſiſtence, and the materials of pleaſure.

WHERE a happy ſyſtem of nations is formed, they do not rely for the continuance of their ſeparate names, and for that of their political independence, on the barriers erected by nature. Mutual jealouſies lead to the maintenance of a balance of power; and this principle, more than the Rhine and the Ocean, than the Alps and the Pyrenees in modern Europe; more than the ſtraits of Thermopylæ, the mountains of Thrace, or the bays of Salamine and Corinth in ancient Greece; tended to prolong the ſeparation, to which the inhabitants of theſe happy climates have owed their felicity as nations, the luſtre of their fame, and their civil accompliſhments.

If we mean to pursue the history of civil society, our attention must be chiefly directed to such examples, and we must here bid farewel to those regions of the earth, on which our species, by the effects of situation or climate, appear to be restrained in their national pursuits, or inferior in the powers of the mind.

SECT. II.

The History of Subordination.

We have hitherto observed mankind, either united together on terms of equality, or disposed to admit of a subordination founded merely on the voluntary respect and attachment which they paid to their leaders; but, in both cases, without any concerted plan of government, or system of laws.

The savage, whose fortune is comprised in his cabin, his fur, and his arms, is satisfied with that provision, and with that degree of security, he himself can procure. He perceives, in treating with his equal, no subject of discussion that should be referred to the decision of a judge; nor does he find in any hand the badges of magistracy, or the ensigns of a perpetual command.

The barbarian, though induced by his admiration of personal qualities, the lustre of a heroic race, or a superiority of fortune, to follow the banners of a leader, and to act a ſubordinate part in his tribe, knows not, that what he performs from choice, is to be made a ſubject of obligation. He acts from affections unacquainted with forms; and when provoked, or when engaged in diſputes, he recurs to the ſword, as the ultimate means of deciſion, in all queſtions of right.

HUMAN affairs, in the mean time, continue their progreſs. What was in one generation a propenſity to herd with the ſpecies, becomes, in the ages which follow, a principle of national union. What was originally an alliance for common defence, becomes a concerted plan of political force; the care of ſubſiſtence becomes an anxiety for accumulating wealth, and the foundation of commercial arts.

MANKIND, in following the preſent ſenſe of their minds, in ſtriving to remove inconveniencies, or to gain apparent and contiguous advantages, arrive at ends which even their imagination could not anticipate, and paſs on, like other animals, in the track of their nature, without perceiving its end. He who firſt ſaid, "I will appropriate this field; I will leave it to my heirs;" did not perceive, that he was laying the foundation of civil laws and political eſtabliſhments. He who firſt ranged himſelf under a leader, did not perceive, that he was ſetting the example of a permanent ſubordination, under the pretence of which, the rapacious were to ſeize his poſſeſſions, and the arrogant to lay claim to his ſervice.

MEN,

MEN, in general, are sufficiently disposed to occupy themselves in forming projects and schemes: but he who would scheme and project for others, will find an opponent in every person who is disposed to scheme for himself. Like the winds, that come we know not whence, and blow whithersoever they list, the forms of society are derived from an obscure and distant origin; they arise, long before the date of philosophy, from the instincts, not from the speculations, of men. The croud of mankind, are directed in their establishments and measures, by the circumstances in which they are placed; and seldom are turned from their way, to follow the plan of any single projector.

EVERY step and every movement of the multitude, even in what are termed enlightened ages, are made with equal blindness to the future; and nations stumble upon establishments, which are indeed the result of human action, but not the execution of any human design *. If Cromwell said, That a man never mounts higher, than when he knows not whither he is going; it may with more reason be affirmed of communities, that they admit of the greatest revolutions where no change is intended, and that the most refined politicians do not always know whither they are leading the state by their projects.

IF we listen to the testimony of modern history, and to that of the most authentic parts of the ancient; if we attend to the practice of nations in every quarter of the world, and in every condition, whether that of the bar-

* De Retz Memoirs.

barian or the poliſhed, we ſhall find very little reaſon to retract this aſſertion. No conſtitution is formed by concert, no government is copied from a plan. The members of a ſmall ſtate contend for equality; the members of a greater, find themſelves claſſed in a certain manner that lays a foundation for monarchy. They proceed from one form of government to another, by eaſy tranſitions, and frequently under old names adopt a new conſtitution. The ſeeds of every form are lodged in human nature; they ſpring up and ripen with the ſeaſon. The prevalence of a particular ſpecies is often derived from an imperceptible ingredient mingled in the ſoil.

We are therefore to receive, with caution, the traditionary hiſtories of ancient legiſlators, and founders of ſtates. Their names have long been celebrated; their ſuppoſed plans have been admired; and what were probably the conſequences of an early ſituation, is, in every inſtance, conſidered as an effect of deſign. An author and a work, like cauſe and effect, are perpetually coupled together. This is the ſimpleſt form under which we can conſider the eſtabliſhment of nations: and we aſcribe to a previous deſign, what came to be known only by experience, what no human wiſdom could foreſee, and what, without the concurring humour and diſpoſition of his age, no authority could enable an individual to execute.

If men, during ages of extenſive reflection, and employed in the ſearch of improvement, are wedded to their inſtitutions; and, labouring under many acknowledged inconveniencies,

inconveniencies, cannot break loose from the trammels of custom; what shall we suppose their humour to have been in the times of Romulus and Lycurgus? They were not surely more disposed to embrace the schemes of innovators, or to shake off the impressions of habit: they were not more pliant and ductile, when their knowledge was less; not more capable of refinement, when their minds were more circumscribed.

We imagine, perhaps, that rude nations must have so strong a sense of the defects under which they labour, and be so conscious that reformations are requisite in their manners, that they must be ready to adopt, with joy, every plan of improvement, and to receive every plausible proposal with implicit compliance. And we are thus inclined to believe, that the harp of Orpheus could effect, in one age, what the eloquence of Plato could not produce in another. We mistake, however, the characteristic of simple ages: mankind then appear to feel the fewest defects, and are then least desirous to enter on reformations.

The reality, in the mean time, of certain establishments at Rome and at Sparta, cannot be disputed: but it is probable, that the government of both these states took its rise from the situation and genius of the people, not from the projects of single men; that the celebrated warrior and statesman, who are considered as the founders of those nations, only acted a superior part among numbers who were disposed to the same institutions;

and that they left to poſterity a renown, pointing them out as the inventors of many practices which had been already in uſe, and which helped to form their own manners and genius, as well as thoſe of their countrymen.

It has been formerly obſerved, that, in many particulars, the cuſtoms of ſimple nations coincide with what is aſcribed to the invention of early ſtateſmen; that the model of republican government, the ſenate, and the aſſembly of the people; that even the equality of property, or the community of goods, were not reſerved to the invention or contrivance of ſingular men.

If we conſider Romulus as the founder of the Roman ſtate, certainly he who killed his brother that he might reign alone, did not deſire to come under reſtraints from the controuling power of the ſenate, nor to refer the councils of his ſovereignty to the deciſion of a collective body. Love of dominion is, by its nature, averſe to conſtraint; and this chieftain, like every leader in a rude age, probably found a claſs of men ready to intrude on his councils, and without whom he could not proceed. He met with occaſions, on which, as at the ſound of a trumpet, the body of the people aſſembled, and took reſolutions, which any individual might in vain diſpute, or attempt to controul; and Rome, which commenced on the general plan of every artleſs ſociety, found laſting improvements in the purſuit of temporary expedients,

and

and digested her political frame in adjusting the pretensions of parties which arose in the state.

Mankind, in very early ages of society, learn to covet riches, and to admire distinction: they have avarice and ambition, and are occasionally led by them to depredation and conquest: but in their ordinary conduct, these motives are balanced or restrained by other habits and other pursuits; by sloth, or intemperance; by personal attachments, or personal animosities; which mislead from the attention to interest. These circumstances render mankind, at times, remiss or outrageous: they prove the source of civil peace or disorder, but disqualify those who are actuated by them, from maintaining any fixed usurpation; slavery and rapine are first threatened from abroad, and war, either offensive or defensive, is the great business of every tribe. The enemy occupy their thoughts; they have no leisure for domestic dissensions. It is the desire of every separate community, however, to secure itself; and in proportion as it gains this object, by strengthening its barrier, by weakening its enemy, or by procuring allies, the individual at home bethinks him of what he may gain or lose for himself: the leader is disposed to enlarge the advantages which belong to his station; the follower becomes jealous of rights which are open to incroachment; and parties who united before, from affection and habit, or from a regard to their common preservation, disagree in supporting their several claims to precedence or profit.

When

When the animofities of faction are thus awakened at home, and the pretenfions of freedom are oppofed to thofe of dominion, the members of every fociety find a new fcene upon which to exert their activity. They had quarrelled, perhaps, on points of intereft; they had balanced between different leaders; but they had never united as citizens, to withftand the encroachments of fovereignty, or to maintain their common rights as a people. If the prince, in this conteft, finds numbers to fupport, as well as to oppofe his pretenfions, the fword which was whetted againft foreign enemies, may be pointed at the bofom of fellow-fubjects, and every interval of peace from abroad, be filled with domeftic war. The facred names of Liberty, Juftice, and Civil Order, are made to refound in public affemblies; and, during the abfence of other alarms, give to fociety, within itfelf, an abundant fubject of ferment and animofity.

If what is related of the little principalities which, in ancient times, were formed in Greece, in Italy, and over all Europe, agrees with the character we have given of mankind under the firft impreffions of property, of intereft, and of hereditary diftinctions; the feditions and domeftic wars which followed in thofe very ftates, the expulfion of their kings, or the queftions which arofe concerning the prerogatives of the fovereign, or privilege of the fubject, are agreeable to the reprefentation which we now give of the firft ftep toward political eftablifhment, and the defire of a legal conftitution.

What

What this constitution may be in its earliest form, depends on a variety of circumstances in the condition of nations: It depends on the extent of the principality in its rude state; on the degree of disparity to which mankind had submitted before they began to dispute its abuses: it depends likewise on what we term *accidents*, the personal character of an individual, or the events of a war.

Every community is originally a small one. That propensity by which mankind at first unite, is not the principle from which they afterwards act in extending the limits of empire. Small tribes, where they are not assembled by common objects of conquest or safety, are even averse to a coalition. If, like the real or fabulous confederacy of the Greeks for the destruction of Troy, many nations combine in pursuit of a single object, they easily separate again, and act anew on the maxims of rival states.

There is, perhaps, a certain national extent, within which the passions of men are easily communicated from one, or a few, to the whole; and there are certain numbers of men who can be assembled, and act in a body. If, while the society is not enlarged beyond this dimension, and while its members are easily assembled, political contentions arise, the state seldom fails to proceed on republican maxims, and to establish democracy. In most rude principalities, the leader derived his prerogative from the lustre of his race, and from the voluntary attachment of his tribe: the people he commanded, were his friends, his ſubjects, and his troops. If we ſuppoſe, upon any change in their manners, that they ceaſe to revere his dignity, that they pretend to equality among themſelves, or are ſeized with a jealouſy of his aſſuming too much, the foundations of his power are already withdrawn. When the voluntary ſubject becomes refractory; when conſiderable parties, or the collective body, chuſe to act for themſelves; the ſmall kingdom, like that of Athens, becomes of courſe a republic.

THE changes of condition, and of manners, which, in the progreſs of mankind, raiſe up to nations a leader and a prince, create, at the ſame time, a nobility, and a variety of ranks, who have, in a ſubordinate degree, their claim to diſtinction. Superſtition, too, may create an order of men, who, under the title of prieſthood, engage in the purſuit of a ſeparate intereſt; who, by their union and firmneſs as a body, and by their inceſſant ambition, deſerve to be reckoned in the liſt of pretenders to power. Theſe different orders of men are the elements of whoſe mixture the political body is generally formed; each draws to its ſide ſome part from the maſs of the people. The people themſelves are a party upon occaſion; and numbers of men, however claſſed and diſtinguiſhed, become, by their jarring pretenſions and ſeparate views, mutual interruptions and checks; and have, by bringing to the national councils the maxims and apprehenſions of a particular order, and by guarding

ing a particular intereſt, a ſhare in adjuſting or preſerving the political form of the ſtate.

THE pretenſions of any particular order, if not checked by ſome collateral power, would terminate in tyranny; thoſe of a prince, in deſpotiſm; thoſe of a nobility or prieſthood, in the abuſes of ariſtocracy; of a populace, in the confuſions of anarchy. Theſe terminations, as they are never the profeſſed, ſo are they ſeldom even the diſguiſed, object of party: but the meaſures which any party purſues, if ſuffered to prevail, will lead, by degrees, to every extreme.

IN their way to the aſcendant they endeavour to gain; and in the midſt of interruptions which oppoſite intereſts mutually give, liberty may have a permanent or a tranſient exiſtence; and the conſtitution may bear a form and a character as various as the caſual combination of ſuch multiplied parts can effect.

To beſtow on communities ſome degree of political freedom, it is perhaps ſufficient, that their members, either ſingly, or as they are involved with their ſeveral orders, ſhould inſiſt on their rights; that under republics, the citizen ſhould either maintain his own equality with firmneſs, or reſtrain the ambition of his fellow-citizen within moderate bounds: that under monarchy, men of every rank ſhould maintain the honours of their private or their public ſtations; and ſacrifice, neither to the impoſitions of a court, nor to the claims of a populace, thoſe dignities which are deſtined, in ſome meaſure, independent of fortune, to give ſtability to the throne, and to procure a reſpect to the ſubject.

AMIDST the contentions of party, the intereſts of the public, even the maxims of juſtice and candour, are ſometimes forgotten; and yet thoſe fatal conſequences which ſuch a meaſure of corruption ſeems to portend, do not unavoidably follow. The public intereſt is often ſecure, not becauſe individuals are diſpoſed to regard it as the end of their conduct, but becauſe each, in his place, is determined to preſerve his own. Liberty is maintained by the continued differences and oppoſitions of numbers, not by their concurring zeal in behalf of equitable government. In free ſtates, therefore, the wiſeſt laws are never, perhaps, dictated by the intereſt and ſpirit of any order of men: they are moved, they are oppoſed, or amended, by different hands; and come at laſt to expreſs that medium and compoſition which contending parties have forced one another to adopt.

WHEN we conſider the hiſtory of mankind in this view, we cannot be at a loſs for the cauſes which, in ſmall communities, threw the balance on the ſide of democracy; which, in ſtates more enlarged in reſpect to territory and numbers of people, gave the aſcendant to monarchy; and which, in a variety of conditions and of different ages, enabled mankind to blend and unite the characters of different forms; and, inſtead of any of the

ſimple

simple constitutions we have mentioned *, to exhibit a medley of all.

In emerging from a state of rudeness and simplicity, men must be expected to act from that spirit of equality, or moderate subordination, to which they have been accustomed. When crouded together in cities, or within the compass of a small territory, they act by contagious passions, and every individual feels a degree of importance proportioned to his figure in the croud, and the smallness of its numbers. The pretenders to power and dominion appear in too familiar a light to impose upon the multitude, and they have no aids at their call, by which they can bridle the refractory humours of a people who resist their pretensions. Theseus, King of Attica, we are told, assembled the inhabitants of its twelve cantons into one city. In this he took an effectual method to unite into one democracy, what were before the separate members of his monarchy, and to hasten the downfall of the regal power.

The monarch of an extensive territory has many advantages in maintaining his station. Without any grievance to his subjects, he can support the magnificence of a royal estate, and dazzle the imagination of his people, by that very wealth which themselves have bestowed. He can employ the inhabitants of one district against those of another; and while the passions that lead to mutiny

* Part 1. sect. 10.

and rebellion, can at any one time ſeize only on a part of his ſubjects, he feels himſelf ſtrong in the poſſeſſion of a general authority. Even the diſtance at which he reſides from many of thoſe who receive his commands, augments the myſterious awe and reſpect which are paid to his government.

WITH theſe different tendencies, accident and corruption, however, joined to a variety of circumſtances, may throw particular ſtates from their bias, and produce exceptions to every general rule. This has actually happened in ſome of the later principalities of Greece, and modern Italy, in Sweden, Poland, and the German empire. But the united ſtates of the Netherlands, and the Swiſs cantons, are perhaps the moſt extenſive communities, which maintaining the union of nations, have, for any conſiderable time, reſiſted the tendency to monarchical government; and Sweden is the only inſtance of a republic eſtabliſhed in a great kingdom on the ruins of monarchy.

THE ſovereign of a petty diſtrict, or a ſingle city, when not ſupported, as in modern Europe, by the contagion of monarchical manners, holds the ſceptre by a precarious tenure, and is perpetually alarmed by the ſpirit of mutiny in his people, is guided by jealouſy, and ſupports himſelf by ſeverity, prevention, and force.

THE popular and ariſtocratical powers in a great nation, as in the caſe of Germany and Poland, may meet with

with equal difficulty in maintaining their pretensions; and in order to avoid their danger on the side of kingly usurpation, are obliged to with-hold from the supreme magistrate even the necessary trust of an executive power.

THE states of Europe, in the manner of their first settlement, laid the foundations of monarchy, and were prepared to unite under regular and extensive governments. If the Greeks, whose progress at home terminated in the establishment of so many independent republics, had under Agamemnon effected a conquest and settlement in Asia, it is probable, that they might have furnished an example of the same kind. But the original inhabitants of any country, forming many separate cantons, come by slow degrees to that coalition and union into which conquering tribes are, in effecting their conquests, or in securing their possessions, hurried at once. Cæsar encountered some hundreds of independent nations in Gaul, whom even their common danger did not sufficiently unite. The German invaders, who settled in the lands of the Romans, made, in the same district, a number of separate establishments, but far more extensive than what the ancient Gauls, by their conjunctions and treaties, or in the result of their wars, could after many ages have reached.

THE seeds of great monarchies, and the roots of extensive dominion, were every where planted with the colonies that divided the Roman empire. We have no exact account

account of the numbers, who, with a ſeeming concert, continued, during ſome ages, to invade and to ſeize this tempting prize. Where they expected reſiſtance, they endeavoured to muſter up a proportionable force; and when they propoſed to ſettle, entire nations removed to ſhare in the ſpoil. Scattered over an extenſive province, where they could not be ſecure, without maintaining their union, they continued to acknowledge the leader under whom they had fought; and, like an army ſent by diviſions into ſeparate ſtations, were prepared to aſſemble whenever occaſion ſhould require their united operations or counſels.

EVERY ſeparate party had its poſt aſſigned, and every ſubordinate chieftain his poſſeſſions, from which he was to provide his own ſubſiſtence, and that of his followers. The model of government was taken from that of a military ſubordination, and a fief was the temporary pay of an officer proportioned to his rank *. There was a claſs of the people deſtined to military ſervice, another to labour, and to cultivate lands for the benefit of their maſters. The officer improved his tenure by degrees, firſt changing a temporary grant into a tenure for his life; and this alſo, upon the obſervance of certain conditions, into a grant including his heirs.

THE rank of the nobles became hereditary in every quarter, and formed a powerful and permanent order of

* See Dr Robertſon's Hiſtory of Scotland, b. I.

men

men in every ſtate. While they held the people in ſervitude, they diſputed the claims of their ſovereign; they withdrew their attendance upon occaſion, or turned their arms againſt him. They formed a ſtrong and inſurmountable barrier againſt a general deſpotiſm in the ſtate; but they were themſelves, by means of their warlike retainers, the tyrants of every little diſtrict, and prevented the eſtabliſhment of order, or any regular applications of law. They took the advantage of weak reigns or minorities, to puſh their incroachments on the ſovereign; or having made the monarchy elective, they by ſucceſſive treaties and ſtipulations, at every election, limited or undermined the monarchical power. The prerogatives of the prince have been, in ſome inſtances, as in that of the German empire in particular, reduced to a mere title; and the national union itſelf preſerved in the obſervance only of a few inſignificant formalities.

WHERE the conteſt of the ſovereign, and of his vaſſals, under hereditary and ample prerogatives annexed to the crown, had a different iſſue, the feudal lordſhips were gradually ſtript of their powers, the nobles were reduced to the ſtate of ſubjects, and obliged to hold their honours, and exerciſe their juriſdictions, in a dependence on the prince. It was his ſuppoſed intereſt to reduce them to a ſtate of equal ſubjection with the people, and to extend his own authority, by reſcuing the labourer and the dependent from the oppreſſions of their immediate ſuperiors.

In this project the princes of Europe have variously succeeded. While they protected the people, and thereby encouraged the practice of commercial and lucrative arts, they paved the way for despotism in the state; and with the same policy by which they relieved the subject from many oppressions, they increased the powers of the crown.

But where the people had by the constitution a representative in the government, and a head, under which they could avail themselves of the wealth they acquired, and of the sense of their personal importance, this policy turned against the crown; it formed a new power to restrain the prerogative, to establish the government of law, and to exhibit a spectacle new in the history of mankind; monarchy mixed with republic, and extensive territory, governed, during some ages, without military force.

Such were the steps by which the nations of Europe have arrived at their present establishments: in some instances, they have come to the possession of legal constitutions; in others, to the exercise of a mitigated despotism; or continue to struggle with the tendency which they severally have to these different extremes.

The progress of empire, in the early ages of Europe, threatened to be rapid, and to bury the independent spirit of nations in that grave which the Ottoman conquerors found for themselves; and for the wretched race they had vanquished. The Romans were led by slow degrees to extend the limits of their empire; every new acquisition was the result of a tedious war, and required the sending of colonies, and a variety of measures, to secure any new possession. But the feudal superior being animated, from the moment he had gained an establishment, with a desire of extending his territory, and of enlarging the list of his vassals, made frequent annexation of new provinces, merely by bestowing investiture, and received independent states, without any material innovation in the form of their policy, as the subjects of his growing dominion.

SEPARATE principalities were, like the parts of an engine, ready to be joined, and, like the materials of a building, ready to be erected. They were in the result of their struggles put together or taken asunder with facility. The independence of weak states was preserved only by the mutual jealousies of the strong, or by the general attention of all to maintain a balance of power.

THE happy system of policy on which European states have proceeded in preserving this balance; the degree of moderation which is, in adjusting their treaties, become habitual even to victorious and powerful monarchies, does honour to mankind, and may give hopes of a lasting felicity to be derived from a prepossession, never, perhaps, equally strong in any former period, or among any number of nations, that the first conquering people will ruin themselves, as well as their rivals.

It is in such states, perhaps, as in a fabric of a large dimension, that we can perceive most distinctly the several parts of which a political body consists; and observe that concurrence or opposition of interests, which serve to unite or to separate different orders of men, and lead them, by maintaining their several claims, to establish a variety of political forms. The smallest republics, however, consist of parts similar to these, and of members who are actuated by a similar spirit. They furnish examples of government diversified by the casual combinations of parties, and by the different advantages with which those parties engage in the conflict.

In every society there is a casual subordination, independent of its formal establishment, and frequently adverse to its constitution. While the administration and the people speak the language of a particular form, and seem to admit no pretensions to power, without a legal nomination in one instance, or without the advantage of hereditary honours in another, this casual subordination, possibly arising from the distribution of property, or from some other circumstance that bestows unequal degrees of influence, gives the state its tone, and fixes its character.

The plebeian order at Rome having been long considered as of an inferior condition, and excluded from the higher offices of magistracy, had sufficient force, as a body, to get this invidious distinction removed; but the individual still acting under the impressions of a subordi-

nate

nate rank, gave in every competition his suffrage to a patrician, whose protection he had experienced, and whose personal authority he felt. By this means, the ascendency of the patrician families was, for a certain period, as regular as it could be made by the avowed maxims of aristocracy; but the higher offices of state being gradually shared by plebeians, the effects of former distinctions were prevented or weakened. The laws that were made to adjust the pretensions of different orders were easily eluded. The populace became a faction, and their alliance was the surest road to dominion. Clodius, by a pretended adoption into a plebeian family, was qualified to become tribune of the people; and Cæsar, by espousing the cause of this faction, made his way to usurpation and tyranny.

In such fleeting and transient scenes, forms of government are only modes of proceeding, in which every subsequent age may differ from the former. Faction is ever ready to seize all occasional advantages; and mankind, when in hazard from any party, seldom find a better protection than that of its rival. Cato united with Pompey in opposition to Cæsar, and guarded against nothing so much as that reconciliation of parties, which was in effect to be a combination of different leaders against the freedom of the republic. This illustrious personage stood distinguished in his age like a man among children, and was raised above his opponents, as much by the justness of his understanding, and the extent of

his

his penetration, as he was by the manly fortitude and disinterestedness with which he strove to baffle the designs of a vain and childish ambition, that was operating to the ruin of mankind.

ALTHOUGH free constitutions of government seldom or never take their rise from the scheme of any single projector, yet are they often preserved by the vigilance, activity, and zeal, of single men. Happy are they who understand and who chuse this object of care; and happy it is for mankind when it is not chosen too late. It has been reserved to signalize the lives of a Cato or a Brutus, on the eve of fatal revolutions; to foster in secret the indignation of Thrasea and Helvidius; and to occupy the reflections of speculative men in times of corruption. But even in such late and ineffectual examples, it was happy to know, and to value, an object which is so important to mankind. The pursuit, and the love of it, however unsuccessful, has thrown a lustre on human nature.

SECT. III.

Of National Objects in general, and of Establishments and Manners relating to them.

WHILE the mode of subordination is casual, and forms of government take their rise, chiefly from the manner in which the members of a state have been originally classed, and from a variety of circumstances that procure to particular orders of men a sway in their country, there are certain objects that claim the attention of every government, that lead the apprehensions and the reasonings of mankind in every society, and that not only furnish an employment to statesmen, but in some measure direct the community to those institutions, under the authority of which the magistrate holds his power. Such are the national defence, the distribution of justice, the preservation and internal prosperity of the state. If these objects be neglected, we must apprehend that the very scene in which parties contend for power, for privilege, or equality, must disappear, and society itself no longer exist.

THE consideration due to these objects will be pleaded in every public assembly, and will produce, in every political contest, appeals to that common sense and opinion of mankind, which, struggling with the private views

views of individuals, and the claims of party, may be considered as the great legislator of nations.

THE measures required for the attainment of most national objects, are connected together, and must be jointly pursued: they are often the same. The force which is prepared for defence against foreign enemies, may be likewise employed to keep the peace at home: the laws made to secure the rights and liberties of the people, may serve as encouragements to population and commerce: and every community, without considering how its objects may be classed or distinguished by speculative men, is, in every instance, obliged to assume or to retain that form which is best fitted to preserve its advantages, or to avert its misfortunes.

NATIONS, however, like private men, have their favourite ends, and their principal pursuits, which diversify their manners, as well as their establishments. They even attain to the same ends by different means; and, like men who make their fortune by different professions, retain the habits of their principal calling in every condition at which they arrive. The Romans became wealthy in pursuing their conquests; and probably, for a certain period, increased the numbers of mankind, while their disposition to war seemed to threaten the earth with desolation. Some modern nations proceed to dominion and enlargement on the maxims of commerce; and while they only intend to accumulate riches at home, continue to gain an imperial ascendant abroad.

THE

THE characters of the warlike and the commercial are variouſly combined: they are formed in different degrees by the influence of circumſtances that more or leſs frequently give riſe to war, and excite the deſire of conqueſt; of circumſtances that leave a people in quiet to improve their domeſtic reſources, or to purchaſe, by the fruits of their induſtry, from foreigners, what their own ſoil and their climate deny.

THE members of every community are more or leſs occupied with matters of ſtate, in proportion as their conſtitution admits them to a ſhare in the government, and ſummons up their attention to objects of a public nature. A people are cultivated or unimproved in their talents, in proportion as thoſe talents are employed in the practice of arts, and in the affairs of ſociety: they are improved or corrupted in their manners, in proportion as they are encouraged and directed to act on the maxims of freedom and juſtice, or as they are degraded into a ſtate of meanneſs and ſervitude. But whatever advantages are obtained, or whatever evils are avoided, by nations, in any of theſe important reſpects, are generally conſidered as mere occaſional incidents: they are ſeldom admitted among the objects of policy, or entered among the reaſons of ſtate.

WE hazard being treated with ridicule, when we require political eſtabliſhments, merely to cultivate the talents of men, and to inſpire the ſentiments of a liberal mind: we muſt offer ſome motive of intereſt, or ſome hopes of external advantage, to animate the purſuits, or to direct the meaſures, of ordinary men. They would be brave, ingenious, and eloquent, only from neceſſity, or for the ſake of profit: they magnify the uſes of wealth, population, and the other reſources of war; but often forget that theſe are of no conſequence without the direction of able capacities, and without the ſupports of a national vigour. We may expect, therefore, to find among ſtates the bias to a particular policy, taken from the regards to public ſafety; from the deſire of ſecuring perſonal freedom, or private property; ſeldom from the conſideration of moral effects, or from a view to the genius of mankind.

SECT. IV.

Of Population and Wealth.

WHEN we imagine what the Romans muſt have felt when the tidings came that the flower of their city had periſhed at Cannæ; when we think of what the orator had in his mind when he ſaid, "That "the youth among the people was like the ſpring a-"mong the ſeaſons;" when we hear of the joy with which the huntſman and the warrior is adopted, in America, to ſuſtain the honours of the family and the nation; we are made to feel the moſt powerful motives to regard the increaſe and preſervation of our fellow-citizens. Intereſt, affection,

affection, and views of policy, combine to recommend this object; and it is treated with entire neglect only by the tyrant who miſtakes his own advantage, by the ſtateſman who trifles with the charge committed to his care, or by the people who are become corrupted, and who conſider their fellow-ſubjects as rivals in intereſt, and competitors in their lucrative purſuits.

Among rude ſocieties, and among ſmall communities in general, who are engaged in frequent ſtruggles and difficulties, the preſervation and increaſe of their members is a moſt important object. The American rates his defeat from the numbers of men he has loſt, or he eſtimates his victory from the priſoners he has made; not from his having remained the maſter of a field, or from his being driven from a ground on which he encountered his enemy. A man with whom he can aſſociate in all his purſuits, whom he can embrace as his friend; in whom he finds an object to his affections, and an aid in his ſtruggles, is to him the moſt precious acceſſion of fortune.

Even where the friendſhip of particular men is out of the queſtion, the ſociety, being occupied in forming a party that may defend itſelf, and annoy its enemy, finds no object of greater moment than the increaſe of its numbers. Captives who may be adopted, or children of either ſex who may be reared for the public, are accordingly conſidered as the richeſt ſpoil of an enemy. The practice of the Romans in admitting the vanquiſhed to ſhare in the privileges of their city, the rape of the Sabines, and the ſubſequent coalition with that people, were not ſingular or uncommon examples in the hiſtory of mankind. The ſame policy has been followed, and was natural and obvious where-ever the ſtrength of a ſtate conſiſted in the arms of a few, and where men were valued in themſelves, diſtinct from the conſideration of eſtate or of fortune.

In rude ages, therefore, while mankind ſubſiſt in ſmall diviſions, it ſhould appear, that if the earth be thinly peopled, this defect does not ariſe from a diſregard to numbers on the part of ſtates. It is even probable, that the moſt effectual courſe that could be taken to increaſe the ſpecies, would be, to prevent the coalition of nations, and to oblige mankind to act in ſuch ſmall bodies as would make the preſervation of their numbers a principal object of their care. This alone, it is true, would not be ſufficient: we muſt probably add the encouragement for rearing families, which mankind enjoy under a favourable policy, and the means of ſubſiſtence which they owe to the practice of arts.

The mother is unwilling to increaſe her offspring, and is ill provided to rear them, where ſhe herſelf is obliged to undergo great hardſhips in the ſearch of her food. In North America, we are told, that ſhe joins to the reſerves of a cold or a moderate temperament, the abſtinencies to which ſhe ſubmits from the conſideration of this difficulty. In her apprehenſion, it is matter of prudence,

dence, and of conscience, to bring one child to the condition of feeding on venison, and of following on foot, before she will hazard a new burden in travelling the woods.

In warmer latitudes, by the different temperament, perhaps, which the climate bestows, and by a greater facility in procuring subsistence, the numbers of mankind increase, while the object itself is neglected; and the commerce of the sexes, without any concern for population, is made a subject of mere debauch. In some places, we are told, it is even made the object of a barbarous policy, to defeat or to restrain the intentions of nature. In the island of Formosa, the males are prohibited to marry before the age of forty; and females, if pregnant before the age of thirty-six, have an abortion procured by order of the magistrate, who employs a violence that endangers the life of the mother, together with that of the child*.

In China, the permission given to parents to kill or to expose their children, was probably meant as a relief from the burden of a numerous offspring. But notwithstanding what we hear of a practice so repugnant to the human heart, it has not, probably, the effects in restraining population, which it seems to threaten; but, like many other institutions, has an influence the reverse of what it seemed to portend. The parents marry with this means of relief in their view, and the children are saved.

* Collection of Dutch voyages.

However important the object of population may be held by mankind, it will be difficult to find, in the history of civil policy, any wise or effectual establishments solely calculated to obtain it. The practice of rude or feeble nations is inadequate, or cannot surmount the obstacles which are found in their manner of life. The growth of industry, the endeavours of men to improve their arts, to extend their commerce, to secure their possessions, and to establish their rights, are indeed the most effectual means to promote population: but they arise from a different motive; they arise from regards to interest and personal safety. They are intended for the benefit of those who exist, not to procure the increase of their numbers.

It is, in the mean time, of importance to know, that where a people are fortunate in their political establishments, and successful in the pursuits of industry, their population is likely to grow in proportion. Most of the other devices thought of for this purpose, only serve to frustrate the expectations of mankind, or to mislead their attention.

In planting a colony, in striving to repair the occasional wastes of pestilence or war, the immediate contrivance of statesmen may be useful; but if in reasoning on the increase of mankind in general, we overlook their freedom, and their happiness, our aids to population become weak and ineffectual. They only lead us to work on the surface, or to pursue a shadow, while we neglect the substantial concern; and in a decaying state, make us tamper with palliatives, while the roots of an evil are ſuffered to remain. Octavius revived or inforced the laws that related to population at Rome: but it may be ſaid of him, and of many ſovereigns in a ſimilar ſituation, that they adminiſter the poiſon, while they are deviſing the remedy; and bring a damp and a palſy on the principles of life, while they endeavour, by external applications to the ſkin, to reſtore the bloom of a decayed and a ſickly body.

It is indeed happy for mankind, that this important object is not always dependent on the wiſdom of ſovereigns, or the policy of ſingle men. A people intent on freedom, find for themſelves a condition in which they may follow the propenſities of nature with a more ſignal effect, than any which the councils of ſtate could deviſe. When ſovereigns, or projectors, are the ſuppoſed maſters of this ſubject, the beſt they can do, is to be cautious of hurting an intereſt they cannot greatly promote, and of making breaches they cannot repair.

"When nations were divided into ſmall territories, "and petty commonwealths, where each man had his "houſe and his field to himſelf, and each county had its "capital free and independent; what a happy ſituation "for mankind," ſays Mr Hume, "how favourable to "induſtry and agriculture, to marriage and to popula- "tion!" Yet here were probably no ſchemes of the ſtateſman for rewarding the married, or for puniſhing the ſingle; for inviting foreigners to ſettle, or for prohi-

biting

biting the departure of natives. Every citizen finding a poſſeſſion ſecure, and a proviſion for his heirs, was not diſcouraged by the gloomy fears of oppreſſion or want: and where every other function of nature was free, that which furniſhed the nurſery could not be reſtrained. Nature has required the powerful to be juſt; but ſhe has not otherwiſe intruſted the preſervation of her works to their viſionary plans. What fewel can the ſtateſman add to the fires of youth? Let him only not ſmother it, and the effect is ſecure. Where we oppreſs or degrade mankind with one hand, it is vain, like Octavius, to hold out in the other, the baits of marriage, or the whip to barrenneſs. It is vain to invite new inhabitants from abroad, while thoſe we already poſſeſs are made to hold their tenure with uncertainty; and to tremble, not only under the proſpect of a numerous family, but even under that of a precarious and doubtful ſubſiſtence for themſelves. The arbitrary ſovereign, who has made this the condition of his ſubjects, owes the remains of his people to the powerful inſtincts of nature, not to any device of his own.

MEN will croud where the ſituation is tempting, and, in a few generations, will people every country to the meaſure of its means of ſubſiſtence. They will even increaſe under circumſtances that portend a decay. The frequent wars of the Romans, and of many a thriving community; even the peſtilence, and the market for ſlaves, find their ſupply, if, without deſtroying the ſource, the drain become regular; and if an iſſue is made for the

the offspring, without unſettling the families from which they ariſe. Where a happier proviſion is made for mankind, the ſtateſman, who by premiums to marriage, by allurements to foreigners, or by confining the natives at home, apprehends, that he has made the numbers of his people to grow, is often like the fly in the fable, who admired its ſucceſs, in turning the wheel, and in moving the carriage: he has only accompanied what was already in motion; he has daſhed with his oar, to haſten the cataract; and waved with his fan, to give ſpeed to the winds.

PROJECTS of mighty ſettlement, and of ſudden population, however ſucceſsful in the end, are always expenſive to mankind. Above a hundred thouſand peaſants, we are told, were yearly driven, like ſo many cattle, to Peterſburgh, in the firſt attempts to repleniſh that ſettlement, and yearly periſhed for want of ſubſiſtence *. The Indian only attempts to ſettle in the neighbourhood of the plantain †, and while his family increaſes, he adds a tree to the walk.

IF the plantain, the cocoa, or the palm, were ſufficient to maintain an inhabitant, the race of men in the warmer climates might become as numerous as the trees of the foreſt. But in many parts of the earth, from the nature of the climate, and the ſoil, the ſpontaneous pro-

* Strachlenberg.

† Dampier

duce being next to nothing; the means of ſubſiſtence are the fruits only of labour and ſkill. If a people, while they retain their frugality, increaſe their induſtry, and improve their arts, their numbers muſt grow in proportion. Hence it is, that the cultivated fields of Europe are more peopled than the wilds of America, or the plains of Tartary.

But even the increaſe of mankind which attends the accumulation of wealth, has its limits. The *neceſſary of life* is a vague and a relative term: it is one thing in the opinion of the ſavage; another in that of the poliſhed citizen: it has a reference to the fancy, and to the habits of living. While arts improve, and riches increaſe; while the poſſeſſions of individuals, or their proſpects of gain, come up to their opinion of what is required to ſettle a family, they enter on its cares with alacrity. But when the poſſeſſion, however redundant, falls ſhort of the ſtandard, and a fortune ſuppoſed ſufficient for marriage is attained with difficulty, population is checked, or begins to decline. The citizen, in his own apprehenſion, returns to the ſtate of the ſavage; his children, he thinks, muſt periſh for want; and he quits a ſcene overflowing with plenty, becauſe he has not the fortune which his ſuppoſed rank, or his wiſhes, require. No ultimate remedy is applied to this evil, by merely accumulating wealth; for rare and coſtly materials, whatever theſe are, continue to be ſought; and if ſilks and pearl are made common, men will begin to covet ſome new decorations, which the wealthy alone can procure. If they are indulged in their humour, their demands are repeated:

peated: For it is the continual increaſe of riches, not any meaſure attained, that keeps the craving imagination at eaſe.

MEN are tempted to labour, and to practiſe lucrative arts, by motives of intereſt. Secure to the workman the fruit of his labour, give him the proſpects of independence or freedom, the public has found a faithful miniſter in the acquiſition of wealth, and a faithful ſteward in hoarding what he has gained. The ſtateſman in this, as in the caſe of population itſelf, can do little more than avoid doing miſchief. It is well, if, in the beginnings of commerce, he knows how to repreſs the frauds to which it is ſubject. Commerce, if continued, is the branch in which men committed to the effects of their own experience, are leaſt apt to go wrong.

THE trader, in rude ages, is ſhort-ſighted, fraudulent, and mercenary; but in the progreſs and advanced ſtate of his art, his views are enlarged, his maxims are eſtabliſhed: he becomes punctual, liberal, faithful, and enterpriſing; and in the period of general corruption, he alone has every virtue, except the force to defend his acquiſitions. He needs no aid from the ſtate, but its protection; and is often in himſelf its moſt intelligent and reſpectable member. Even in China, we are informed, where pilfering, fraud, and corruption, are the reigning practice with all the other orders of men, the great merchant is ready to give, and to procure confidence: while his countrymen act on the plans and under the reſtric-

 tions

tions of a police adjuſted to knaves, he acts on the reaſons of trade, and the maxims of mankind.

If population be connected with national wealth, liberty and perſonal ſecurity is the great foundation of both: and if this foundation be laid in the ſtate, nature has ſecured the increaſe and the induſtry of its members; the one by deſires the moſt ardent in the human frame; the other by a conſideration the moſt uniform and conſtant of any that poſſeſſes the mind. The great object of policy, therefore, with reſpect to both, is, to ſecure to the family its means of ſubſiſtence and ſettlement; to protect the induſtrious in the purſuit of his occupation; to reconcile the reſtrictions of police, and the ſocial affections of mankind, with their ſeparate and intereſted purſuits.

In matters of particular profeſſion, induſtry, and trade, the experienced practitioner is the maſter, and every general reaſoner is a novice. The object in commerce is to make the individual rich; the more he gains for himſelf, the more he augments the wealth of his country. If a protection be required, it muſt be granted; if crimes and frauds be committed, they muſt be repreſſed; and government can pretend to no more. When the refined politician would lend an active hand, he only multiplies interruptions and grounds of complaint; when the merchant forgets his own intereſt to lay plans for his country, the period of viſion and chimera is near, and the ſolid baſis of commerce withdrawn. He might

be

be told, perhaps, that while he purſues his advantage, and gives no cauſe of complaint, the intereſt of commerce is ſafe.

THE general police of France, proceeding on a ſuppoſition that the exportation of corn muſt drain the country where it has grown, had, till of late, laid that branch of commerce under a ſevere prohibition. The Engliſh landholder and the farmer had credit enough to obtain a premium for exportation, to favour the ſale of their commodity; and the event has ſhewn, that private intereſt is a better patron of commerce and plenty, than the refinements of ſtate. One nation lays the refined plan of a ſettlement on the continent of North America, and truſts little to the conduct of traders and ſhort-ſighted men; another leaves men to find their own poſition in a ſtate of freedom, and to think for themſelves. The active induſtry and the limited views of the one, made a thriving ſettlement; the great projects of the other were ſtill in idea.

BUT I willingly quit a ſubject in which I am not much converſant, and ſtill leſs engaged by the views with which I write. Speculations on commerce and wealth have been delivered by the ableſt writers, who have left nothing ſo important to be offered on the ſubject, as the general caution, not to conſider theſe articles as making the ſum of national felicity, or the principal object of any ſtate.

ONE nation, in ſearch of gold and of precious metals, neglect the domeſtic ſources of wealth, and become dependent on their neighbours for the neceſſaries of life: another ſo intent on improving their internal reſources, and on increaſing their commerce, that they become dependent on foreigners for the defence of what they acquire. It is even painful in converſation to find the intereſts of trade give the tone to our reaſonings, and to find a ſubject perpetually offered as the great buſineſs of national councils, to which any interpoſition of government is ſeldom, with propriety, applied, or never beyond the protection it affords.

WE complain of a want of public ſpirit; but whatever may be the effect of this error in practice, in ſpeculation it is none of our faults: we reaſon perpetually for the public; but the want of national views were frequently better than the poſſeſſion of thoſe we expreſs: we would have nations, like a company of merchants, think of nothing but the increaſe of their ſtock; aſſemble to deliberate on profit and loſs; and, like them too, intruſt their protection to a force which they do not poſſeſs in themſelves.

BECAUSE men, like other animals, are maintained in multitudes, where the neceſſaries of life are amaſſed, and the ſtore of wealth is enlarged, we drop our regards for the happineſs, the moral and political character of a people; and anxious for the herd we would propagate, carry our views no farther than the ſtall and the paſture. We

forget

forget that the few have often made a prey of the many; that to the poor there is nothing ſo enticing as the coffers of the rich; and that when the price of freedom comes to be paid, the heavy ſword of the victor may fall into the oppoſite ſcale.

WHATEVER be the actual conduct of nations in this matter, it is certain, that many of our arguments would hurry us, for the ſake of wealth and of population, into a ſcene where mankind being expoſed to corruption, are unable to defend their poſſeſſions; and where they are, in the end, ſubject to oppreſſion and ruin. We cut off the roots, while we would extend the branches, and thicken the foliage.

IT is poſſibly from an opinion that the virtues of men are ſecure, that ſome who turn their attention to public affairs, think of nothing but the numbers and wealth of a people: it is from a dread of corruption, that others think of nothing but how to preſerve the national virtues. Human ſociety has great obligations to both. They are oppoſed to one another only by miſtake; and even when united, have not ſtrength ſufficient to combat the wretched party, that refers every object to perſonal intereſt, and that cares not for the ſafety or increaſe of any ſtock but its own.

SECT. V.

Of National Defence and Conqueſt.

IT is impoſſible to aſcertain how much of the policy of any ſtate has a reference to war, or to national ſafety. " Our legiſlator," ſays the Cretan in Plato, " thought that nations were by nature in a ſtate of hoſti-" lity: he took his meaſures accordingly; and obſer-" ving that all the poſſeſſions of the vanquiſhed pertain " to the victor, he held it ridiculous to propoſe any be-" nefit to his country, before he had provided that it " ſhould not be conquered."

CRETE, which is ſuppoſed to have been a model of military policy, is commonly conſidered as the original from which the celebrated laws of Lycurgus were copied. Mankind, it ſeems, in every inſtance, muſt have ſome palpable object to direct their proceedings, and muſt have a view to ſome point of external utility, even in the choice of their virtues. The diſcipline of Sparta was military; and a ſenſe of its uſe in the field, more than the force of unwritten and traditionary laws, or the ſuppoſed engagement of the public faith obtained by the lawgiver, may have induced this people to perſevere in the obſervance of many rules, which to other nations

tions do not appear necessary, except in the presence of an enemy.

EVERY institution of this singular people gave a lesson of obedience, of fortitude, and of zeal for the public: but it is remarkable that they chose to obtain, by their virtues alone, what other nations are fain to buy with their treasure; and it is well known, that, in the course of their history, they came to regard their discipline merely on account of its moral effects. They had experienced the happiness of a mind courageous, disinterested, and devoted to its best affections; and they studied to preserve this character in themselves, by resigning the interests of ambition, and the hopes of military glory, even by sacrificing the numbers of their people.

IT was the fate of Spartans who escaped from the field, not of those who perished with Cleombrotus at Leuctra, that filled the cottages of Lacedemon with mourning and serious reflection *: it was the fear of having their citizens corrupted abroad, by intercourse with servile and mercenary men, that made them quit the station of leaders in the Persian war, and leave Athens, during fifty years, to pursue, unrivalled, that career of ambition and profit, by which she made such acquisitions of power and of wealth †.

* Xenophon.

† Thucydides, book 1.

We have had occaſion to obſerve, that in every rude ſtate, the great buſineſs is war; and that in barbarous times, mankind, being generally divided into ſmall parties, are engaged in almoſt perpetual hoſtilities. This circumſtance gives the military leader a continued aſcendant in his country, and inclines every people, during warlike ages, to monarchical government.

The conduct of an army can leaſt of all ſubjects be divided: and we may be juſtly ſurpriſed to find, that the Romans, after many ages of military experience, and after having recently felt the arms of Hannibal, in many encounters, aſſociated two leaders at the head of the ſame army, and left them to adjuſt their pretenſions, by taking the command, each a day in his turn. The ſame people, however, on other occaſions, thought it expedient to ſuſpend the exerciſe of every ſubordinate magiſtracy, and in the time of great alarms, to intruſt all the authority of the ſtate in the hands of one perſon.

Republics have generally found it neceſſary, in the conduct of war, to place great confidence in the executive branch of their government. When a conſul at Rome had proclaimed his levies, and adminiſtered the military oath, he became from that moment maſter of the public treaſury, and of the lives of thoſe who were under his command *. The axe and the rods were no longer a mere badge of magiſtracy, or an empty pageant, in the

* Polybius.

hands

hands of the lictor: they were, at the command of the father, ftained with the blood of his own children ; and fell, without appeal, on the mutinous and the difobedient of every condition.

In every free ftate, there is a perpetual neceffity to diftinguifh the maxims of martial law from thofe of the civil; and he who has not learned to give an implicit obedience, where the ftate has given him a military leader, and to refign his perfonal freedom in the field, from the fame magnanimity with which he maintains it in the political deliberations of his country, has yet to learn the moft important leffon of civil fociety, and is only fit to occupy a place in a rude, or in a corrupted ftate, where the principles of mutiny and of fervility being joined, the one or the other is frequently adopted in the wrong place.

From a regard to what is neceffary in war, nations inclined to popular or ariftocratical government, have had recourfe to eftablifhments that bordered on monarchy. Even where the higheft office of the ftate was in common times adminiftered by a plurality of perfons, the whole power and authority belonging to it was, on particular occafions, committed to one; and upon great alarms, when the political fabric was fhaken or endangered, a monarchical power has been applied, like a prop, to fecure the ftate againft the rage of the tempeft. Thus were the dictators occafionally named at Rome, and the ftadtholders in the United Provinces ; and thus, in mixed governments, the royal prerogative is occaſionally enlarged, by the temporary ſuſpenſion of laws *, and the barriers of liberty appear to be removed, in order to veſt a dictatorial power in the hands of the king.

Had mankind, therefore, no view but to warfare, it is probable that they would continue to prefer monarchical government to any other; or at leaſt that every nation, in order to procure ſecret and united councils, would intruſt the executive power with unlimited authority. But, happily for civil ſociety, men have objects of a different ſort: and experience has taught, that although the conduct of armies requires an abſolute and undivided command; yet a national force is beſt formed, where numbers of men are inured to equality; and where the meaneſt citizen may conſider himſelf, upon occaſion, as deſtined to command as well as to obey. It is here that the dictator finds a ſpirit and a force prepared to ſecond his councils; it is here too that the dictator himſelf is formed, and that numbers of leaders are preſented to the public choice; it is here that the proſperity of a ſtate is independent of ſingle men, and that a wiſdom which never dies, with a ſyſtem of military arrangements permanent and regular, can, even under the greateſt miſfortunes, prolong the national ſtruggle. With this advantage, the Romans, finding a number of diſtinguiſhed leaders ariſe in ſucceſſion, were at all times almoſt equally prepared to contend with their enemies of Aſia

* In Britain, by the ſuſpenſion of the *Habeas corpus*.

or Africa; while the fortune of thoſe enemies, on the contrary, depended on the caſual appearance of ſingular men, of a Mithridates, or of a Hannibal.

THE ſoldier, we are told, has his point of honour, and a faſhion of thinking, which he wears with his ſword. This point of honour, in free and uncorrupted ſtates, is a zeal for the public; and war to them, is an operation of paſſions, not the mere purſuit of a calling. Its good and its ill effects are felt in extremes: the friend is made to experience the warmeſt proofs of attachment; the enemy the ſevereſt effects of animoſity. On this ſyſtem the celebrated nations of antiquity made war under their higheſt attainments of civility, and under their greateſt degrees of refinement.

IN ſmall and rude ſocieties, the individual finds himſelf attacked in every national war; and none can propoſe to devolve his defence on another. "The King "of Spain is a great prince," ſaid an American chief to the governor of Jamaica, who was preparing a body of troops to join in an enterpriſe againſt the Spaniards: "do you propoſe to make war upon ſo great a "king with ſo ſmall a force?" Being told that the forces he ſaw were to be joined by troops from Europe, and that the governor could then command no more: "Who "are theſe then," ſaid the American, "who form this "croud of ſpectators? are they not your people? and "why do you not all go forth to ſo great a war?" He was anſwered, That the ſpectators were merchants, and

other

other inhabitants, who took no part in the ſervice: " Would they be merchants ſtill," continued this ſtateſman, " if the King of Spain was to attack you here? " For my part, I do not think that merchants ſhould be " permitted to live in any country: when I go to war, I " leave no body at home but the women." It ſhould ſeem that this ſimple warrior conſidered merchants as a kind of neutral perſons, who took no part in the quarrels of their country; and that he did not know how much war itſelf may be made a ſubject of traffic; what mighty armies may be put in motion from behind the counter; how often human blood is, without any national animoſity, bought and ſold for bills of exchange; and how often the prince, the nobles, and the ſtateſmen, in many a poliſhed nation, might, in his account, be conſidered as merchants.

In the progreſs of arts and of policy, the members of every ſtate are divided into claſſes; and in the commencement of this diſtribution, there is no diſtinction more ſerious than that of the warrior and the pacific inhabitant; no more is required to place men in the relation of maſter and ſlave. Even when the rigours of an eſtabliſhed ſlavery abate, as they have done in modern Europe, in conſequence of a protection, and a property, allowed to the mechanic and labourer, this diſtinction ſerves ſtill to ſeparate the noble from the baſe, and to point out that claſs of men who are deſtined to reign and to domineer in their country.

It was certainly never foreseen by mankind, that in the pursuit of refinement, they were to reverse this order; or even that they were to place the government, and the military force of nations, in different hands. But is it equally unforseen, that the former order may again take place? and that the pacific citizen, however distinguished by privilege and rank, must one day bow to the person with whom he has intrusted his sword. If such revolutions should actually follow, will this new master revive in his own order the spirit of the noble and the free? Will he renew the characters of the warrior and the statesman? Will he restore to his country the civil and military virtues? I am afraid to reply. Montesquieu observes, that the government of Rome, even under the emperors, became, in the hands of the troops, elective and republican: but the Fabii or the Bruti were heard of no more, after the prætorian bands became the republic.

We have enumerated some of the heads under which a people, as they emerge from barbarity, may come to be classed. Such are, the nobility, the people, the adherents of the prince; and even the priesthood have not been forgotten: when we arrive at times of refinement, the army must be joined to the list. The departments of civil government and of war being severed, and the preeminence being given to the statesman, the ambitious will naturally devolve the military service on those who are contented with a subordinate station. They who have the greatest share in the division of fortune, and the greatest interest in defending their country, having re-

signed

ſigned the ſword, muſt pay for what they have ceaſed to perform; and armies, not only at a diſtance from home, but in the very boſom of their country, are ſubſiſted by pay. A diſcipline is invented to inure the ſoldier to perform, from habit, and from the fear of puniſhment, thoſe hazardous duties, which the love of the public, or a national ſpirit, no longer inſpire.

When we conſider the breach that ſuch an eſtabliſhment makes in the ſyſtem of national virtues, it is unpleaſant to obſerve, that moſt nations who have run the career of civil arts, have, in ſome degree, adopted this meaſure. Not only ſtates, which either have wars to maintain, or precarious poſſeſſions to defend at a diſtance; not only a prince jealous of his authority, or in haſte to gain the advantage of diſcipline, are diſpoſed to employ foreign troops, or to keep ſtanding armies; but even republics, with little of the former occaſion, and none of the motives which prevail in monarchy, have been found to tread in the ſame path.

If military arrangements occupy ſo conſiderable a place in the domeſtic policy of nations, the actual conſequences of war are equally important in the hiſtory of mankind. Glory and ſpoil were the earlieſt ſubject of quarrels; a conceſſion of ſuperiority, or a ranſom, were the prices of peace. The love of ſafety, and the deſire of dominion, equally lead mankind to wiſh for acceſſions of ſtrength. Whether as victors or as vanquiſhed, they tend to a coalition; and powerful nations conſidering a province,

vince, or a fortreſs acquired on their frontier, as ſo much gained, are perpetually intent on extending their limits.

THE maxims of conqueſt are not always to be diſtinguiſhed from thoſe of ſelf-defence. If a neighbouring ſtate be dangerous, if it be frequently troubleſome, it is a maxim founded in the conſideration of ſafety, as well as of conqueſt, That it ought to be weakened or diſarmed: If, being once reduced, it be diſpoſed to renew the conteſt, it muſt from thenceforward be governed in form. Rome never avowed any other maxims of conqueſt; and ſhe every where ſent her inſolent armies, under the ſpecious pretence of procuring to herſelf and her allies a laſting peace, which ſhe alone would reſerve the power to diſturb.

THE equality of thoſe alliances which the Grecian ſtates formed againſt each other, maintained, for a time, their independence and ſeparation; and that time was the ſhining and the happy period of their ſtory. It was prolonged more by the vigilance and conduct which they ſeverally applied, than by the moderation of their councils, or by any peculiarities of domeſtic policy which arreſted their progreſs. The victors were ſometimes contented, with merely changing to a reſemblance of their own forms the government of the ſtates they ſubdued. What the next ſtep might have been in the progreſs of impoſitions, is hard to determine. But when we conſider, that one party fought for the impoſition of tributes, another for the aſcendant in war, it cannot be doubted,

 that

that the Athenians, from a national ambition, and from the deſire of wealth, and the Spartans, though they originally only meant to defend themſelves, and their allies, were both, at laſt, equally willing to become the maſters of Greece; and were preparing for each other at home, that yoke, which both, together with their confederates, were obliged to receive from abroad.

In the conqueſts of Philip, the deſire of ſelf-preſervation and ſecurity ſeemed to be blended with the ambition natural to princes. He turned his arms ſucceſſively to the quarters on which he found himſelf hurt, from which he had been alarmed or provoked: and when he had ſubdued the Greeks, he propoſed to lead them againſt their ancient enemy of Perſia. In this he laid the plan which was carried into execution by his ſon.

The Romans, become the maſters of Italy, and the conquerors of Carthage, had been alarmed on the ſide of Macedon, and were led to croſs a new ſea in ſearch of a new field, on which to exerciſe their military force. In proſecution of their wars, from the earlieſt to the lateſt date of their hiſtory, without intending the very conqueſts they made, perhaps without foreſeeing what advantage they were to reap from the ſubjection of diſtant provinces, or in what manner they were to govern their new acquiſitions, they ſtill proceeded to ſeize what came ſucceſſively within their reach; and, ſtimulated by a policy which engaged them in perpetual wars, which led to perpetual victory and acceſſions of territory, they extended

tended the frontier of a ſtate, which, but a few centuries before, had been confined within the ſkirts of a village, to the Euphrates, the Danube, the Weſer, the Forth, and the Ocean.

It is vain to affirm, that the genius of any nation is adverſe to conqueſt. Its real intereſts indeed moſt commonly are ſo; but every ſtate which is prepared to defend itſelf, and to obtain victories, is likewiſe in hazard of being tempted to conquer.

In Europe, where mercenary and diſciplined armies are every where formed, and ready to traverſe the earth, where, like a flood pent up by ſlender banks, they are only reſtrained by political forms, or a temporary balance of power; if the ſluices ſhould break, what inundations may we not expect to behold? Effeminate kingdoms and empires are ſpread from the ſea of Corea to the Atlantic ocean. Every ſtate, by the defeat of its troops, may be turned into a province; every army oppoſed in the field to-day may be hired to-morrow; and every victory gained, may give the acceſſion of a new military force to the victor.

The Romans, with inferior arts of communication both by ſea and land, maintained their dominion in a conſiderable part of Europe, Aſia, and Africa, over fierce and intractable nations: What may not the fleets and armies of Europe, with the acceſs they have by commerce to every part of the world, and the facility of their conveyance, effect, if that ruinous maxim should prevail, That the grandeur of a nation is to be estimated from the extent of its territory; or, That the interest of any particular people consists in reducing their neighbours to servitude?

SECT. VI.

Of Civil Liberty.

IF war, either for depredation or defence, were the principal object of nations, every tribe would, from its earliest state, aim at the condition of a Tartar horde; and in all its successes would hasten to the grandeur of a Tartar empire. The military leader would supersede the civil magistrate; and preparations to fly with all their possessions, or to pursue with all their forces, would, in every society, make the sum of their public arrangements.

HE who first on the banks of the Wolga, or the Jenisca, had taught the Scythian to mount the horse, to move his cottage on wheels, to harass his enemy alike by his attacks and his flights, to handle at full speed the lance and the bow, and when beat from the field, to leave his arrows in the wind to meet his pursuer; he who had taught his countrymen to use the same animal for every purpose of the dairy, the shambles, and the field; would be esteemed the founder of his nation; or, like Ceres and Bacchus

Bacchus among the Greeks, would be invested with the honours of a god, as the reward of his useful inventions. Amidst such institutions, the names and atchievements of Hercules and Jason might have been transmitted to posterity; but those of Lycurgus or Solon, the heroes of political society, could have gained no reputation, either fabulous or real, in the records of fame.

EVERY tribe of warlike barbarians may entertain among themselves the strongest sentiments of affection and honour, while they carry to the rest of mankind the aspect of banditti and robbers *. They may be indifferent to interest, and superior to danger; but our sense of humanity, our regard to the rights of nations, our admiration of civil wisdom and justice, even our effeminacy itself, make us turn away with contempt, or with horror, from a scene which exhibits so few of our good qualities, and which serve so much to reproach our weakness.

IT is in conducting the affairs of civil society, that mankind find the exercise of their best talents, as well as the object of their best affections. It is in being grafted on the advantages of civil society, that the art of war is brought to perfection; that the resources of armies, and the complicated springs to be touched in their conduct, are best understood. The most celebrated warriors were also citizens: Opposed to a Roman, or a Greek, the

* D'Arvieux's Hist. of the Arabs.

chieftain

chieftain of Thrace, of Germany, or Gaul, was a novice. The native of Pella learned the principles of his art from Epaminondas and Pelopidas.

If nations, as hath been obſerved in the preceding ſection, muſt adjuſt their policy on the proſpect of war from abroad, they are equally bound to provide for the attainment of peace at home. But there is no peace in the abſence of juſtice. It may ſubſiſt with diviſions, diſputes, and contrary opinions; but not with the commiſſion of wrongs. The injurious, and the injured, are, as implied in the very meaning of the terms, in a ſtate of hoſtility.

Where men enjoy peace, they owe it either to their mutual regards and affections, or to the reſtraints of law. Thoſe are the happieſt ſtates which procure peace to their members by the firſt of theſe methods: But it is ſufficiently uncommon to procure it even by the ſecond. The firſt would with-hold the occaſions of war and of competition: The ſecond adjuſts the pretenſions of men by ſtipulations and treaties. Sparta taught her citizens not to regard intereſt: Other free nations ſecure the intereſt of their members, and conſider this as a principal part of their rights.

Law is the treaty to which members of the ſame community have agreed, and under which the magiſtrate and the ſubject continue to enjoy their rights, and to maintain the peace of ſociety. The deſire of lucre is the great motive to injuries: law therefore has a principal reference to property. It would aſcertain the different methods

by

by which property may be acquired, as by prescription, conveyance, and succession; and it makes the necessary provisions for rendering the possession of property secure.

BESIDE avarice, there are other motives from which men are unjust; such are pride, malice, envy, and revenge. The law would eradicate the principles themselves, or at least prevent their effects.

FROM whatever motive wrongs are committed, there are different particulars in which the injured may suffer. He may suffer in his goods, in his person, or in the freedom of his conduct. Nature has made him master of every action which is not injurious to others. The laws of his particular society intitle him perhaps to a determinate station, and bestow on him a certain share in the government of his country. An injury, therefore, which in this respect puts him under any unjust restraint, may be called an infringement of his political rights.

WHERE the citizen is supposed to have rights of property and of station, and is protected in the exercise of them, he is said to be free; and the very restraints by which he is hindered from the commission of crimes, are a part of his liberty. No person is free, where any person is suffered to do wrong with impunity. Even the despotic prince on his throne, is not an exception to this general rule. He himself is a slave, the moment he pretends that force should decide any contest. The disregard he throws on the rights of his people recoils on himself; and

in

in the general uncertainty of all conditions, there is no tenure more precarious than his own.

FROM the different particulars to which men refer, in ſpeaking of liberty, whether to the ſafety of the perſon and the goods, the dignity of rank, or the participation of political importance, as well as from the different methods by which their rights are ſecured, they are led to differ in the interpretation of the term; and every people is apt to imagine, that its ſignification is to be found only among themſelves.

SOME having thought, that the unequal diſtribution of wealth is unjuſt, required a new diviſion of property, as the foundation of freedom. This ſcheme is ſuited to democratical government; and in ſuch only it has been admitted with any degree of effect.

NEW ſettlements, like that of the people of Iſrael, and ſingular eſtabliſhments, like thoſe of Sparta and Crete, have furniſhed examples of its actual execution; but in moſt other ſtates, even the democratical ſpirit could attain no more than to prolong the ſtruggle for Agrarian laws; to procure, on occaſion, the expunging of debts; and to keep the people in mind, under all the diſtinctions of fortune, that they ſtill had a claim to equality.

THE citizen at Rome, at Athens, and in many republics, contended for himſelf, and his order. The Agrarian law was moved and debated for ages: it ſerved to awaken

awaken the mind; it nouriſhed the ſpirit of equality, and furniſhed a field on which to exert its force; but was never eſtabliſhed with any of its other and more formal effects.

MANY of the eſtabliſhments which ſerve to defend the weak from oppreſſion, contribute, by ſecuring the poſſeſſion of property, to favour its unequal diviſion, and to increaſe the aſcendant of thoſe from whom the abuſes of power may be feared. Thoſe abuſes were felt very early both at Athens and Rome *.

IT has been propoſed to prevent the exceſſive accumulation of wealth in particular hands, by limiting the increaſe of private fortunes, by prohibiting entails, and by with-holding the right of primogeniture in the ſucceſſion of heirs. It has been propoſed to prevent the ruin of moderate eſtates, and to reſtrain the uſe, and conſequently the deſire, of great ones, by ſumptuary laws. Theſe different methods are more or leſs conſiſtent with the intereſts of commerce, and may be adopted, in different degrees, by a people whoſe national object is wealth: and they have their degree of effect, by inſpiring moderation, or a ſenſe of equality, and by ſtifling the paſſions by which mankind are prompted to mutual wrongs.

* Plutarch in the life of Solon.——Livy.

It appears to be, in a particular manner, the object of sumptuary laws, and of the equal division of wealth, to prevent the gratification of vanity, to check the ostentation of superior fortune, and, by this means, to weaken the desire of riches, and to preserve in the breast of the citizen, that moderation and equity which ought to regulate his conduct.

This end is never perfectly attained in any state where the unequal division of property is admitted, and where fortune is allowed to bestow distinction and rank. It is indeed difficult, by any methods whatever, to shut up this source of corruption. Of all the nations whose history is known with certainty, the design itself, and the manner of executing it, appear to have been understood in Sparta alone.

There property was indeed acknowledged by law; but in consequence of certain regulations and practices, the most effectual, it seems, that mankind have hitherto found out. The manners that prevail among simple nations before the establishment of property, were in some measure preserved *; the passion for riches was, during many ages, suppressed; and the citizen was made to consider himself as the property of his country, not as the owner of a private estate.

* See part 2. sect. 2.

It was held ignominious either to buy or to ſell the patrimony of a citizen. Slaves were, in every family, intruſted with the care of its effects, and freemen were ſtrangers to lucrative arts; juſtice was eſtabliſhed on a contempt of the ordinary allurement to crimes; and the preſervatives of civil liberty applied by the ſtate, were the diſpoſitions that were made to prevail in the hearts of its members.

The individual was relieved from every ſolicitude that could ariſe on the head of his fortune; he was educated, and he was employed for life in the ſervice of the public; he was fed at a place of common reſort, to which he could carry no diſtinction but that of his talents and his virtues; his children were the wards and the pupils of the ſtate; he himſelf was taught to be a parent, and a director to the youth of his country, not the anxious father of a ſeparate family.

This people, we are told, beſtowed ſome care in adorning their perſons, and were known from afar by the red or the purple they wore; but could not make their equipage, their buildings, or their furniture, a ſubject of fancy, or of what we call *taſte*. The carpenter and the houſe-builder were reſtricted to the uſe of the axe and the ſaw: their workmanſhip muſt have been ſimple, and probably, in reſpect to its form, continued for ages the ſame. The ingenuity of the artiſt was employed in cultivating his own nature, not in adorning the habitations of his fellow-citizens.

On this plan, they had ſenators, magiſtrates, leaders of armies, and miniſters of ſtate; but no men of fortune. Like the heroes of Homer, they diſtributed honours by the meaſure of the cup and the platter. A citizen, who, in his political capacity, was the arbiter of Greece, thought himſelf honoured by receiving a double portion of plain entertainment at ſupper. He was active, penetrating, brave, diſintereſted, and generous; but his eſtate, his table, and his furniture, might, in our eſteem, have marred the luſtre of all his virtues. Neighbouring nations, however, applied for commanders to this nurſery of ſtateſmen and warriors, as we apply for the practitioners of every art to the countries in which they excel; for cooks to France, and for muſicians to Italy.

After all, we are, perhaps, not ſufficiently inſtructed in the nature of the Spartan laws and inſtitutions, to underſtand in what manner all the ends of this ſingular ſtate were obtained; but the admiration paid to its people, and the conſtant reference of contemporary hiſtorians to their avowed ſuperiority, will not allow us to queſtion the facts. "When I obſerved," ſays Xenophon, "that this nation, though not the moſt populous, was the "moſt powerful ſtate of Greece, I was ſeized with won-"der, and with an earneſt deſire to know by what arts "it attained its pre-eminence; but when I came to the "knowledge of its inſtitutions, my wonder ceaſed.—— "As one man excels another, and as he who is at pains "to cultivate his mind, muſt ſurpaſs the perſon who "neglects it; ſo the Spartans ſhould excel every nation,

"being

" being the only ſtate in which virtue is ſtudied as the
" object of government."

THE ſubjects of property, conſidered with a view to ſubſiſtence, or even to enjoyment, have little effect in corrupting mankind, or in awakening the ſpirit of competition and of jealouſy; but conſidered with a view to diſtinction and honour, where fortune conſtitutes rank, they excite the moſt vehement paſſions, and abſorb all the ſentiments of the human ſoul: they reconcile avarice and meanneſs with ambition and vanity; and lead men through the practice of ſordid and mercenary arts to the poſſeſſion of a ſuppoſed elevation and dignity.

WHERE this ſource of corruption, on the contrary, is effectually ſtopped, the citizen is dutiful, and the magiſtrate upright; any form of government may be wiſely adminiſtered; places of truſt are likely to be well ſupplied; and by whatever rule office and power are beſtowed, it is likely that all the capacity and force that ſubſiſts in the ſtate will come to be employed in its ſervice: for on this ſuppoſition, experience and abilities are the only guides and the only titles to public confidence; and if citizens be ranged into ſeparate claſſes, they become mutual checks by the difference of their opinions, not by the oppoſition of their intereſted deſigns.

WE may eaſily account for the cenſures beſtowed on the government of Sparta, by thoſe who conſidered it merely on the ſide of its forms. It was not calculated to

prevent

prevent the practice of crimes, by balancing against each other the selfish and partial dispositions of men; but to inspire the virtues of the soul, to procure innocence by the absence of criminal inclinations, and to derive its internal peace from the indifference of its members to the ordinary motives of strife and disorder. It were trifling to seek for its analogy to any other constitution of state, in which its principal characteristic and distinguishing feature is not to be found. The collegiate sovereignty, the senate, and the ephori, had their counterparts in other republics, and a resemblance has been found in particular to the government of Carthage *: but what affinity of consequence can be found between a state whose sole object was virtue, and another whose principal object was wealth; between a people whose associated kings, being lodged in the same cottage, had no fortune but their daily food; and a commercial republic, in which a proper estate was required as a necessary qualification for the higher offices of state?

Other petty commonwealths expelled kings, when they became jealous of their designs, or after having experienced their tyranny; here the hereditary succession of kings was preserved: other states were afraid of the intrigues and cabals of their members in competition for dignities; here solicitation was required as the only condition upon which a place in the senate was obtained. A supreme inquisitorial power was, in the persons of the

* Aristotle.

ephori,

ephori, ſafely committed to a few men, who were drawn by lot, and without diſtinction, from every order of the people: and if a contraſt to this, as well as to many other articles of the Spartan policy, be required, it may be found in the general hiſtory of mankind.

But Sparta, under every ſuppoſed error of its form, proſpered for ages, by the integrity of its manners, and by the character of its citizens. When that integrity was broken, this people did not languiſh in the weakneſs of nations ſunk in effeminacy. They fell into the ſtream by which other ſtates had been carried in the torrent of violent paſſions, and in the outrage of barbarous times. They ran the career of other nations, after that of ancient Sparta was finiſhed: They built walls, and began to improve their poſſeſſions, after they ceaſed to improve their people; and on this new plan, in their ſtruggle for political life, they ſurvived the ſyſtem of ſtates that periſhed under the Macedonian dominion: They lived to act with another which aroſe in the Achæan league; and were the laſt community of Greece that became a village in the empire of Rome.

If it ſhould be thought we have dwelt too long on the hiſtory of this ſingular people, it may be remembered, in excuſe, that they alone, in the language of Xenophon, made virtue an object of ſtate.

We muſt be contented to derive our freedom from a different ſource; to expect juſtice from the limits which are

are ſet to the powers of the magiſtrate, and to rely for protection on the laws which are made to ſecure the eſtate, and the perſon of the ſubject. We live in ſocieties, where men muſt be rich, in order to be great; where pleaſure itſelf is often purſued from vanity; where the deſire of a ſuppoſed happineſs ſerves to inflame the worſt of paſſions, and is itſelf the foundation of miſery; where public juſtice, like fetters applied to the body, may, without inſpiring the ſentiments of candour and equity, prevent the actual commiſſion of crimes.

MANKIND come under this deſcription the moment they are ſeized with their paſſions for riches and power. But their deſcription in every inſtance is mixed: in the beſt there is an alloy of evil; in the worſt a mixture of good. Without any eſtabliſhments to preſerve their manners, beſides penal laws, and the reſtraints of police, they derive, from inſtinctive feelings, a love of integrity and candour, and, from the very contagion of ſociety itſelf, an eſteem for what is honourable and praiſe-worthy. They derive, from their union, and joint oppoſition to foreign enemies, a zeal for their own community, and courage to maintain its rights. If the frequent neglect of virtue as a political object, tend to diſcredit the underſtandings of men, its luſtre, and its frequency, as a ſpontaneous offspring of the heart, will reſtore the honours of our nature.

IN every caſual and mixed ſtate of the national manners, the ſafety of every individual, and his political conſequence,

ſequence, depends much on himſelf, but more on the party to which he is joined. For this reaſon, all who feel a common intereſt, are apt to unite in parties; and, as far as that intereſt requires, mutually ſupport each other.

WHERE the citizens of any free community are of different orders, each order has a peculiar ſet of claims and pretenſions: relatively to the other members of the ſtate, it is a party; relatively to the differences of intereſt among its own members, it may admit of numberleſs ſubdiviſions. But in every ſtate there are two intereſts very readily apprehended; that of a prince and his adherents, that of a nobility, or of any temporary faction, oppoſed to the people.

WHERE the ſovereign power is reſerved by the collective body, it appears unneceſſary to think of additional eſtabliſhments for ſecuring the rights of the citizen. But it is difficult, if not impoſſible, for the collective body to exerciſe this power in a manner that ſuperſedes the neceſſity of every other political caution.

IF popular aſſemblies aſſume every function of government; and if, in the ſame tumultuous manner in which they can, with great propriety, expreſs their feelings, the ſenſe of their rights, and their animoſity to foreign or domeſtic enemies, they pretend to deliberate on points of national conduct, or to decide queſtions of equity and juſtice; the public is expoſed to manifold inconveniencies; and popular governments would, of all others, be the moſt ſubject to errors in adminiſtration, and to weakneſs in the execution of public meaſures.

To avoid theſe diſadvantages, the people are always contented to delegate part of their powers. They eſtabliſh a ſenate to debate, and to prepare, if not to determine, queſtions that are brought to the collective body for a final reſolution. They commit the executive power to ſome council of this ſort, or to a magiſtrate who preſides in their meetings. Under the uſe of this neceſſary and common expedient, even while democratical forms are moſt carefully guarded, there is one party of the few, another of the many. One attacks, the other defends; and they are both ready to aſſume in their turns. But though, in reality, a great danger to liberty ariſes on the part of the people themſelves, who, in times of corruption, are eaſily made the inſtruments of uſurpation and tyranny; yet, in the ordinary aſpect of government, the executive carries an air of ſuperiority, and the rights of the people ſeem always expoſed to incroachment.

Though on the day that the Roman people aſſembled in their tribes, the ſenators mixed with the croud, and the conſul was no more than the ſervant of the multitude; yet, when this awful meeting was diſſolved, the ſenators met to preſcribe buſineſs for their ſovereign, and the conſul went armed with the axe and the rods, to teach every Roman, in his ſeparate capacity, the ſubmiſſion which he owed to the ſtate.

Thus,

THUS, even where the collective body is ſovereign, they are aſſembled only occaſionally: and though on ſuch occaſions they determine every queſtion relative to their rights and their intereſts as a people, and can aſſert their freedom with irreſiſtible force; yet they do not think themſelves, nor are they in reality, ſafe, without a more conſtant and more uniform power operating in their favour.

THE multitude is every where ſtrong; but requires, for the ſafety of its members, when ſeparate as well as when aſſembled, a head to direct and to employ its ſtrength. For this purpoſe, the ephori, we are told, were eſtabliſhed at Sparta, the council of a hundred at Carthage, and the tribunes at Rome. So prepared, the popular party has, in many inſtances, been able to cope with its adverſaries, and has even trampled on the powers, whether ariſtocratical or monarchical, with which it would have been otherwiſe unequally matched. The ſtate, in ſuch caſes, commonly ſuffered by the delays, interruptions, and confuſions, which popular leaders, from private envy, or a prevailing jealouſy of the great, ſeldom failed to create in the proceedings of government.

WHERE the people, as in ſome larger communities, have only a ſhare in the legiſlature, they cannot overwhelm the collateral powers, who having likewiſe a ſhare, are in condition to defend themſelves: Where they act only by their repreſentatives, their force may be uniformly

 employed.

employed. And they may make part in a conſtitution of government more laſting than any of thoſe in which the people poſſeſſing or pretending to the entire legiſlature, are, when aſſembled, the tyrants, and, when diſperſed, the ſlaves, of a diſtempered ſtate. In governments properly mixed, the popular intereſt, finding a counterpoiſe in that of the prince or of the nobles, a balance is actually eſtabliſhed between them, in which the public freedom and the public order are made to conſiſt.

From ſome ſuch caſual arrangement of different intereſts, all the varieties of mixed government proceed; and on the degree of conſideration which every ſeparate intereſt can procure to itſelf, depends the equity of the laws they enact, and the neceſſity they are able to impoſe, of adhering ſtrictly to the terms of law in its execution. States are accordingly unequally qualified to conduct the buſineſs of legiſlation, and unequally fortunate in the completeneſs, and regular obſervance, of their civil code.

In democratical eſtabliſhments, citizens, feeling themſelves poſſeſſed of the ſovereignty, are not equally anxious, with the ſubject of other governments, to have their rights explained, or ſecured, by actual ſtatute. They truſt to perſonal vigour, to the ſupport of party, and to the ſenſe of the public.

If the collective body perform the office of judge, as well as of legiſlator, they ſeldom think of deviſing rules for their own direction, and are found ſtill more ſeldom to fol-

low

low any determinate rule, after it is made. They difpenfe, at one time, with what they enacted at another; and in their judicative, perhaps even more than in their legiflative, capacity, are guided by paffions and partialities that arife from circumftances of the cafe before them.

But under the fimpleft governments of a different fort, whether ariftocracy or monarchy, there is a neceffity for law, and there are a variety of interefts to be adjufted in framing every ftatute. The fovereign wifhes to give ftability and order to adminiftration, by exprefs and promulgated rules. The fubject wifhes to know the conditions and limits of his duty. He acquiefces, or he revolts, according as the terms on which he is made to live with the fovereign, or with his fellow-fubjects, are, or are not, confiftent with the fenfe of his rights.

Neither the monarch, nor the council of nobles, where either is poffeffed of the fovereignty, can pretend to govern, or to judge at difcretion. No magiftrate, whether temporary or hereditary, can with fafety neglect that reputation for juftice and equity, from which his authority, and the refpect that is paid to his perfon, are in a great meafure derived. Nations, however, have been fortunate in the tenor, and in the execution of their laws, in proportion as they have admitted every order of the people, by reprefentation or otherwife, to an actual fhare of the legiflature. Under eftablifhments of this fort, law is literally a treaty, to which the parties concern-

ed

ed have agreed, and have given their opinion in ſettling its terms. The intereſts to be affected by a law, are likewiſe conſulted in making it. Every claſs propounds an objection, ſuggeſts an addition or an amendment of its own. They proceed to adjuſt, by ſtatute, every ſubject of controverſy: and while they continue to enjoy their freedom, they continue to multiply laws, and to accumulate volumes, as if they could remove every poſſible ground of diſpute, and were ſecure of their rights, merely by having put them in writing.

ROME and England, under their mixed governments, the one inclining to democracy, the other to monarchy, have proved the great legiſlators among nations. The firſt has left the foundation, and great part of the ſuperſtructure of its civil code, to the continent of Europe: the other, in its iſland, has carried the authority and government of law to a point of perfection, which they never before attained in the hiſtory of mankind.

UNDER ſuch favourable eſtabliſhments, known cuſtoms, the practice and deciſions of courts, as well as poſitive ſtatutes, acquire the authority of laws; and every proceeding is conducted by ſome fixed and determinate rule. The beſt and moſt effectual precautions are taken for the impartial application of rules to particular caſes; and it is remarkable, that, in the two examples we have mentioned, a ſurpriſing coincidence is found in the ſingular methods of their juriſdiction. The people in both reſerved in a manner the office of judgement to themſelves, and brought the deciſion of civil rights, or of criminal queſtions, to the tribunal of peers, who, in judging of their fellow-citizens, preſcribed a condition of life for themſelves.

It is not in mere laws, after all, that we are to look for the ſecurities to juſtice, but in the powers by which thoſe laws have been obtained, and without whoſe conſtant ſupport they muſt fall to diſuſe. Statutes ſerve to record the rights of a people, and ſpeak the intention of parties to defend what the letter of the law has expreſſed: but without the vigour to maintain what is acknowledged as a right, the mere record, or the feeble intention, is of little avail.

A populace rouſed by oppreſſion, or an order of men poſſeſſed of a temporary advantage, have obtained many charters, conceſſions, and ſtipulations, in favour of their claims; but where no adequate preparation was made to preſerve them, the written articles were often forgotten, together with the occaſion on which they were framed.

The hiſtory of England, and of every free country, abounds with the example of ſtatutes enacted when the people or their repreſentatives aſſembled, but never executed when the crown or the executive was left to itſelf. The moſt equitable laws on paper are conſiſtent with the utmoſt deſpotiſm in adminiſtration. Even the form of trial by juries in England had its authority in law, while

while the proceedings of courts were arbitrary and oppreſſive.

We muſt admire, as the key-ſtone of civil liberty, the ſtatute which forces the ſecrets of every priſon to be revealed, the cauſe of every commitment to be declared, and the perſon of the accuſed to be produced, that he may claim his enlargement, or his trial, within a limited time. No wiſer form was ever oppoſed to the abuſes of power. But it requires a fabric no leſs than the whole political conſtitution of Great Britain, a ſpirit no leſs than the refractory and turbulent zeal of this fortunate people, to ſecure its effects.

If even the ſafety of the perſon, and the tenure of property, which may be ſo well defined in the words of a ſtatute, depend, for their preſervation, on the vigour and jealouſy of a free people, and on the degree of conſideration which every order of the ſtate maintains for itſelf; it is ſtill more evident, that what we have called the political freedom, or the right of the individual to act in his ſtation for himſelf and the public, cannot be made to reſt on any other foundation. The eſtate may be ſaved, and the perſon releaſed, by the forms of a civil procedure; but the rights of the mind cannot be ſuſtained by any other force but its own.

SECT.

SECT. VII.

Of the History of Arts.

WE have already obſerved, that art is natural to man; and that the ſkill he acquires after many ages of practice, is only the improvement of a talent he poſſeſſed at the firſt. Vitruvius finds the rudiments of architecture in the form of a Scythian cottage. The armourer may find the firſt productions of his calling in the ſling and the bow; and the ſhip-wright of his in the canoe of the ſavage. Even the hiſtorian and the poet may find the original eſſays of their arts in the tale, and the ſong, which celebrate the wars, the loves, and the adventures of men in their rudeſt condition.

DESTINED to cultivate his own nature, or to mend his ſituation, man finds a continual ſubject of attention, ingenuity, and labour. Even where he does not propoſe any perſonal improvement, his faculties are ſtrengthened by thoſe very exerciſes in which he ſeems to forget himſelf: his reaſon and his affections are thus profitably engaged in the affairs of ſociety; his invention and his ſkill are exerciſed in procuring his accommodations and his food; his particular purſuits are preſcribed to him by circumſtances of the age and of the country in which he lives: in one ſituation he is occupied with wars and political deliberations; in another, with the care of his

 intereſt,

intereſt, of his perſonal eaſe, or conveniency. He ſuits his means to the ends he has in view; and, by multiplying contrivances, proceeds, by degrees, to the perfection of his arts. In every ſtep of his progreſs, if his ſkill be increaſed, his deſire muſt likewiſe have time to extend: and it would be as vain to ſuggeſt a contrivance of which he ſlighted the uſe, as it would be to tell him of bleſſings which he could not command.

Ages are generally ſuppoſed to have borrowed from thoſe who went before them, and nations to have derived their portion of learning or of art from abroad. The Romans are thought to have learned from the Greeks, and the moderns of Europe from both. In this imagination we frequently proceed ſo far as to admit of nothing original in the practice or manners of any people. The Greek was a copy of the Egyptian, and even the Egyptian was an imitator, though we have loſt ſight of the model on which he was formed.

It is known, that men improve by example and intercourſe; but in the caſe of nations, whoſe members excite and direct each other, why ſeek from abroad the origin of arts, of which every ſociety, having the principles in itſelf, only requires a favourable occaſion to bring them to light? When ſuch occaſion preſents itſelf to any people, they generally ſeize it; and while it continues, they improve the inventions to which it gave riſe among themſelves, or they willingly copy from others: but they never employ their own invention, nor

look

look abroad, for instruction on subjects that do not lie in the way of their common pursuits; they never adopt a refinement of which they have not discovered the use.

INVENTIONS, we frequently observe, are accidental; but it is probable, that an accident which escapes the artist in one age, may be seized by one who succeeds him, and who is better apprised of its use. Where circumstances are favourable, and where a people is intent on the objects of any art, every invention is preserved, by being brought into general practice; every model is studied, and every accident is turned to account. If nations actually borrow from their neighbours, they probably borrow only what they are nearly in a condition to have invented themselves.

ANY singular practice of one country, therefore, is seldom transferred to another, till the way be prepared by the introduction of similar circumstances. Hence our frequent complaints of the dullness or obstinacy of mankind, and of the dilatory communication of arts, from one place to another. While the Romans adopted the arts of Greece, the Thracians and Illyrians continued to behold them with indifference. Those arts were, during one period, confined to the Greek colonies, and during another, to the Roman. Even where they were spread by a visible intercourse, they were still received by independent nations with the slowness of invention. They made a progress not more rapid at Rome than they had done at Athens; and they passed to the extremities of the Roman empire, only in company with new colonies, and joined to Italian policy.

THE modern race, who came abroad to the possession of cultivated provinces, retained the arts they had practised at home: the new master hunted the boar, or pastured his herds, where he might have raised a plentiful harvest: he built a cottage in the view of a palace: he buried, in one common ruin, the edifices, sculptures, paintings, and libraries, of the former inhabitant: he made a settlement upon a plan of his own, and opened anew the source of inventions, without perceiving from a distance to what length their progress might lead his posterity. The cottage of the present race, like that of the former, by degrees enlarged its dimensions; public buildings acquired a magnificence in a new taste. Even this taste came, in a course of ages, to be exploded, and the people of Europe recurred to the models which their fathers destroyed, and wept over the ruins which they could not restore.

THE literary remains of antiquity were studied and imitated, after the original genius of modern nations had broke forth: the rude efforts of poetry in Italy and Provence, resembled those of the Greeks and the ancient Romans. How far the merit of our works might, without the aid of their models, have risen by successive improvements, or whether we have gained more by imitation than we have lost by quitting our native system of thinking, and

our

our vein of fable, must be left to conjecture. We are certainly indebted to them for the materials, as well as the form, of many of our compositions; and without their example, the strain of our literature, together with that of our manners and policy, would have been different from what they at present are. This much however may be said with assurance, that although the Roman and the modern literature savour alike of the Greek original, yet mankind in either instance would not have drank of this fountain, unless they had been hastening to open springs of their own.

SENTIMENT and fancy, the use of the hand or the head, are not inventions of particular men; and the flourishing of arts that depend on them, are, in the case of any people, a proof rather of political felicity at home, than of any instruction received from abroad, or of any natural superiority in point of industry or talents.

WHEN the attentions of men are turned toward particular subjects, when the acquisitions of one age are left entire to the next, when every individual is protected in his place, and left to pursue the suggestion of his wants, devices accumulate; and it is difficult to find the original of any art. The steps which lead to perfection are many; and we are at a loss on whom to bestow the greatest share of our praise; on the first or on the last who may have bore a part in the progress.

SECT. VIII.

Of the History of Literature.

IF we may rely on the general obſervations contained in the laſt ſection, the literary, as well as mechanical arts, being a natural produce of the human mind, will riſe ſpontaneouſly where-ever men are happily placed; and in certain nations it is not more neceſſary to look abroad for the origin of literature, than it is for the ſuggeſtion of any of the pleaſures or exerciſes in which mankind, under a ſtate of proſperity and freedom, are ſufficiently inclined to indulge themſelves.

WE are apt to conſider arts as foreign and adventitious to the nature of man: but there is no art that did not find its occaſion in human life, and that was not, in ſome one or other of the ſituations in which our ſpecies is found, ſuggeſted as a means for the attainment of ſome uſeful end. The mechanic and commercial arts took their riſe from the love of property, and were encouraged by the proſpects of ſafety and of gain: the literary and liberal arts took their riſe from the underſtanding, the fancy, and the heart. They are mere exerciſes of the mind in ſearch of its peculiar pleaſures and occupations; and are promoted by circumſtances that ſuffer the mind to enjoy itſelf.

MEN are equally engaged by the paſt, the preſent, and the future, and are prepared for every occupation that gives ſcope to their powers. Productions therefore, whether of narration, fiction, or reaſoning, that tend to employ the imagination, or move the heart, continue for ages a ſubject of attention, and a ſource of delight. The memory of human tranſactions being preſerved in tradition or writing, is the natural gratification of a paſſion that conſiſts of curioſity, admiration, and the love of amuſement.

BEFORE many books are written, and before ſcience is greatly advanced, the productions of mere genius are ſometimes complete: the performer requires not the aid of learning where his deſcription or ſtory relates to near and contiguous objects; where it relates to the conduct and characters of men with whom he himſelf has acted, and in whoſe occupations and fortunes he himſelf has borne a part.

WITH this advantage, the poet is the firſt to offer the fruits of his genius, and to lead in the career of thoſe arts by which the mind is deſtined to exhibit its imaginations, and to expreſs its paſſions. Every tribe of barbarians have their paſſionate or hiſtoric rhymes, which contain the ſuperſtition, the enthuſiaſm, and the admiration of glory, with which the breaſts of men, in the earlieſt ſtate of ſociety, are poſſeſſed. They delight in verſe-compoſitions, either becauſe the cadence of numbers is natural to the language of ſentiment, or becauſe, not having the advantage of writing, they are obliged to bring the ear in aid of the memory, in order to facilitate the repetition, and inſure the preſervation of their works.

WHEN we attend to the language which ſavages employ on any ſolemn occaſion, it appears that man is a poet by nature. Whether at firſt obliged by the mere defects of his tongue, and the ſcantineſs of proper expreſſions, or ſeduced by a pleaſure of the fancy in ſtating the analogy of its objects, he clothes every conception in image and metaphor. "We have planted the tree of peace," ſays an American orator; "we have buried the "axe under its roots: we will henceforth repoſe under "its ſhade; we will join to brighten the chain that binds "our nations together." Such are the collections of metaphor which thoſe nations employ in their public harangues. They have likewiſe already adopted thoſe lively figures, and that daring freedom of language, which the learned have afterwards found ſo well fitted to expreſs the rapid tranſitions of the imagination, and the ardours of a paſſionate mind.

IF we are required to explain, how men could be poets, or orators, before they were aided by the learning of the ſcholar and the critic? we may inquire, in our turn, how bodies could fall by their weight, before the laws of gravitation were recorded in books? Mind, as well as body, has laws, which are exemplified in the practice of men,

men, and which the critic collects only after the example has shewn what they are.

Occasioned, probably, by the physical connection we have mentioned, between the emotions of a heated imagination, and the impressions received from music and pathetic sounds, every tale among rude nations is repeated in verse, and is made to take the form of a song. The early history of all nations is uniform in this particular. Priests, statesmen, and philosophers, in the first ages of Greece, delivered their instructions in poetry, and mixed with the dealers in music and heroic fable.

It is not so surprising, however, that poetry should be the first species of composition in every nation, as it is, that a style apparently so difficult, and so far removed from ordinary use, should be almost as universally the first to attain its maturity. The most admired of all poets lived beyond the reach of history, almost of tradition. The artless song of the savage, the heroic legend of the bard, have sometimes a magnificent beauty, which no change of language can improve, and no refinements of the critic reform.

Under the supposed disadvantage of a limited knowledge, and a rude apprehension, the simple poet has impressions that more than compensate the defects of his skill. The best subjects of poetry, the characters of the violent and the brave, the generous and the intrepid, great dangers, trials of fortitude and fidelity, are exhibited within his view, or are delivered in traditions which animate like truth, because they are equally believed: He is not engaged in recalling, like Virgil or Tasso, the sentiments or scenery of an age remote from his own: he needs not be told by the critic *, to recollect what another would have thought, or in what manner another would have expressed his conception. The simple passions, friendship, resentment, and love, are the movements of his own mind, and he has no occasion to copy. Simple and vehement in his conceptions and feelings, he knows no diversity of thought, or of style, to mislead or to exercise his judgement. He delivers the emotions of the heart, in words suggested by the heart: for he knows no other. And hence it is, that while we admire the judgement and invention of Virgil, and of other later poets, these terms appear misapplied to Homer. Though intelligent, as well as sublime, in his conceptions, we cannot anticipate the lights of his understanding, nor the movements of his heart: he appears to speak from inspiration, not from invention; and to be guided in the choice of his thoughts and expressions by a supernatural instinct, not by reflection.

THE language of early ages, is in one respect, simple and confined; in another, it is varied and free: it allows liberties, which, to the poet of after times, are denied.

* See Longinus.

In rude ages men are not separated by distinctions of rank or profession. They live in one manner, and speak one dialect. The bard is not to chuse his expression among the singular accents of different conditions. He has not to guard his language from the peculiar errors of the mechanic, the peasant, the scholar, or the courtier, in order to find that elegant propriety, and just elevation, which is free from the vulgar of one class, the pedantic of the second, or the flippant of the third. The name of every object, and of every sentiment, is fixed; and if his conception has the dignity of nature, his expression will have a purity which does not depend on his choice.

With this apparent confinement in the choice of his words, he is at liberty to break through the ordinary modes of construction; and in the form of a language not established by rules, may find for himself a cadence agreeable to the tone of his mind. The liberty he takes, while his meaning is striking, and his language is raised, appears an improvement, not a trespass on grammar. He delivers a style to the ages that follow, and becomes a model from which his posterity judge.

But whatever may be the early disposition of mankind to poetry, or the advantages they possess in cultivating this species of literature; whether the early maturity of poetical compositions arise from their being the first studied, or from their having a charm to engage persons of the liveliest genius, who are best qualified to improve the eloquence of their native tongue; it is a remarkable fact, that, not only in countries where every vein of composition was original, and was opened in the order of natural succession; but even at Rome, and in modern Europe, where the learned began early to practise on foreign models, we have poets of every nation, who are perused with pleasure, while the prose writers of the same ages are neglected.

As Sophocles and Euripides preceded the historians and moralists of Greece, not only Nævius and Ennius, who wrote the Roman history in verse, but Lucilius, Plautus, Terence, and we may add Lucretius, were prior to Cicero, Sallust, or Cæsar. Dante and Petrarch went before any good prose writer in Italy; Corneille and Racine brought on the fine age of prose compositions in France; and we had in England, not only Chaucer and Spenser, but Shakespear and Milton, while our attempts in history or science were yet in their infancy; and deserve our attention, only for the sake of the matter they treat.

HILLANICUS, who is reckoned among the first prose writers in Greece, and who immediately preceded, or was the contemporary of Herodotus, set out with declaring his intention to remove from history the wild representations, and extravagant fictions, with which it had been disgraced by the poets *. The want of records or

* Quoted by Demetrius Phalerius.

authorities,

authorities, relating to any distant transactions, may have hindered him, as it did his immediate successor, from giving truth all the advantage it might have reaped from this transition to prose. There are, however, ages in the progress of society, when such a proposition must be favourably received. When men become occupied on the subjects of policy, or commercial arts, they wish to be informed and instructed, as well as moved. They are interested by what was real in past transactions. They build on this foundation, the reflections and reasonings they apply to present affairs, and wish to receive information on the subject of different pursuits, and of projects in which they begin to be engaged. The manners of men, the practice of ordinary life, and the form of society, furnish their subjects to the moral and political writer. Mere ingenuity, justness of sentiment, and correct representation, though conveyed in ordinary language, are understood to constitute literary merit, and by applying to reason more than to the imagination and passions, meet with a reception that is due to the instruction they bring.

THE talents of men come to be employed in a variety of affairs, and their inquiries directed to different subjects. Knowledge is important in every department of civil society, and requisite to the practice of every art. The science of nature, morals, politics, and history, find their several admirers; and even poetry itself, which retains its former station in the region of warm imagina-

tion

tion and enthusiastic passion, appears in a growing variety of forms.

MATTERS have proceeded so far, without the aid of foreign examples, or the direction of schools. The cart of Thespis was changed into a theatre, not to gratify the learned, but to please the Athenian populace: and the prize of poetical merit was decided by this populace equally before and after the invention of rules. The Greeks were unacquainted with every language but their own; and if they became learned, it was only by studying what they themselves had produced: the childish mythology, which they are said to have copied from Asia, was equally of little avail in promoting their love of arts, or their success in the practice of them.

WHEN the historian is struck with the events he has witnessed, or heard; when he is excited to relate them by his reflections or his passions; when the statesman, who is required to speak in public, is obliged to prepare for every remarkable appearance in studied harangues; when conversation becomes extensive and refined; and when the social feelings and reflections of men are committed to writing, a system of learning may arise from the bustle of an active life. Society itself is the school, and its lessons are delivered in the practice of real affairs. An author writes from observations he has made on his subject, not from the suggestion of books; and every production carries the mark of his character as a man, not of his mere proficiency as a student or scholar. It

may

may be made a queſtion, whether the trouble of ſeeking for diſtant models, and of wading for inſtruction, through dark alluſions and languages unknown, might not have quenched his fire, and rendered him a writer of a very inferior claſs.

If ſociety may thus be conſidered as a ſchool for letters, it is probable that its leſſons are varied in every ſeparate ſtate, and in every age. For a certain period, the ſevere applications of the Roman people to policy and war ſuppreſſed the literary arts, and appear to have ſtifled the genius even of the hiſtorian and the poet. The inſtitutions of Sparta gave a profeſſed contempt for whatever was not connected with the practical virtues of a vigorous and reſolute ſpirit: the charms of imagination, and the parade of language, were by this people claſſed with the arts of the cook and the perfumer: their ſongs in praiſe of fortitude are mentioned by ſome writers; and collections of their witty ſayings and repartees are ſtill preſerved: they indicate the virtues and the abilities of an active people, not their proficiency in ſcience or literary taſte. Poſſeſſed of what was eſſential to happineſs in the virtues of the heart, they had a diſcernment of its value, unimbarraſſed by the numberleſs objects on which mankind in general are ſo much at a loſs to adjuſt their eſteem: fixed in their own apprehenſion, they turned a ſharp edge on the follies of mankind. "When will you "begin to practiſe it?" was the queſtion of a Spartan to a perſon who, in an advanced age of life, was ſtill occupied with queſtions on the nature of virtue.

WHILE this people confined their ſtudies to one queſtion, How to improve and to preſerve the courage and the diſintereſted affections of the human heart? their rivals the Athenians gave a ſcope to refinement on every object of reflection or paſſion. By the rewards, either of profit or of reputation, which they beſtowed on every effort of ingenuity employed in miniſtering to the pleaſure, the decoration, or the conveniency of life; by the variety of conditions in which their citizens were placed; by their inequalities of fortune, and their ſeveral purſuits in war, politics, commerce, and lucrative arts, they awakened whatever was either good or bad in the natural diſpoſitions of men. Every road to eminence was opened: eloquence, fortitude, military ſkill, envy, detraction, faction, and treaſon, even the muſe herſelf, was courted to beſtow importance among a buſy, acute, and turbulent people.

FROM this example, we may ſafely conclude, that although buſineſs is ſometimes a rival to ſtudy, retirement and leiſure are not the principal requiſites to the improvement, perhaps not even to the exerciſe, of literary talents. The moſt ſtriking exertions of imagination and ſentiment have a reference to mankind: they are excited by the preſence and intercourſe of men: they have moſt vigour when actuated in the mind by the operation

of

of its principal springs, by the emulations, the friendships, and the oppositions, which subsist among a forward and aspiring people. Amidst the great occasions which put a free, and even a licentious, society in motion, its members become capable of every exertion; and the same scenes which gave employment to Themistocles and Thrasybulus, inspired, by contagion, the genius of Sophocles and Plato. The petulant and the ingenuous find an equal scope to their talents; and literary monuments become the repositories of envy and folly, as well as of wisdom and virtue.

GREECE, divided into many little states, and agitated, beyond any spot on the globe, by domestic contentions and foreign wars, set the example in every species of literature. The fire was communicated to Rome; not when the state ceased to be warlike, and had discontinued her political agitations, but when she mixed the love of refinement and of pleasure with her national pursuits, and indulged an inclination to study in the midst of ferments, occasioned by the wars and pretensions of opposite factions. It was revived in modern Europe among the turbulent states of Italy, and spread to the North, together with the spirit which shook the fabric of the Gothic policy: it rose while men were divided into parties, under civil or religious denominations, and when they were at variance on subjects held the most important and sacred.

We may be ſatisfied, from the example of many ages, that liberal endowments beſtowed on learned ſocieties, and the leiſure with which they were furniſhed for ſtudy, are not the likelieſt means to excite the exertions of genius: even ſcience itſelf, the ſuppoſed offspring of leiſure, pined in the ſhade of monaſtic retirement. Men at a diſtance from the objects of uſeful knowledge, untouched by the motives that animate an active and a vigorous mind, could produce only the jargon of a technical language, and accumulate the impertinence of academical forms.

To ſpeak or to write juſtly from an obſervation of nature, it is neceſſary to have felt the ſentiments of nature. He who is penetrating and ardent in the conduct of life, will probably exert a proportional force and ingenuity in the exerciſe of his literary talents: and although writing may become a trade, and require all the application and ſtudy which are beſtowed on any other calling; yet the principal requiſites in this calling are, the ſpirit and ſenſibility of a vigorous mind.

In one period, the ſchool may take its light and direction from active life; in another, it is true, the remains of an active ſpirit are greatly ſupported by literary monuments, and by the hiſtory of tranſactions that preſerve the examples and the experience of former and of better times. But in whatever manner men are formed for great efforts of elocution or conduct, it appears

pears the most glaring of all other deceptions, to look for the accomplishments of a human character in the mere attainments of speculation, whilst we neglect the qualities of fortitude and public affection, which are so necessary to render our knowledge an article of happiness or of use.

PART FOURTH.

Of Confequences that refult from the Advancement of Civil and Commercial Arts.

SECT. I.

Of the Separation of Arts and Profeffions.

IT is evident, that, however urged by a fenfe of neceffity, and a defire of convenience, or favoured by any advantages of fituation and policy, a people can make no great progrefs in cultivating the arts of life, until they have feparated, and committed to different perfons, the feveral tafks, which require a peculiar fkill and attention. The favage, or the barbarian, who muft build and plant, and fabricate for himfelf, prefers, in the interval of great alarms and fatigues, the enjoyments of floth to the improvement of his fortune: he is, perhaps, by the diverfity of his wants, difcouraged from induftry; or, by his divided attention, prevented from acquiring

acquiring ſkill in the management of any particular ſubject.

THE enjoyment of peace, however, and the proſpect of being able to exchange one commodity for another, turns, by degrees, the hunter and the warrior into a tradeſman and a merchant. The accidents which diſtribute the means of ſubſiſtence unequally, inclination, and favourable opportunities, aſſign the different occupations of men; and a ſenſe of utility leads them, without end, to ſubdivide their profeſſions.

THE artiſt finds, that the more he can confine his attention to a particular part of any work, his productions are the more perfect, and grow under his hands in the greater quantities. Every undertaker in manufacture finds, that the more he can ſubdivide the taſks of his workmen, and the more hands he can employ on ſeparate articles, the more are his expences diminiſhed, and his profits increaſed. The conſumer too requires, in every kind of commodity, a workmanſhip more perfect than hands employed on a variety of ſubjects can produce; and the progreſs of commerce is but a continued ſubdiviſion of the mechanical arts.

EVERY craft may ingroſs the whole of a man's attention, and has a myſtery which muſt be ſtudied or learned by a regular apprenticeſhip. Nations of tradeſmen come to conſiſt of members who, beyond their own particular trade, are ignorant of all human affairs, and who may contribute to the preſervation and enlargement of their commonwealth, without making its intereſt an object of their regard or attention. Every individual is diſtinguiſhed by his calling, and has a place to which he is fitted. The ſavage, who knows no diſtinction but that of his merit, of his ſex, or of his ſpecies, and to whom his community is the ſovereign object of affection, is aſtoniſhed to find, that in a ſcene of this nature, his being a man does not qualify him for any ſtation whatever: he flies to the woods with amazement, diſtaſte, and averſion.

By the ſeparation of arts and profeſſions, the ſources of wealth are laid open; every ſpecies of material is wrought up to the greateſt perfection, and every commodity is produced in the greateſt abundance. The ſtate may eſtimate its profits and its revenues by the number of its people. It may procure, by its treaſure, that national conſideration and power, which the ſavage maintains at the expence of his blood.

The advantage gained in the inferior branches of manufacture by the ſeparation of their parts, ſeem to be equalled by thoſe which ariſe from a ſimilar device in the higher departments of policy and war. The ſoldier is relieved from every care but that of his ſervice; ſtateſmen divide the buſineſs of civil government into ſhares; and the ſervants of the public, in every office, without being ſkilful in the affairs of ſtate, may ſucceed, by obſerving forms which are already eſtabliſhed on the experience of others. They are made, like the parts of an engine, to concur to a purpoſe,

purpose, without any concert of their own: and, equally blind with the trader to any general combination, they unite with him, in furnishing to the state its resources, its conduct, and its force.

THE artifices of the beaver, the ant, and the bee, are ascribed to the wisdom of nature. Those of polished nations are ascribed to themselves, and are supposed to indicate a capacity superior to that of rude minds. But the establishments of men, like those of every animal, are suggested by nature, and are the result of instinct, directed by the variety of situations in which mankind are placed. Those establishments arose from successive improvements that were made, without any sense of their general effect; and they bring human affairs to a state of complication, which the greatest reach of capacity with which human nature was ever adorned, could not have projected; nor even when the whole is carried into execution, can it be comprehended in its full extent.

WHO could anticipate, or even enumerate, the separate occupations and professions by which the members of any commercial state are distinguished; the variety of devices which are practised in separate cells, and which the artist, attentive to his own affair, has invented, to abridge or to facilitate his separate task? In coming to this mighty end, every generation, compared to its predecessors, may have appeared to be ingenious; compared to its followers, may have appeared to be dull: and human ingenuity, whatever heights it may have gained in a ſucceſſion of ages, continues to move with an equal pace, and to creep in making the laſt as well as the firſt ſtep of commercial or civil improvement.

It may even be doubted, whether the meaſure of national capacity increaſes with the advancement of arts. Many mechanical arts, indeed, require no capacity; they ſucceed beſt under a total ſuppreſſion of ſentiment and reaſon; and ignorance is the mother of induſtry as well as of ſuperſtition. Reflection and fancy are ſubject to err; but a habit of moving the hand, or the foot, is independent of either. Manufactures, accordingly, proſper moſt, where the mind is leaſt conſulted, and where the workſhop may, without any great effort of imagination, be conſidered as an engine, the parts of which are men.

The foreſt has been felled by the ſavage without the the uſe of the axe, and weights have been raiſed without the aid of the mechanical powers. The merit of the inventor, in every branch, probably deſerves a preference to that of the performer; and he who invented a tool, or could work without its aſſiſtance, deſerved the praiſe of ingenuity in a much higher degree than the mere artiſt, who, by its aſſiſtance, produces a ſuperior work.

But if many parts in the practice of every art, and in the detail of every department, require no abilities, or actually tend to contract and to limit the views of the mind, there are others which lead to general reflections, and to enlargement of thought. Even in manufacture, the

the genius of the maſter, perhaps, is cultivated, while that of the inferior workman lies waſte. The ſtateſman may have a wide comprehenſion of human affairs, while the tools he employs are ignorant of the ſyſtem in which they are themſelves combined. The general officer may be a great proficient in the knowledge of war, while the ſoldier is confined to a few motions of the hand and the foot. The former may have gained, what the latter has loſt; and being occupied in the conduct of diſciplined armies, may practiſe on a larger ſcale, all the arts of preſervation, of deception, and of ſtratagem, which the ſavage exerts in leading a ſmall party, or merely in defending himſelf.

THE practitioner of every art and profeſſion may afford matter of general ſpeculation to the man of ſcience; and thinking itſelf, in this age of ſeparations, may become a peculiar craft. In the buſtle of civil purſuits and occupations, men appear in a variety of lights, and ſuggeſt matter of inquiry and fancy, by which converſation is enlivened, and greatly enlarged. The productions of ingenuity are brought to the market; and men are willing to pay for whatever has a tendency to inform or amuſe. By this means the idle, as well as the buſy, contribute to forward the progreſs of arts, and beſtow on poliſhed nations that air of ſuperior ingenuity, under which they appear to have gained the ends that were purſued by the ſavage in his foreſt, knowledge, order, and wealth.

SECT. II.

Of the Subordination consequent to the Separation of Arts and Professions.

THERE is one ground of ſubordination in the difference of natural talents and diſpoſitions; a ſecond in the unequal diviſion of property; and a third, not leſs ſenſible, in the habits which are acquired by the practice of different arts.

SOME employments are liberal, others mechanic. They require different talents, and inſpire different ſentiments; and whether or not this be the cauſe of the preference we actually give, it is certainly reaſonable to form our opinion of the rank that is due to men of certain profeſſions and ſtations, from the influence of their manner of life in cultivating the powers of the mind, or in preſerving the ſentiments of the heart.

THERE is an elevation natural to man, by which he would be thought, in his rudeſt ſtate, however urged by neceſſity, to riſe above the conſideration of mere ſubſiſtence, and the regards of intereſt: He would appear to act only from the heart, in its engagements of friendſhip, or oppoſition; he would ſhew himſelf only upon occaſions of danger or difficulty, and leave ordinary cares to the weak or the ſervile.

THE

THE same apprehensions, in every situation, regulate his notions of meanness or of dignity. In that of polished society, his desire to avoid the character of sordid, makes him conceal his regard for what relates merely to his preservation or his livelihood. In his estimation, the beggar, who depends upon charity; the labourer, who toils that he may eat; the mechanic, whose art requires no exertion of genius, are degraded by the object they pursue, and by the means they employ to attain it. Professions requiring more knowledge and study; proceeding on the exercise of fancy, and the love of perfection; leading to applause as well as to profit, place the artist in a superior class, and bring him nearer to that station in which men are supposed to be highest; because in it they are bound to no task; because they are left to follow the disposition of the mind, and to take that part in society, to which they are led by the sentiments of the heart, or by the calls of the public.

THIS last was the station, which, in the distinction betwixt freemen and slaves, the citizens of every ancient republic strove to gain, and to maintain for themselves. Women, or slaves, in the earliest ages, had been set apart for the purposes of domestic care, or bodily labour; and in the progress of lucrative arts, the latter were bred to mechanical professions, and were even intrusted with merchandise for the benefit of their masters. Freemen would be understood to have no object beside those of politics and war. In this manner, the honours of one half of the species were sacrificed to those of the other;

as ſtones from the ſame quarry are buried in the foundation, to ſuſtain the blocks which happen to be hewn for the ſuperior parts of the pile. In the midſt of our encomiums beſtowed on the Greeks and the Romans, we are, by this circumſtance, made to remember, that no human inſtitution is perfect.

IN many of the Grecian ſtates, the benefits ariſing to the free from this cruel diſtinction, were not conferred equally on all the citizens. Wealth being unequally divided, the rich alone were exempted from labour; the poor were reduced to work for their own ſubſiſtence: intereſt was a reigning paſſion in both, and the poſſeſſion of ſlaves, like that of any other lucrative property, became an object of avarice, not an exemption from ſordid attentions. The entire effects of the inſtitution were obtained, or continued to be enjoyed for any conſiderable time, at Sparta alone. We feel its injuſtice; we ſuffer for the helot, under the ſeverities and unequal treatment to which he was expoſed: but when we think only of the ſuperior order of men in this ſtate; when we attend to that elevation and magnanimity of ſpirit, for which danger had no terror, intereſt no means to corrupt; when we conſider them as friends, or as citizens, we are apt to forget, like themſelves, that ſlaves have a title to be treated like men.

WE look for elevation of ſentiment, and liberality of mind, among thoſe orders of citizens, who, by their condition, and their fortunes, are relieved from ſordid cares

and

and attentions. This was the description of a free man at Sparta; and if the lot of a slave among the ancients was really more wretched than that of the indigent labourer and the mechanic among the moderns, it may be doubted, whether the superior orders, who are in possession of consideration and honours, do not proportionally fail in the dignity which befits their condition. If the pretensions to equal justice and freedom should terminate in rendering every class equally servile and mercenary, we make a nation of helots, and have no free citizens.

In every commercial state, notwithstanding any pretension to equal rights, the exaltation of a few must depress the many. In this arrangement, we think that the extreme meanness of some classes must arise chiefly from the defect of knowledge, and of liberal education; and we refer to such classes, as to an image of what our species must have been in its rude and uncultivated state. But we forget how many circumstances, especially in populous cities, tend to corrupt the lowest orders of men. Ignorance is the least of their failings. An admiration of wealth unpossessed, becoming a principle of envy, or of servility; a habit of acting perpetually with a view to profit, and under a sense of subjection; the crimes to which they are allured, in order to feed their debauch, or to gratify their avarice, are examples, not of ignorance, but of corruption and baseness. If the savage has not received our instructions, he is likewise unacquainted with our vices. He knows no superior, and cannot be servile; he

knows

knows no diſtinctions of fortune, and cannot be envious; he acts from his talents in the higheſt ſtation which human ſociety can offer, that of the counſellor, and the ſoldier of his country. Toward forming his ſentiments, he knows all that the heart requires to be known; he can diſtinguiſh the friend whom he loves, and the public intereſt which awakens his zeal.

THE principal objections to democratical or popular government, are taken from the inequalities which ariſe among men in the reſult of commercial arts. And it muſt be confeſſed, that popular aſſemblies, when compoſed of men whoſe diſpoſitions are ſordid, and whoſe ordinary applications are illiberal, however they may be intruſted with the choice of their maſters and leaders, are certainly, in their own perſons, unfit to command. How can he who has confined his views to his own ſubſiſtence or preſervation, be intruſted with the conduct of nations? Such men, when admitted to deliberate on matters of ſtate, bring to its councils confuſion and tumult, or ſervility and corruption; and ſeldom ſuffer it to repoſe from ruinous factions, or the effect of reſolutions ill formed or ill conducted.

THE Athenians retained their popular government under all theſe defects. The mechanic was obliged, under a penalty, to appear in the public market-place, and to hear debates on the ſubjects of war, and of peace. He was tempted by pecuniary rewards, to attend on the trial of civil and criminal cauſes. But notwithſtanding an

exerciſe

exercise tending so much to cultivate their talents, the indigent came always with minds intent upon profit, or with the habits of an illiberal calling. Sunk under the sense of their personal disparity and weakness, they were ready to resign themselves entirely to the influence of some popular leader, who flattered their passions, and wrought on their fears; or, actuated by envy, they were ready to banish from the state whomsoever was respectable and eminent in the superior order of citizens: and whether from their neglect of the public at one time, or their male-administration at another, the sovereignty was every moment ready to drop from their hands.

THE people, in this case, are, in fact, frequently governed by one, or a few, who know how to conduct them. Pericles possessed a species of princely authority at Athens; Crassus, Pompey, and Cæsar, either jointly or successively, possessed for a considerable period the sovereign direction at Rome.

WHETHER in great or in small states, democracy is preserved with difficulty, under the disparities of condition, and the unequal cultivation of the mind, which attend the variety of pursuits, and applications, that separate mankind in the advanced state of commercial arts. In this, however, we do but plead against the form of democracy, after the principle is removed; and see the absurdity of pretensions to equal influence and consideration, after the characters of men have ceased to be similar.

SECT. III.

Of the Manners of Poliſhed and Commercial Nations.

MANKIND, when in their rude ſtate, have a great uniformity of maners; but when civilized, they are engaged in a variety of purſuits; they tread on a larger field, and ſeparate to a greater diſtance. If they be guided, however, by ſimilar diſpoſitions, and by like ſuggeſtions of nature, they will probably, in the end, as well as in the beginning of their progreſs, continue to agree in many particulars; and while communities admit, in their members, that diverſity of ranks and profeſſions which we have already deſcribed, as the conſequence or the foundation of commerce, they will reſemble each other in many effects of this diſtribution, and of other circumſtances in which they nearly concur.

UNDER every form of government, ſtateſmen endeavour to remove the dangers by which they are threatened from abroad, and the diſturbances which moleſt them at home. By this conduct, if ſucceſsful, they in a few ages gain an aſcendant for their country; eſtabliſh a frontier at a diſtance from its capital; they find, in the mutual deſires of tranquillity, which come to poſſeſs mankind, and in thoſe public eſtabliſhments which tend to keep the peace of ſociety, a reſpite from foreign wars, and a relief from domeſtic diſorders. They learn to decide every conteſt

test without tumult, and to secure, by the authority of law, every citizen in the possession of his personal rights.

In this condition, to which thriving nations aspire, and which they in some measure attain, mankind having laid the basis of safety, proceed to erect a superstructure suitable to their views. The consequence is various in different states; even in different orders of men of the same community; and the effect to every individual corresponds with his station. It enables the statesman and the soldier to settle the forms of their different procedure; it enables the practitioner in every profession to pursue his separate advantage; it affords the man of pleasure a time for refinement, and the speculative, leisure for literary conversation or study.

In this scene, matters that have little reference to the active pursuits of mankind, are made subjects of inquiry, and the exercise of sentiment and reason itself becomes a profession. The songs of the bard, the harangues of the statesman and the warrior, the tradition and the story of ancient times, are considered as the models, or the earliest production, of so many arts, which it becomes the object of different professions to copy or to improve. The works of fancy, like the subjects of natural history, are distinguished into classes and species; the rules of every particular kind are distinctly collected; and the library is stored, like the warehouse, with the finished manufacture of different arts, who, with the aids of the grammarian and the critic, aſpire, each in his particular way, to inſtruct the head, or to move the heart.

Every nation is a motley aſſemblage of different characters, and contains, under any political form, ſome examples of that variety, which the humours, tempers, and apprehenſions of men, ſo differently employed, are likely to furniſh. Every profeſſion has its point of honour, and its ſyſtem of manners; the merchant his punctuality and fair dealing; the ſtateſman his capacity and addreſs; the man of ſociety, his good-breeding and wit. Every ſtation has a carriage, a dreſs, a ceremonial, by which it is diſtinguiſhed, and by which it ſuppreſſes the national character under that of the rank, or of the individual.

This deſcription may be applied equally to Athens and Rome, to London and Paris. The rude or the ſimple obſerver would remark the variety he ſaw in the dwellings and in the occupations of different men, not in the aſpect of different nations. He would find, in the ſtreets of the ſame city, as great a diverſity, as in the territory of a ſeparate people. He could not pierce through the cloud that was gathered before him, nor ſee how the tradeſman, mechanic, or ſcholar, of one country, ſhould differ from thoſe of another. But the native of every province can diſtinguiſh the foreigner; and when he himſelf travels, is ſtruck with the aſpect of a ſtrange country, the moment he paſſes the bounds of his own. The air of the perſon, the tone of the voice, the idiom of lan-

guage,

guage, and the ſtrain of converſation, whether pathetic or languid, gay or ſevere, are no longer the ſame.

MANY ſuch differences may ariſe among poliſhed nations, from the effects of climate, or from ſources of faſhion, that are ſtill more unaccountable and obſcure; but the principal diſtinctions on which we can reſt, are derived from the part a people are obliged to act in their national capacity; from the objects placed in their view by the ſtate; or from the conſtitution of government, which preſcribing the terms of ſociety to its ſubjects, has a great influence in forming their apprehenſions and habits.

THE Roman people, deſtined to acquire wealth by conqueſt, and by the ſpoil of provinces; the Carthaginians, intent on the returns of merchandiſe, and the produce of commercial ſettlements, muſt have filled the ſtreets of their ſeveral capitals with men of a different diſpoſition and aſpect. The Roman laid hold of his ſword when he wiſhed to be great, and the ſtate found her armies prepared in the dwellings of her people. The Carthaginian retired to his counter on a ſimilar project; and, when the ſtate was alarmed, or had reſolved on a war, lent of his profits to purchaſe an army abroad.

THE member of a republic, and the ſubject of a monarchy, muſt differ; becauſe they have different parts aſſigned to them by the forms of their country: the one deſtined to live with his equals, or, by his perſonal talents and character, to contend for pre-eminence; the other, born to a determinate ſtation, where any pretence to equality creates a confuſion, and where nought but precedence is ſtudied. Each, when the inſtitutions of his country are mature, may find in the laws a protection to his perſonal rights; but thoſe rights themſelves are differently underſtood, and with a different ſet of opinions, give riſe to a different temper of mind. The republican muſt act in the ſtate, to ſuſtain his pretenſions; he muſt join a party, in order to be ſafe; he muſt form one, in order to be great. The ſubject of monarchy refers to his birth for the honour he claims; he waits on a court, to ſhew his importance; and holds out the enſigns of dependence and favour, to gain him eſteem with the public.

If national inſtitutions, calculated for the preſervation of liberty, inſtead of calling upon the citizen to act for himſelf, and to maintain his rights, ſhould give a ſecurity, requiring, on his part, no perſonal attention or effort; this ſeeming perfection of government might weaken the bands of ſociety, and, upon maxims of independence, ſeparate and eſtrange the different ranks it was meant to reconcile. Neither the parties formed in republics, nor the courtly aſſemblies which meet in monarchical governments, could take place, where the ſenſe of a mutual dependence ſhould ceaſe to ſummon their members together. The reſorts for commerce might be frequented, and mere amuſement might be purſued in the croud, while the private dwelling became a retreat for reſerve, averſe to the trouble ariſing from regards and attentions, which it might be part of the political creed to

believe

believe of no consequence, and a point of honour to hold in contempt.

THIS humour is not likely to grow either in republics or monarchies: it belongs more properly to a mixture of both; where the administration of justice may be better secured; where the subject is tempted to look for equality, but where he finds only independence in its place; and where he learns, from a spirit of equality, to hate the very distinctions to which, on account of their real importance, he pays a remarkable deference.

IN either of the separate forms of republic or monarchy, or in acting on the principles of either, men are obliged to court their fellow-citizens, and to employ parts and address to improve their fortunes, or even to be safe. They find in both a school for discernment and penetration; but in the one, are taught to overlook the merits of a private character, for the sake of abilities that have weight with the public; and in the other, to overlook great and respectable talents, for the sake of qualities engaging or pleasant in the scene of entertainment, and private society. They are obliged, in both, to adapt themselves with care to the fashion and manners of their country. They find no place for caprice or singular humours. The republican must be popular, and the courtier polite. The first must think himself well placed in every company; the other must chuse his resorts, and desire to be distinguished only where the society itself is esteemed. With his inferiors, he takes an air of protection;

tion; and suffers, in his turn, the same air to be taken with himself. It did not, perhaps, require in a Spartan, who feared nothing but a failure in his duty, who loved nothing but his friend and the state, so constant a guard on himself to support his character, as it frequently does in the subject of a monarchy, to adjust his expence and his fortune to the desires of his vanity, and to appear in a rank as high as his birth, or ambition, can possibly reach.

THERE is no particular, in the mean time, in which we are more frequently unjust, than in applying to the individual the supposed character of his country; or more frequently misled, than in taking our notion of a people from the example of one, or a few of their members. It belonged to the constitution of Athens, to have produced a Cleon, and a Pericles; but all the Athenians were not, therefore, like Cleon, or Pericles. Themistocles and Aristides lived in the same age; the one advised what was profitable; the other told his country what was just.

SECT.

SECT. IV.

The same subject continued.

THE law of Nature, with respect to nations, is the same that it is with respect to individuals: it gives to the collective body a right to preserve themselves; to employ, undisturbed, the means of life; to retain the fruits of labour; to demand the observance of stipulations and contracts. In the case of violence, it condemns the aggressor, and establishes, on the part of the injured, the right of defence, and a claim to retribution. Its applications, however, admit of disputes, and give rise to variety in the apprehension, as well as the practice of mankind.

NATIONS have agreed universally, in distinguishing right from wrong; in exacting the reparation of injuries by consent or by force. They have always reposed, in a certain degree, on the faith of treaties; but have acted as if force were the ultimate arbiter in all their disputes, and the power to defend themselves, the surest pledge of their safety. Guided by these common apprehensions, they have differed from one another, not merely in points of form, but in points of the greatest importance, respecting the usage of war, the effects of captivity, and the rights of conquest and victory.

When a number of independent communities have been frequently involved in wars, and have had their ſtated alliances and oppoſitions, they adopt cuſtoms which they make the foundation of rules, or of laws, to be obſerved, or alledged, in all their mutual tranſactions. Even in war itſelf, they would follow a ſyſtem, and plead for the obſervance of forms in their very operations for mutual deſtruction.

The ancient ſtates of Greece and Italy derived their manners in war from the nature of their republican government; thoſe of modern Europe, from the influence of monarchy, which, by its prevalence in this part of the world, has a great effect on nations, even where it is not the form eſtabliſhed. Upon the maxims of this government, we apprehend a diſtinction between the ſtate and its members, as that between the King and the people, which renders war an operation of policy, not of popular animoſity. While we ſtrike at the public intereſt, we would ſpare the private; and we carry a reſpect and conſideration for individuals, which often ſtops the iſſues of blood in the ardour of victory, and procures to the priſoner of war a hoſpitable reception in the very city which he came to deſtroy. Theſe practices are ſo well eſtabliſhed, that ſcarcely any provocation on the part of an enemy, or any exigence of ſervice, can excuſe a treſpaſs on the ſuppoſed rules of humanity, or ſave the leader who commits it from becoming an object of deteſtation and horror.

To this, the general practice of the Greeks and the Romans was opposite. They endeavoured to wound the state by destroying its members, by desolating its territory, and by ruining the possessions of its subjects. They granted quarter only to inslave, or to bring the prisoner to a more solemn execution; and an enemy, when disarmed, was, for the most part, either sold in the market, or killed, that he might never return to strengthen his party. When this was the issue of war, it was no wonder, that battles were fought with desperation, and that every fortress was defended to the last extremity. The game of human life went upon a high stake, and was played with a proportional zeal.

THE term *barbarian*, in this state of manners, could not be employed by the Greeks or the Romans in that sense in which we use it; to characterise a people regardless of commercial arts; profuse of their own lives, and of those of others; vehement in their attachment to one society, and implacable in their antipathy to another. This, in a great and shining part of their history, was their own character, as well as that of some other nations, whom, upon this very account, we distinguish by the appellations of *barbarous* or *rude*.

IT has been observed, that those celebrated nations are indebted, for a great part of their estimation, not to the matter of their history, but to the manner in which it has been delivered, and to the capacity of their historians, and other writers. Their story has been told by men who knew how to draw our attention on the proceedings of the underſtanding and of the heart, more than on the detail of facts; and who could exhibit characters to be admired and loved, in the midſt of actions which we ſhould now univerſally hate or condemn. Like Homer, the model of Grecian literature, they could make us forget the horrors of a vindictive, cruel, and remorſeleſs proceeding towards an enemy, in behalf of the ſtrenuous conduct, the courage, and vehement affections, with which the hero maintained the cauſe of his friend and of his country.

Our manners are ſo different, and the ſyſtem upon which we regulate our apprehenſions, in many things, ſo oppoſite, that no leſs could make us endure the practice of ancient nations. Were that practice recorded by the mere journaliſt, who retains only the detail of events, without throwing any light on the character of the actors; who, like the Tartar hiſtorian, tells only what blood was ſpilt in the field, and how many inhabitants were maſſacred in the city; we ſhould never have diſtinguiſhed the Greeks from their barbarous neighbours, nor have thought, that the character of civility pertained even to the Romans, till very late in their hiſtory, and in the decline of their empire.

It would, no doubt, be pleaſant to ſee the remarks of ſuch a traveller as we ſometimes ſend abroad to inſpect the manners of mankind, left, unaſſiſted by hiſtory, to collect the character of the Greeks from the ſtate of their

country,

country, or from their practice in war. "This country," he might say, "compared to ours, has an air of barren-
" ness and desolation. I saw upon the road troops of la-
" bourers, who were employed in the fields; but no
" where the habitations of the master and the landlord.
" It was unsafe, I was told, to reside in the country; and
" the people of every district crouded into towns to find
" a place of defence. It is indeed impossible, that they
" can be more civilized, till they have established some
" regular government, and have courts of justice to hear
" their complaints. At present, every town, nay, I may
" say, every village, acts for itself, and the greatest dis-
" orders prevail. I was not indeed molested; for you
" must know, that they call themselves nations, and do
" all their mischief under the pretence of war.

" I do not mean to take any of the liberties of travel-
" lers, nor to vie with the celebrated author of the
" voyage to Lilliput; but cannot help endeavouring to
" communicate what I felt on hearing them speak
" of their territory, their armies, their revenue, treaties,
" and alliances. Only imagine the church-wardens
" and constables of Highgate or Hampstead turned
" statesmen and generals, and you will have a tolerable
" conception of this singular country. I passed through
" one state, where the best house in the capital would
" not lodge the meanest of your labourers, and where
" your very beggars would not chuse to dine with the
" King; and yet they are thought a great nation, and
" have no less than two kings. I saw one of them; but

" ſuch a potentate! he had ſcarcely cloaths to his back; " and for his Majeſty's table, he was obliged to go to the " eating-houſe with his ſubjects. They have not a ſingle " farthing of money; and I was obliged to get food at " the public expence, there being none to be had in the " market. You will imagine, that there muſt have been " a ſervice of plate, and great attendance, to wait up- " on the illuſtrious ſtranger; but my fare was a meſs of " ſorry pottage, brought me by a naked ſlave, who left " me to deal with it as I thought proper: and even this " I was in continual danger of having ſtoln from me by " the children, who are as vigilant to ſeize opportunities, " and as dextrous in ſnatching their food, as any ſtar- " ved greyhound you ever ſaw. The miſery of the " whole people, in ſhort, as well as my own, while I " ſtaid there, was beyond deſcription. You would " think that their whole attention were to torment " themſelves as much as they can: they are even diſ- " pleaſed with one of their kings for being well liked. " He had made a preſent, while I was there, of a cow " to one favourite, and of a waiſtcoat to another*; and " it was publicly ſaid, that this method of gaining " friends was robbing the public. My landlord told " me very gravely, that a man ſhould come under no " obligation that might weaken the love which he owes " to his country; nor form any perſonal attachment be- " yond the mere habit of living with his friend, and of " doing him a kindneſs when he can.

* Plutarch, in the life of Ageſilaus.

" I

" I asked him once, Why they did not, for their own
" sakes, enable their kings to assume a little more state?
" Because, says he, we intend them the happiness of li-
" ving with men. When I found fault with their hou-
" ses, and said in particular, that I was surprised they
" did not build better churches; What would you be
" then, says he, if you found religion in stone walls?
" This will suffice for a sample of our conversation; and
" sententious as it was, you may believe I did not stay
" long to profit by it.

" THE people of this place are not quite so stupid.
" There is a pretty large square of a market-place, and
" some tolerable buildings; and, I am told, they have
" some barks and lighters employed in trade, which
" they likewise, upon occasion, muster into a fleet, like
" my Lord Mayor's shew. But what pleases me most, is,
" that I am likely to get a passage from hence, and bid
" farewell to this wretched country. I have been at some
" pains to observe their ceremonies of religion, and to
" pick up curiosities. I have copied some inscriptions,
" as you will see when you come to peruse my journal,
" and will then judge, whether I have met with enough to
" compensate the fatigues and bad entertainment to which
" I have submitted. As for the people, you will believe,
" from the specimen I have given you, that they could not
" be very engaging company: though poor and dirty,
" they still pretend to be proud; and a fellow who is
" not worth a groat, is above working for his liveli-
" hood. They come abroad barefooted, and without

" any

" any cover to the head, wrapt up in the coverlets " under which you would imagine they had ſlept. They " throw all off, and appear like ſo many naked canni- " bals, when they go to violent ſports and exerciſes; at " which they highly value feats of dexterity and ſtrength. " Brawny limbs, and muſcular arms, the faculty of " ſleeping out all nights, of faſting long, and of putting " up with any kind of food, are thought genteel ac- " compliſhments. They have no ſettled government " that I could learn; ſometimes the mob, and ſometimes " the better ſort, do what they pleaſe: they meet in " great crouds in the open air, and ſeldom agree about " any thing. If a fellow has preſumption enough, and " a loud voice, he can make a great figure. There was " a tanner here, ſome time ago, who, for a while, car- " ried every thing before him. He cenſured ſo loudly " what others had done, and talked ſo big of what " might be performed, that he was ſent out at laſt to " make good his words, and to curry the enemy inſtead " of his leather *. You will imagine, perhaps, that he " was preſſed for a recruit; no;——he was ſent to com- " mand the army. They are indeed ſeldom long of one " mind, except in their readineſs to haraſs their neigh- " bours. They go out in bodies, and rob, pillage, and " murder where-ever they come." So far may we ſup- poſe our traveller to have written; and upon a recollec- tion of the reputation which thoſe nations have acquired

* Thucydides, lib. 4.——Ariſtophanes.

at a diſtance, he might have added, perhaps, "That he "could not underſtand how ſcholars, fine gentlemen, "and even women, ſhould combine to admire a people, "who ſo little reſemble themſelves."

To form a judgement of the character from which they acted in the field, and in their competitions with neighbouring nations, we muſt obſerve them at home. They were bold and fearleſs in their civil diſſenſions; ready to proceed to extremities, and to carry their debates to the deciſion of force. Individuals ſtood diſtinguiſhed by their perſonal ſpirit and vigour, not by the valuation of their eſtates, or the rank of their birth. They had a perſonal elevation founded on the ſenſe of equality, not of precedence. The general of one campaign was, during the next, a private ſoldier, and ſerved in the ranks. They were ſolicitous to acquire bodily ſtrength; becauſe, in the uſe of their weapons, battles were a trial of the ſoldier's ſtrength, as well as of the leader's conduct. The remains of their ſtatuary, ſhews a manly grace, an air of ſimplicity and eaſe, which being frequent in nature, were familiar to the artiſt. The mind, perhaps, borrowed a confidence and force, from the vigour and addreſs of the body; their eloquence and ſtyle bore a reſemblance to the carriage of the perſon. The underſtanding was chiefly cultivated in the practice of affairs. The moſt reſpectable perſonages were obliged to mix with the croud, and derived their degree of aſcendency, only from their conduct, their eloquence, and perſonal vigour. They had no forms of expreſſion,

to

to mark a ceremonious and guarded reſpect. Invective proceeded to railing, and the groſſeſt terms were often employed by the moſt admired and accompliſhed orators. Quarrelling had no rules but the immediate dictates of paſſion, which ended in words of reproach, in violence, and blows. They fortunately went always unarmed; and to wear a ſword in times of peace, was among them the mark of a barbarian. When they took arms in the diviſions of faction, the prevailing party ſupported itſelf by expelling their opponents, by proſcriptions, and bloodſhed. The uſurper endeavoured to maintain his ſtation by the moſt violent and prompt executions. He was oppoſed, in his turn, by conſpiracies and aſſaſſinations, in which the moſt reſpectable citizens were ready to uſe the dagger.

SUCH was the character of their ſpirit, in its occaſional ferments at home; and it burſt commonly with a ſuitable violence and force, againſt their foreign rivals and enemies. The amiable plea of humanity was little regarded by them in the operations of war. Cities were razed, or inſlaved; the captive ſold, mutilated, or condemned to die.

WHEN viewed on this ſide, the ancient nations have but a ſorry plea for eſteem with the inhabitants of modern Europe, who profeſs to carry the civilities of peace into the practice of war; and who value the praiſe of indiſcriminate lenity at a higher rate than even that of military prioweſs, or the love of their country. And yet they

they have, in other respects, merited and obtained our praise. Their ardent attachment to their country; their contempt of suffering, and of death, in its cause; their manly apprehensions of personal independence, which rendered every individual, even under tottering establishments, and imperfect laws, the guardian of freedom to his fellow-citizens; their activity of mind; in short, their penetration, the ability of their conduct, and force of their spirit, have gained them the first rank among nations.

If their animosities were great, their affections were proportionate: they, perhaps, loved, where we only pity; and were stern and inexorable, where we are not merciful, but only irresolute. After all, the merit of a man is determined by his candour and generosity to his associates, by his zeal for national objects, and by his vigour in maintaining political rights; not by moderation alone, which proceeds frequently from indifference to national and public interests, and which serves to relax the nerves on which the force of a private as well as a public character depends.

When under the Macedonian and the Roman monarchies, a nation came to be considered as the estate of a prince, and the inhabitants of a province to be regarded as a lucrative property, the possession of territory, not the destruction of its people, became the object of conquest. The pacific citizen had little concern in the quarrels of sovereigns; the violence of the soldier was reſtrained by diſcipline. He fought, becauſe he was taught to carry arms, and to obey: he ſometimes ſhed unneceſſary blood in the ardour of victory; but, except in the caſe of civil wars, had no paſſions to excite his animoſity beyond the field and the day of battle. Leaders judged of the objects of an enterpriſe, and they arreſted the ſword when theſe were obtained.

In the modern nations of Europe, where extent of territory admits of a diſtinction between the ſtate and its ſubjects, we are accuſtomed to think of the individual with compaſſion, ſeldom of the public with zeal. We have improved on the laws of war, and on the lenitives which have been deviſed to ſoften its rigours; we have mingled politeneſs with the uſe of the ſword; we have learned to make war under the ſtipulations of treaties and cartels, and truſt to the faith of an enemy whoſe ruin we meditate. Glory is more ſucceſsfully obtained by ſaving and protecting, than by deſtroying the vanquiſhed: and the moſt amiable of all objects is, in appearance, attained; the employing of force, only for the obtaining of juſtice, and for the preſervation of national rights.

This is, perhaps, the principal characteriſtic, on which, among modern nations, we beſtow the epithets of *civilized* or of *poliſhed*. But we have ſeen, that it did not accompany the progreſs of arts among the Greeks, nor keep pace with the advancement of policy, literature, and philoſophy. It did not await the returns of learning and politeneſs among the moderns; it was found

found in early periods of our hiſtory, and diſtinguiſhed, perhaps, more than at preſent, the manners of ages otherwiſe rude and undiſciplined. A King of France, priſoner in the hands of his enemies, was treated, about four hundred years ago, with as much diſtinction and courteſy, as a crowned head, in the like circumſtances, could poſſibly expect in this age of politeneſs *. The Prince of Conde, defeated and taken in the battle of Dreux, ſlept at night in the ſame bed with his enemy the Duke of Guiſe †.

If the moral of popular traditions, and the taſte of fabulous legends, which are the production or entertainment of particular ages, are likewiſe ſure indications of their notions and characters, we may preſume, that the foundation of what is now held to be the law of war, and of nations, was laid in the manners of Europe, together with the ſentiments which are expreſſed in the tales of chivalry, and of gallantry. Our ſyſtem of war differs not more from that of the Greeks, than the favourite characters of our early romance differed from thoſe of the Iliad, and of every ancient poem. The hero of the Greek fable, endued with ſuperior force, courage, and addreſs, takes every advantage of an enemy, to kill with ſafety to himſelf; and actuated by a deſire of ſpoil, or by a principle of revenge, is never ſtayed in his progreſs by interruptions of remorſe or com-

* Hume's Hiſtory of England.

† Davila.

paſſion. Homer, who, of all poets, knew beſt how to exhibit the emotions of a vehement affection, ſeldom attempts to excite commiſeration. Hector falls unpitied, and his body is inſulted by every Greek.

Our modern fable, or romance, on the contrary, generally couples an object of pity, weak, oppreſſed, and defenceleſs, with an object of admiration, brave, generous, and victorious; or ſends the hero abroad in ſearch of mere danger, and of occaſions to prove his valour. Charged with the maxims of a refined courteſy, to be obſerved even towards an enemy; and of a ſcrupulous honour, which will not ſuffer him to take any advantages by artifice or ſurpriſe; indifferent to ſpoil, he contends only for renown, and employs his valour to reſcue the diſtreſſed, and to protect the innocent. If victorious, he is made to riſe above nature as much in his generoſity and gentleneſs, as in his military proweſs and valour.

It may be difficult, upon ſtating this contraſt between the ſyſtem of ancient and modern fable, to aſſign, among nations equally rude, equally addicted to war, and equally fond of military glory, the origin of apprehenſions on the point of honour, ſo different, and ſo oppoſite. The hero of Greek poetry proceeds on the maxims of animoſity and hoſtile paſſion. His maxims in war are like thoſe which prevail in the woods of America. They require him to be brave, but they allow him to practiſe againſt his enemy every ſort of deception.

The

The hero of modern romance professes a contempt of stratagem, as well as of danger, and unites in the same person, characters and dispositions seemingly opposite; ferocity with gentleness, and the love of blood with sentiments of tenderness and pity.

THE system of chivalry, when completely formed, proceeded on a marvellous respect and veneration to the fair sex, on forms of combat established, and on a supposed junction of the heroic and sanctified character. The formalities of the duel, and a kind of judicial challenge, were known among the ancient Celtic nations of Europe. The Germans, even in their native forests, paid a kind of devotion to the female sex. The Christian religion injoined meekness and compassion to barbarous ages. These different principles combined together, may have served as the foundation of a system, in which courage was directed by religion and love, and the warlike and gentle were united together. When the characters of the hero and the saint were mixed, the mild spirit of Christianity, though often turned into venom by the bigotry of opposite parties, though it could not always subdue the ferocity of the warrior, nor suppress the admiration of courage and force, may have confirmed the apprehensions of men in what was to be held meritorious and splendid in the conduct of their quarrels.

IN the early and traditionary history of the Greeks and the Romans, rapes were assigned as the most frequent occaſions of war; and the ſexes were, no doubt, at all times, equally important to each other. The enthuſiaſm of love is moſt powerful in the neighbourhood of Aſia and Africa; and beauty, as a poſſeſſion, was probably more valued by the countrymen of Homer, than it was by thoſe of Amadis de Gaul, or by the authors of modern gallantry. “ What wonder,” ſays the old Priam, when Helen appeared, “ that nations ſhould contend for “ the poſſeſſion of ſo much beauty ?” This beauty, indeed, was poſſeſſed by different lovers; a ſubject on which the modern hero had many refinements, and ſeemed to ſoar in the clouds. He adored at a reſpectful diſtance, and employed his valour to captivate the admiration, not to gain the poſſeſſion of his miſtreſs. A cold and unconquerable chaſtity was ſet up, as an idol to be worſhipped, in the toils, the ſufferings, and the combats of the hero and the lover.

THE feudal eſtabliſhments, by the high rank to which they elevated certain families, no doubt greatly favoured this romantic ſyſtem. Not only the luſtre of a noble deſcent, but the ſtately caſtle beſet with battlements and towers, ſerved to inflame the imagination, and create a veneration for the daughter and the ſiſter of gallant chiefs, whoſe point of honour it was to be inacceſſible and chaſte, and who could perceive no merit but that of the high-minded and the brave, nor be approached in any other accents than thoſe of gentleneſs and reſpect.

WHAT

WHAT was originally ſingular in theſe apprehenſions, was, by the writer of romance, turned to extravagance; and under the title of chivalry was offered a model of conduct, even in common affairs: the fortunes of nations were directed by gallantry; and human life, on its greateſt occaſions, became a ſcene of affectation and folly. Warriors went forth to realize the legends they had ſtudied; princes and leaders of armies dedicated their moſt ſerious exploits to a real or to a fancied miſtreſs.

BUT whatever was the origin of notions, often ſo lofty and ſo ridiculous, we cannot doubt of their laſting effects on our manners. The point of honour, the prevalence of gallantry in our converſations, and on our theatres, many of the opinions which the vulgar apply even to the conduct of war; their notion, that the leader of an army, being offered battle upon equal terms, is diſhonoured by declining it, are undoubtedly remains of this antiquated ſyſtem: and chivalry, uniting with the genius of our policy, has probably ſuggeſted thoſe peculiarities in the law of nations, by which modern ſtates are diſtinguiſhed from the ancient. And if our rule in meaſuring degrees of politeneſs and civilization is to be taken from hence, or from the advancement of commercial arts, we ſhall be found to have greatly excelled any of the celebrated nations of antiquity.

PART FIFTH.

Of the Decline of Nations.

SECT. I.

Of supposed National Eminence, and of the Vicissitudes of Human Affairs.

NO nation is so unfortunate as to think itself inferior to the rest of mankind: few are even willing to put up with the claim to equality. The greater part having chosen themselves, as at once, the judges and the models of what is excellent in their kind, are first in their own opinion, and give to others consideration or eminence, so far only as they approach to their own condition. One nation is vain of the personal character, or of the learning, of a few of its members; another, of its policy, its wealth, its tradesmen, its gardens, and its buildings; and they who have nothing to boast, are vain, because they are ignorant. The Russians, before the reign of Peter the Great, thought themselves possessed

ſed of every national honour, and held the *Nemei*, or *dumb nations*, (the name which they beſtowed on their weſtern neighbours of Europe), in a proportional degree of contempt *. The map of the world, in China, was a ſquare plate, the greater part of which was occupied by the provinces of this great empire, leaving on its ſkirts a few obſcure corners, into which the wretched remainder of mankind were ſuppoſed to be driven. "If you "have not the uſe of our letters, nor the knowledge of "our books," ſaid the learned Chineſe to the European miſſionary, "what literature, or what ſcience, can you "have †?"

THE term *poliſhed*, if we may judge from its etymology, originally referred to the ſtate of nations in reſpect to their laws and government. In its later applications, it refers no leſs to their proficiency in the liberal and mechanical arts, in literature, and in commerce. But whatever may be its application, it appears, that if there were a name ſtill more reſpectable than this, every nation, even the moſt barbarous, or the moſt corrupted, would aſſume it; and beſtow its reverſe where they conceived a diſlike, or apprehended a difference. The names of *alien*, or *foreigner*, are ſeldom pronounced without ſome degree of intended reproach. That of *barbarian*, in uſe with one arrogant people, and that of *genteel*,

* Strahlenberg.

† Gemelli Carceri.

with another, only served to distinguish the stranger, whose language and pedigree differed from theirs.

EVEN where we pretend to found our opinions on reason, and to justify our preference of one nation to another, we frequently bestow our esteem on circumstances which do not relate to national character, and which have little tendency to promote the welfare of mankind. Conquest, or great extent of territory, however peopled, and great wealth, however distributed or employed, are titles upon which we indulge our own, and the vanity of other nations, as we do that of private men on the score of their fortunes and honours. We even sometimes contend, whose capital is the most overgrown; whose king has the most absolute power; and at whose court the bread of the subject is consumed in the most senseless riot. These indeed are the notions of vulgar minds; but it is impossible to determine, how far the notions of vulgar minds may lead mankind.

THERE have certainly been very few examples of states, who have, by arts or policy, improved the original dispositions of human nature, or endeavoured, by wise and effectual precautions, to prevent its corruption. Affection, and force of mind, which are the band and the strength of communities, were the inspiration of God, and original attributes in the nature of man. The wisest policy of nations, except in a very few instances, has tended, we may suspect, rather to maintain the peace of society, and to repress the external effects of bad

passions,

passions, than to strengthen the disposition of the heart itself to justice and goodness. It has tended, by introducing a variety of arts, to exercise the ingenuity of men, and by engaging them in a variety of pursuits, inquiries, and studies, to inform, but frequently to corrupt the mind. It has tended to furnish matter of distinction and vanity; and by incumbering the individual with new subjects of personal care, to substitute the anxiety he entertains for himself, instead of the confidence and the affection he should entertain for his fellow-creatures.

WHETHER this suspicion be just or no, we are come to point at circumstances tending to verify, or to disprove it: and if to understand the real felicity of nations be of importance, it is certainly so likewise, to know what are those weaknesses, and those vices, by which men not only mar this felicity, but in one age forfeit all the external advantages they had gained in a former.

THE wealth, the aggrandizement and power of nations, are commonly the effects of virtue; the loss of these advantages, is often a consequence of vice.

WERE we to suppose men to have succeeded in the discovery and application of every art by which states are preserved, and governed; to have attained, by efforts of wisdom and magnanimity, the admired establishments and advantages of a civilized and flourishing people; the subsequent part of their history, containing, according to vulgar apprehenſion, a full diſplay of thoſe fruits in maturity, of which they had till then carried only the bloſſom, and the firſt formation, ſhould, ſtill more than the former, merit our attention, and excite our admiration.

THE event, however, has not correſponded to this expectation. The virtues of men have ſhone moſt during their ſtruggles, not after the attainment of their ends. Thoſe ends themſelves, though attained by virtue, are frequently the cauſes of corruption and vice. Mankind, in aſpiring to national felicity, have ſubſtituted arts which increaſe their riches, inſtead of thoſe which improve their nature. They have entertained admiration of themſelves, under the titles of *civilized* and of *poliſhed*, where they ſhould have been affected with ſhame; and even where they have for a while acted on maxims tending to raiſe, to invigorate, and to preſerve the national character, they have, ſooner or later, been diverted from their object, and fallen a prey to misfortune, or to the neglects which proſperity itſelf had encouraged.

WAR, which furniſhes mankind with a principal occupation of their reſtleſs ſpirit, ſerves, by the variety of its events, to diverſify their fortunes. While it opens to one tribe or ſociety, the way to eminence, and leads to dominion, it brings another to ſubjection, and cloſes the ſcene of their national efforts. The celebrated rivalſhip of Carthage and Rome was, in both parties, the natural

natural exercise of an ambitious spirit, impatient of opposition, or even of equality. The conduct and the fortune of leaders, held the balance for some time in suspense; but to whichever side it had inclined, a great nation was to fall; a seat of empire, and of policy, was to be removed from its place; and it was then to be determined, whether the Syriac or the Latin should contain the erudition that was, in future ages, to occupy the studies of the learned.

STATES have been thus conquered from abroad, before they gave any signs of internal decay, even in the midst of prosperity, and in the period of their greatest ardour for national objects. Athens, in the height of her ambition, and of her glory, received a fatal wound, in striving to extend her maritime power beyond the Grecian seas. And nations of every description, formidable by their rude ferocity, respected for their discipline and military experience, when advancing, as well as when declining, in their strength, fell a prey, by turns, to the ambition and arrogant spirit of the Romans. Such examples may excite and alarm the jealousy and caution of states; the presence of similar dangers may exercise the talents of politicians and statesmen; but mere reverses of fortune are the common materials of history, and must long since have ceased to create our surprise.

DID we find, that nations advancing from small beginnings, and arrived at the possession of arts which lead to dominion, became secure of their advantages, in proportion

proportion as they were qualified to gain them; that they proceeded in a course of uninterrupted felicity, till they were broke by external calamities; and that they retained their force, till a more fortunate or vigorous power arose to depress them; the subject in speculation could not be attended with many difficulties, nor give rise to many reflections. But when we observe among nations a kind of spontaneous return to obscurity and weakness; when, in spite of perpetual admonitions of the danger they run, they suffer themselves to be subdued, in one period, by powers which could not have entered into competition with them in a former, and by forces which they had often baffled and despised; the subject becomes more curious, and its explanation more difficult.

THE fact itself is known in a variety of different examples. The empire of Asia was, more than once, transferred from the greater to the inferior power. The states of Greece, once so warlike, felt a relaxation of their vigour, and yielded the ascendant they had disputed with the monarchs of the east, to the forces of an obscure principality, become formidable in a few years, and raised to eminence under the conduct of a single man. The Roman empire, which stood alone for ages; which had brought every rival under subjection, and saw no power from whom a competition could be feared, sunk at last before an artless and contemptible enemy. Abandoned to inroad, to pillage, and at last to conquest, on her frontier, she decayed in all her extremities, and shrunk

on

on every side. Her territory was dismembered, and whole provinces gave way, like branches fallen down with age, not violently torn by superior force. The spirit with which Marius had baffled and repelled the attacks of barbarians in a former age, the civil and military force with which the consul and his legions had extended this empire, were now no more. The Roman greatness, doomed to sink as it rose, by slow degrees, was impaired in every encounter. It was reduced to its original dimensions, within the compass of a single city; and depending for its preservation on the fortune of a siege, it was extinguished at a blow; and the brand, which had filled the world with its flames, sunk like a taper in the socket.

SUCH appearances have given rise to a general apprehension, that the progress of societies to what we call the heights of national greatness, is not more natural, than their return to weakness and obscurity, is necessary and unavoidable. The images of youth, and of old age, are applied to nations; and communities, like single men, are supposed to have a period of life, and a length of thread, which is spun by the fates in one part uniform and strong, in another weakened and shattered by use; to be cut, when the destined æra is come, and to make way for a renewal of the emblem in the case of those who arise in succession. Carthage, being so much older than Rome, had felt her decay, says Polybius, so much the sooner: and the survivor too, he foresaw, carried in her bosom the seeds of mortality.

THE image indeed is apposite, and the history of mankind renders the application familiar. But it must be obvious, that the case of nations, and that of individuals, are very different. The human frame has a general course; it has, in every individual, a frail contexture, and a limited duration; it is worn by exercise, and exhausted by a repetition of its functions: But in a society, whose constituent members are renewed in every generation, where the race seems to enjoy perpetual youth, and accumulating advantages, we cannot, by any parity of reason, expect to find imbecilities connected with mere age and length of days.

THE subject is not new, and reflections will croud upon every reader. The notions, in the mean time, which we entertain, even in speculation, upon a subject so important, cannot be entirely fruitless to mankind; and however little the labours of the speculative may influence the conduct of men, one of the most pardonable errors a writer can commit, is to believe that he is about to do a great deal of good. But leaving the care of effects to others, we proceed to consider the grounds of inconstancy among mankind, the sources of internal decay, and the ruinous corruptions to which nations are liable, in the supposed condition of accomplished civility.

SECT.

SECT. II.

Of the Temporary Efforts and Relaxations of the National Spirit.

FROM what we have already obſerved on the general characteriſtics of human nature, it has appeared, that man is not made for repoſe. In him, every amiable and reſpectable quality is an active power, and every ſubject of commendation an effort. If his errors and his crimes are the movements of an active being, his virtues and his happineſs conſiſt likewiſe in the employment of his mind; and all the luſtre which he caſts around him, to captivate or engage the attention of his fellow-creatures, like the flame of a meteor, ſhines only while his motion continues: the moments of reſt and of obſcurity are the ſame. We know, that the taſks aſſigned him frequently may exceed, as well as come ſhort of his powers; that he may be agitated too much, as well as too little; but cannot aſcertain a preciſe medium between the ſituations in which he would be haraſſed, and thoſe in which he would fall into languor. We know, that he may be employed on a great variety of ſubjects, which occupy different paſſions; and that, in conſequence of habit, he becomes reconciled to very different ſcenes. All we can determine in general is, that whatever be the ſubjects with which he is engaged, the frame of his nature requires him to be occupied, and his happineſs requires him to be juſt.

We are now to inquire, why nations ceaſe to be eminent; and why ſocieties which have drawn the attention of mankind by great examples of magnanimity, conduct, and national ſucceſs, ſhould ſink from the height of their honours, and yield, in one age, the palm which they had won in a former. Many reaſons will probably occur. One may be taken from the fickleneſs and inconſtancy of mankind, who become tired of their purſuits and exertions, even while the occaſions that gave riſe to thoſe purſuits, in ſome meaſure continue: Another, from the change of ſituations, and the removal of objects which ſerved to excite their ſpirit.

The public ſafety, and the relative intereſts of ſtates; political eſtabliſhments, the pretenſions of party, commerce, and arts, are ſubjects which engage the attention of nations. The advantages gained in ſome of theſe particulars, determine the degree of national proſperity. The ardour and vigour with which they are at any one time purſued, is the meaſure of a national ſpirit. When thoſe objects ceaſe to animate, nations may be ſaid to languiſh; when they are during any conſiderable time neglected, ſtates muſt decline, and their people degenerate.

In the moſt forward, enterpriſing, inventive, and induſtrious nations, this ſpirit is fluctuating; and they who continue longeſt to gain advantages, or to preſerve them, have periods of remiſſneſs, as well as of ardour. The deſire of public ſafety, is, at all times, a powerful motive of conduct; but it operates moſt, when combined with occaſional paſſions, when provocations inflame, when ſucceſſes encourage, or mortifications exaſperate.

A whole people, like the individuals of whom they are compoſed, act under the influence of temporary humours, ſanguine hopes, or vehement animoſities. They are diſpoſed, at one time, to enter on national ſtruggles with vehemence; at another, to drop them from mere laſſitude and diſguſt. In their civil debates and contentions at home, they are occaſionally ardent or remiſs. Epidemical paſſions ariſe or ſubſide, on trivial, as well as important, grounds. Parties are ready, at one time, to take their names, and the pretence of their oppoſitions, from mere caprice or accident; at another time, they ſuffer the moſt ſerious occaſions to paſs in ſilence. If a vein of literary genius be caſually opened, or a new ſubject of diſquiſition be ſtarted, real or pretended diſcoveries ſuddenly multiply, and every converſation is inquiſitive and animated. If a new ſource of wealth be found, or a proſpect of conqueſt be offered, the imaginations of men are inflamed, and whole quarters of the globe are ſuddenly engaged in ruinous or in ſucceſsful adventures.

COULD we recall the ſpirit that was exerted, or enter into the views that were entertained, by our anceſtors, when they burſt, like a deluge, from their ancient ſeats, and poured into the Roman empire, we ſhould probably, after their firſt ſucceſſes, at leaſt, find a ferment in the minds of men, for which no attempt was too arduous, no difficulties inſurmountable.

THE ſubſequent ages of enterpriſe in Europe, were thoſe in which the alarm of enthuſiaſm was rung, and the followers of the croſs invaded the Eaſt, to plunder a country, and to recover a ſepulchre; thoſe in which the people in different ſtates contended for freedom, and aſſaulted the fabric of civil or religious uſurpation; that in which having found means to croſs the Atlantic, and to double the cape of Good Hope, the inhabitants of one half the world were let looſe on the other, and parties from every quarter, wading in blood, and at the expence of every crime, and of every danger, traverſed the earth in ſearch of gold.

EVEN the weak and the remiſs are rouſed to enterpriſe, by the contagion of ſuch remarkable ages; and ſtates which have not in their form the principles of a continued exertion, either favourable or adverſe to the welfare of mankind, may have paroxyſms of ardour, and a temporary appearance of national vigour. In the caſe of ſuch nations, indeed, the returns of moderation are but a relapſe to obſcurity, and the preſumption of one age is turned to dejection in that which ſucceeds.

BUT

But in the caſe of ſtates that are fortunate in their domeſtic policy, even madneſs itſelf may, in the reſult of violent convulſions, ſubſide into wiſdom; and a people return to their ordinary mood, cured of their follies, and wiſer by experience: or, with talents improved, in conducting the very ſcenes which frenzy had opened, they may then appear beſt qualified to purſue with ſucceſs the object of nations. Like the ancient republics, immediately after ſome alarming ſedition, or like the kingdom of Great Britain, at the cloſe of its civil wars, they retain the ſpirit of activity, which was recently awakened, and are equally vigorous in every purſuit, whether of policy, learning, or arts. From having appeared on the brink of ruin, they paſs to the greateſt proſperity.

Men engage in purſuits with degrees of ardour not proportioned to the importance of their object. When they are ſtated in oppoſition, or joined in confederacy, they only wiſh for pretences to act. They forget, in the heat of their animoſities, the ſubject of their controverſy; or they ſeek, in their formal reaſonings concerning it, only a diſguiſe for their paſſions. When the heart is inflamed, no conſideration can repreſs its ardour; when its fervour ſubſides, no reaſoning can excite, and no eloquence awaken, its former emotions.

The continuance of emulation among ſtates, muſt depend on the degree of equality by which their forces are balanced; or on the incentives by which either party, ty, or all, are urged to continue their ſtruggles. Long intermiſſions of war, ſuffer, equally in every period of civil ſociety, the military ſpirit to languiſh. The reduction of Athens by Lyſander, ſtruck a fatal blow at the inſtitutions of Lycurgus; and the quiet poſſeſſion of Italy, happily, perhaps, for mankind, had almoſt put an end to the military progreſs of the Romans. After ſome years of repoſe, Hannibal found Italy unprepared for his onſet, and the Romans in a diſpoſition likely to drop, on the banks of the Po, that martial ambition, which, being rouſed by the ſenſe of a new danger, afterwards carried them to the Euphrates and the Rhine.

STATES even diſtinguiſhed for military prowefs, ſometimes lay down their arms from laſſitude, and are weary of fruitleſs contentions: but if they maintain the ſtation of independent communities, they will have frequent occaſions to recall, and exert their vigour. Even under popular governments, men ſometimes drop the conſideration of their political rights, and appear at times remiſs or ſupine; but if they have reſerved the power to defend themſelves, the intermiſſion of its exerciſe cannot be of long duration. Political rights, when neglected, are always invaded; and alarms from this quarter muſt frequently come to renew the attention of parties. The love of learning, and of arts, may change its purſuits, or droop for a ſeaſon; but while men are poſſeſſed of freedom, and while the exerciſes of ingenuity are not ſuperſeded, the public may proceed, at different

times.

times, with unequal fervour; but its progreſs is ſeldom altogether diſcontinued, or the advantages gained in one age are ſeldom entirely loſt to the following.

If we would find the cauſes of final corruption, we muſt examine thoſe revolutions of ſtate that remove or with-hold the objects of every ingenious ſtudy, or liberal purſuit; that deprive the citizen of occaſions to act as the member of a public; that cruſh his ſpirit; that debaſe his ſentiments, and diſqualify his mind for affairs.

S E C T. III.

Of Relaxations in the National Spirit incident to Polifhed Nations.

IMPROVING nations, in the courfe of their advancement, have to ftruggle with foreign enemies, to whom they bear an extreme animofity, and with whom, in many conflicts, they contend for their exiftence as a people. In certain periods too, they feel in their domeftic policy inconveniencies and grievances, which beget an eager impatience; and they apprehend reformations and new eftablifhments, from which they have fanguine hopes of national happinefs. In early ages, every art is imperfect, and fufceptible of many improvements. The firft principles of every fcience are yet fecrets to be difcovered, and to be fucceffively publifhed with applaufe and triumph.

WE may fancy to ourfelves, that in ages of progrefs, the human race, like fcouts gone abroad on the difcovery of fertile lands, having the world open before them, are prefented at every ftep with the appearance of novelty. They enter on every new ground with expectation and joy: They engage in every enterprife with the ardour of men, who believe they are going to arrive at national

national felicity, and permanent glory; and forget past disappointments amidst the hopes of future success. From mere ignorance, rude minds are intoxicated with every passion; and partial to their own condition, and to their own pursuits, they think that every scene is inferior to that in which they are placed. Roused alike by success, and by misfortune, they are sanguine, ardent, and precipitant; and leave to the more knowing ages which succeed them, monuments of imperfect skill, and of rude execution in every art; but they leave likewise the marks of a vigorous and ardent spirit, which their successors are not always qualified to sustain, or to imitate.

THIS may be admitted, perhaps, as a fair description of prosperous societies, at least during certain periods of their progress. The spirit with which they advance may be unequal, in different ages, and may have its paroxysms, and intermissions, arising from the inconstancy of human passions, and from the casual appearance or removal of occasions that excite them. But does this spirit, which for a time continues to carry on the project of civil and commercial arts, find a natural pause in the termination of its own pursuits? May the business of civil society be accomplished, and may the occasion of farther exertion be removed? Do continued disappointments reduce sanguine hopes, and familiarity with objects blunt the edge of novelty? Does experience itself cool the ardour of the mind? May the society be again compared to the individual? And may it be suspected, although the vigour of a nation, like that of a natural body, does not waſte by a phyſical decay, that yet it may ſicken for want of exerciſe, and die in the cloſe of its own exertions? May ſocieties, in the completion of all their deſigns, like men in years, who diſregard the amuſements, and are inſenſible to the paſſions, of youth, become cold and indifferent to objects that uſed to animate in a ruder age? And may a poliſhed community be compared to a man, who having executed his plan, built his houſe, and made his ſettlement; who having, in ſhort, exhauſted the charms of every ſubject, and waſted all his ardour, ſinks into languor and liſtleſs indifference? If ſo, we have found at leaſt another ſimile to our purpoſe. But it is probable, that here too, the reſemblance is imperfect; and the inference that would follow, like that of moſt arguments drawn from analogy, tends rather to amuſe the fancy, than to give any real information on the ſubject to which it refers.

THE materials of human art are never entirely exhauſted, and the applications of induſtry are never at an end. The national ardour is not, at any particular time, proportioned to the occaſion there is for activity; nor curioſity, to the extent of ſubject that remains to be ſtudied.

THE ignorant and the artleſs, to whom objects of ſcience are new, and who are worſt furniſhed with the conveniencies of life, inſtead of being more active, and more curious, are commonly more quieſcent, and leſs inquiſitive,

quisitive, than the knowing and the polished. When we compare the particulars which occupy mankind in their rude and in their polished condition, they will be found greatly multiplied and enlarged in the last. The questions we have put, however, deserve to be answered; and if, in the advanced ages of society, we do not find the objects of human pursuit removed, or greatly diminished, we may find them at least changed; and in estimating the national spirit, we may find a negligence in one part, but ill compensated by the growing attention which is paid to another.

It is true, in general, that in all our pursuits, there is a termination of trouble, and a point of repose to which we aspire. We would remove this inconvenience, or gain that advantage, that our labours may cease. When I have conquered Italy and Sicily, say Pyrrhus, I shall then enjoy my repose. This termination is proposed in our national as well as in our personal exertions; and in spite of frequent experience to the contrary, is considered at a distance as the height of felicity. But nature has wisely, in most particulars, baffled our project; and placed no where within our reach this visionary blessing of absolute ease. The attainment of one end is but the beginning of a new pursuit; and the discovery of one art is but a prolongation of the thread by which we are conducted to further inquiries, and only hope to escape from the labyrinth.

Among the occupations that may be enumerated, as tending to exercise the invention, and to cultivate the talents of men, are the pursuits of accommodation and wealth, including all the different contrivances which serve to increase manufactures, and to perfect the mechanical arts. But it must be owned, that as the materials of commerce may continue to be accumulated without any determinate limit, so the arts which are applied to improve them, may admit of perpetual refinements. No measure of fortune, or degree of skill, is found to diminish the supposed necessities of human life; refinement and plenty foster new desires, while they furnish the means, or practise the methods, to gratify them.

In the result of commercial arts, inequalities of fortune are greatly increased, and the majority of every people are obliged by necessity, or at least strongly incited by ambition and avarice, to employ every talent they possess. After a history of some thousand years employed in manufacture and commerce, the inhabitants of China are still the most laborious and industrious of any people on the surface of the earth.

Some part of this observation may be extended to the elegant and literary arts. They too have their materials, which cannot be exhausted, and proceed from desires which cannot be satiated. But the respect paid to literary merit is fluctuating, and matter of transient fashion. When learned productions accumulate, the acquisition of of knowledge occupies the time that might be beſtowed on invention. The object of mere learning is attained with moderate or inferior talents, and the growing liſt of pretenders diminiſhes the luſtre of the few who are eminent. When we only mean to learn what others have taught, it is probable, that even our knowledge will be leſs than that of our maſters. Great names continue to be repeated with admiration, after we have ceaſed to examine the foundations of our praiſe; and new pretenders are rejected, not becauſe they fall ſhort of their predeceſſors, but becauſe they do not excel them; or becauſe, in reality, we have, without examination, taken for granted the merit of the firſt, and cannot judge of either.

AFTER libraries are furniſhed, and every path of ingenuity is occupied, we are, in proportion to our admiration of what is already done, prepoſſeſſed againſt farther attempts. We become ſtudents and admirers, inſtead of rivals; and ſubſtitute the knowledge of books, inſtead of the inquiſitive or animated ſpirit in which they were written.

THE commercial and lucrative arts may continue to proſper, but they gain an aſcendant at the expence of other purſuits. The deſire of profit ſtifles the love of perfection. Intereſt cools the imagination, and hardens the heart; and, recommending employments in proportion as they are lucrative, and certain in their gains, it drives

ingenuity,

ingenuity, and ambition itſelf, to the counter and the workſhop.

But apart from theſe conſiderations, the ſeparation of profeſſions, while it ſeems to promiſe improvement of ſkill, and is actually the cauſe why the productions of every art become more perfect as commerce advances; yet in its termination, and ultimate effects, ſerves, in ſome meaſure, to break the bands of ſociety, to ſubſtitute form in place of ingenuity, and to withdraw individuals from the common ſcene of occupation, on which the ſentiments of the heart, and the mind, are moſt happily employed.

Under the *diſtinction* of callings, by which the members of poliſhed ſociety are ſeparated from each other, every individual is ſuppoſed to poſſeſs his ſpecies of talent, or his peculiar ſkill, in which the others are confeſſedly ignorant; and ſociety is made to conſiſt of parts, of which none is animated with the ſpirit of ſociety itſelf. "We ſee in the ſame perſons," ſaid Pericles, "an "equal attention to private and to public affairs; and "in men who have turned to ſeparate profeſſions, a "competent knowledge of what relates to the community; for we alone conſider thoſe who are inattentive "to the ſtate, as perfectly inſignificant." This encomium on the Athenians, was probably offered under an apprehenſion, that the contrary was likely to be charged by their enemies, or might ſoon take place. It happened accordingly, that the buſineſs of ſtate, as well as of war,

came

came to be worse administered at Athens, when these, as well as other applications, became the objects of separate professions; and the history of this people abundantly shewed, that men ceased to be citizens, even to be good poets and orators, in proportion as they came to be distinguished by the profession of these, and other separate crafts.

ANIMALS less honoured than we, have sagacity enough to procure their food, and to find the means of their solitary pleasures; but it is reserved for man to consult, to persuade, to oppose, to kindle in the society of his fellow-creatures, and to lose the sense of his personal interest or safety, in the ardour of his friendships and his oppositions.

WHEN we are involved in any of the divisions into which mankind are separated, under the denominations of a country, a tribe, or an order of men any way affected by common interests, and guided by communicating passions, the mind recognises its natural station; the sentiments of the heart, and the talents of the understanding, find their natural exercise. Wisdom, vigilance, fidelity, and fortitude, are the characters requisite in such a scene, and the qualities which it tends to improve.

IN simple or barbarous ages, when nations are weak, and beset with enemies, the love of a country, of a party, or a faction, are the same. The public is a knot

of

of friends, and its enemies are the rest of mankind. Death, or slavery, are the ordinary evils which they are concerned to ward off; victory and dominion, the objects to which they aspire. Under the sense of what they may suffer from foreign invasions, it is one object, in every prosperous society, to increase its force, and to extend its limits. In proportion as this object is gained, security increases. They who possess the interior districts, remote from the frontier, are unused to alarms from abroad. They who are placed on the extremities, remote from the seats of government, are unused to hear of political interests; and the public becomes an object perhaps too extensive, for the conceptions of either. They enjoy the protection of its laws, or of its armies; and they boast of its splendor, and its power; but the glowing sentiments of public affection, which, in small states, mingle with the tenderness of the parent and the lover, of the friend and the companion, merely by having their object enlarged, lose great part of their force.

THE manners of rude nations require to be reformed. Their foreign quarrels, and domestic dissensions, are the operations of extreme and sanguinary passions. A state of greater tranquillity hath many happy effects. But if nations pursue the plan of enlargement and pacification, till their members can no longer apprehend the common ties of society, nor be engaged by affection in the cause of their country, they must err on the opposite side, and by leaving

leaving too little to agitate the ſpirits of men, bring on ages of languor, if not of decay.

THE members of a community may, in this manner, like the inhabitants of a conquered province, be made to loſe the ſenſe of every connection, but that of kindred or neighbourhood; and have no common affairs to tranſact, but thoſe of trade: Connections, indeed, or tranſactions, in which probity and friendſhip may ſtill take place; but in which the national ſpirit, whoſe ebbs and flows we are now conſidering, cannot be exerted.

WHAT we obſerve, however, on the tendency of enlargement to looſen the bands of political union, cannot be applied to nations who, being originally narrow, never greatly extended their limits, nor to thoſe who, in a rude ſtate, had already the extenſion of a great kingdom.

IN territories of conſiderable extent, ſubject to one government, and poſſeſſed of freedom, the national union, in rude ages, is extremely imperfect. Every diſtrict forms a ſeparate party; and the deſcendents of different families are oppoſed to one another, under the denomination of *tribes* or of *clans*: they are ſeldom brought to act with a ſteady concert; their feuds and animoſities give more frequently the appearance of ſo many nations at war, than of a people united by connections of policy. They acquire a ſpirit, however, in their private diviſions, and in the midſt of a diſorder, otherwiſe hurtful, of which the force, on many occaſions, redounds to the power of the ſtate.

WHATEVER be the national extent, civil order, and regular government, are advantages of the greateſt importance; but it does not follow, that every arrangement made to obtain theſe ends, and which may, in the making, exerciſe and cultivate the beſt qualities of men, is therefore of a nature to produce permanent effects, and to ſecure the preſervation of that national ſpirit from which it aroſe.

WE have reaſon to dread the political refinements of ordinary men, when we conſider, that repoſe, or inaction itſelf, is in a great meaſure their object; and that they would frequently model their governments, not merely to prevent injuſtice and error, but to prevent agitation and buſtle; and by the barriers they raiſe againſt the evil actions of men, would prevent them from acting at all. Every diſpute of a free people, in the opinion of ſuch politicians, amounts to diſorder, and a breach of the national peace. What heart-burnings? What delay to affairs? What want of ſecrecy and diſpatch? What defect of police? Men of ſuperior genius ſometimes ſeem to imagine, that the vulgar have no title to act, or to think. A great prince is pleaſed to ridicule the precaution by which judges in a free country are confined to the ſtrict interpretation of law*.

* Memoirs of Brandenburg.

We easily learn to contract our opinions of what men may, in consistence with public order, be safely permitted to do. The agitations of a republic, and the licence of its members, strike the subjects of monarchy with aversion and disgust. The freedom with which the European is left to traverse the streets and the fields, would appear to a Chinese a sure prelude to confusion and anarchy. "Can men behold their superior and not "tremble? Can they converse without a precise and "written ceremonial? What hopes of peace, if the "streets are not barricaded at an hour? What wild "disorder, if men are permitted in any thing to do "what they please?"

If the precautions which men thus take against each other be necessary to repress their crimes, and do not arise from a corrupt ambition, or from cruel jealousy in their rulers, the proceeding itself must be applauded, as the best remedy of which the vices of men will admit. The viper must be held at a distance, and the tyger chained. But if a rigorous policy, applied to enslave, not to restrain from crimes, has an actual tendency to corrupt the manners, and to extinguish the spirit of nations; if its severities be applied to terminate the agitations of a free people, not to remedy their corruptions; if forms be often applauded as salutary, because they tend merely to silence the voice of mankind, or be condemned as pernicious, because they allow this voice to be heard; we may expect that many of the boasted improvements of civil society, will be mere devices to lay the political ſpirit at reſt, and will chain up the active virtues more than the reſtleſs diſorders of men.

If to any people it be the avowed object of policy, in all its internal refinements, to ſecure the perſon and the property of the ſubject, without any regard to his political character, the conſtitution indeed may be free, but its members may likewiſe become unworthy of the freedom they poſſeſs, and unfit to preſerve it. The effects of ſuch a conſtitution may be to immerſe all orders of men in their ſeparate purſuits of pleaſure, which they may now enjoy with little diſturbance; or of gain, which they may preſerve without any attention to the commonwealth.

If this be the end of political ſtruggles, the deſign, when executed, in ſecuring to the individual his eſtate, and the means of ſubſiſtence, may put an end to the exerciſe of thoſe very virtues that were required in conducting its execution. A man who, in concert with his fellow-ſubjects, contends with uſurpation in defence of his eſtate or his perſon, may find an exertion of great generoſity, and of a vigorous ſpirit; but he who, under political eſtabliſhments, ſuppoſed to be fully confirmed, betakes him, becauſe he is ſafe, to the mere enjoyment of fortune, has in fact turned to a ſource of corruption the very advantages which the virtues of the other procured. Individuals, in certain ages, derive their protection chiefly from the ſtrength of the party to which they adhere; but in times of corruption, they flatter
themſelves,

themselves, that they may continue to derive from the public that safety which, in former ages, they must have owed to their own vigilance and spirit, to the warm attachment of their friends, and to the exercise of every talent which could render them respected, feared, or beloved. In one period, therefore, mere circumstances serve to excite the spirit, and to preserve the manners of men; in another, great wisdom and zeal for the good of mankind on the part of their leaders, are required for the same purposes.

ROME, it may be thought, did not die of a lethargy, nor perish by the remission of her political ardours at home. Her distemper appeared of a nature more violent and acute. Yet if the virtues of Cato and of Brutus found an exercise in the dying hour of the republic, the neutrality, and the cautious retirement of Atticus, found its security in the same tempestuous season; and the great body of the people lay undisturbed, below the current of a storm, by which the superior ranks of men were destroyed. In the minds of the people, the sense of a public was defaced; and even the animosity of faction had subsided: they only could share in the commotion, who were the soldiers of a legion, or the partisans of a leader. But this state fell not into obscurity for want of eminent men. If at the time of which we speak, we look only for a few names distinguished in the history of mankind, there is no period at which the list was more numerous. But those names became distinguished in the contest for dominion, not in the exercise

of

of equal rights: the people was corrupted; the empire of the known world ſtood in need of a maſter.

REPUBLICAN governments, in general, are in hazard of ruin from the aſcendant of particular factions, and from the mutinous ſpirit of a populace, who being corrupted, are no longer fit to ſhare in the adminiſtration of ſtate. But under other eſtabliſhments, where liberty may be more ſucceſsfully attained if men are corrupted, the national vigour declines from the abuſe of that very ſecurity which is procured by the ſuppoſed perfection of public order.

A diſtribution of power and office; an execution of law, by which mutual incroachments and moleſtations are brought to an end; by which the perſon and the property are, without friends, without cabal, without obligation, perfectly ſecured to individuals, does honour to the genius of a nation; and could not have been fully eſtabliſhed, without thoſe exertions of underſtanding and integrity, thoſe trials of a reſolute and vigorous ſpirit, which adorn the annals of a people, and leave to future ages a ſubject of juſt admiration and applauſe. But if we ſuppoſe that the end is attained, and that men no longer act, in the enjoyment of liberty, from liberal ſentiments, or with a view to the preſervation of public manners; if individuals think themſelves ſecure without any attention or effort of their own; this boaſted advantage may be found only to give them an opportunity of enjoying, at leiſure, the conveniencies and

neceſſaries

necessaries of life; or, in the language of Cato, teach them to value their houses, their villas, their statues, and their pictures, at a higher rate than they do the republic. They may be found to grow tired in secret of a free constitution, of which they never cease to boast in their conversation, and which they always neglect in their conduct.

THE dangers to liberty are not the subject of our present consideration; but they can never be greater from any cause than they are from the supposed remissness of a people, to whose personal vigour every constitution, as it owed its establishment, so must continue to owe its preservation. Nor is this blessing ever less secure than it is in the possession of men who think that they enjoy it in safety, and who therefore consider the public only as it presents to their avarice a number of lucrative employments; for the sake of which they may sacrifice those very rights which render themselves objects of management or consideration.

FROM the tendency of these reflections, then, it should appear, that a national spirit is frequently transient, not on account of any incurable distemper in the nature of mankind, but on account of their voluntary neglects and corruptions. This spirit subsisted solely, perhaps, in the execution of a few projects, entered into for the acquisition of territory or wealth; it comes, like a useless weapon, to be laid aside after its end is attained.

ORDINARY

ORDINARY eſtabliſhments terminate in a relaxation of vigour, and are ineffectual to the preſervation of ſtates; becauſe they lead mankind to rely on their arts, inſtead of their virtues, and to miſtake for an improvement of human nature, a mere acceſſion of accommodation, or of riches. Inſtitutions that fortify the mind, inſpire courage, and promote national felicity, can never tend to national ruin.

Is it not poſſible, amidſt our admiration of arts, to find ſome place for theſe? Let ſtateſmen, who are intruſted with the government of nations, reply for themſelves. It is their buſineſs to ſhew, whether they climb into ſtations of eminence, merely to diſplay a paſſion for intereſt, which they had better indulge in obſcurity; and whether they have capacity to underſtand the happineſs of a people, the conduct of whoſe affairs they are ſo willing to undertake.

SECT.

SECT. IV.

The same subject continued.

MEN frequently, while they study to improve their fortunes, neglect themselves; and while they reason for their country, forget the considerations that most deserve their attention. Numbers, riches, and the other resources of war, are highly important: but nations consist of men; and a nation consisting of degenerate and cowardly men, is weak; a nation consisting of vigorous, public-spirited, and resolute men, is strong. The resources of war, where other advantages are equal, may decide a contest; but the resources of war, in hands that cannot employ them, are of no avail.

VIRTUE is a necessary constituent of national strength: capacity, and a vigorous understanding, are no less necessary to sustain the fortune of states. Both are improved by discipline, and by the exercises in which men are engaged. We despise, or we pity, the lot of mankind, while they lived under uncertain establishments, and were obliged to sustain in the same person, the character of the senator, the statesman, and the soldier. Polished nations discover, that any one of these characters is sufficient in one person; and that the ends of each, when disjoined, are more eaſily accompliſhed. The firſt, however, were circumſtances under which nations advanced and proſpered; the ſecond were thoſe in which the ſpirit relaxed, and the nation went to decay.

WE may, with good reaſon, congratulate our ſpecies on their having eſcaped from a ſtate of barbarous diſorder and violence, into a ſtate of domeſtic peace and regular policy; when they have ſheathed the dagger, and diſarmed the animoſities of civil contention; when the weapons with which they contend are the reaſonings of the wiſe, and the tongue of the eloquent. But we cannot, mean-time, help to regret, that they ſhould ever proceed, in ſearch of perfection, to place every branch of adminiſtration behind the counter, and come to employ, inſtead of the ſtateſman and warrior, the mere clerk and accountant.

BY carrying this ſyſtem to its height, men are educacated, who could copy for Cæſar his military inſtructions, or even execute a part of his plans; but none who could act in all the different ſcenes for which the leader himſelf muſt be qualified, in the ſtate and in the field, in times of order or of tumult, in times of diviſion or of unanimity; none who could animate the council when deliberating on ordinary occaſions, or when alarmed by attacks from abroad.

THE policy of China is the moſt perfect model of an arrangement, at which the ordinary refinements of go-

vernment

vernment are aimed; and the inhabitants of this empire possess, in the highest degree, those arts on which vulgar minds make the felicity and greatness of nations to depend. The state has acquired, in a measure unequalled in the history of mankind, numbers of men, and the other resources of war. They have done what we are very apt to admire; they have brought national affairs to the level of the meanest capacity; they have broke them into parts, and thrown them into separate departments; they have clothed every proceeding with splendid ceremonies, and majestical forms; and where the reverence of forms cannot repress disorder, a rigorous and severe police, armed with every species of corporal punishment, is applied to the purpose. The whip, and the cudgel, are held up to all orders of men; they are at once employed, and they are dreaded by every magistrate. A mandarine is whipped, for having ordered a pickpocket to receive too few or too many blows.

Every department of state is made the object of a separate profession, and every candidate for office must have passed through a regular education; and, as in the graduations of the university, must have obtained by his proficiency, or his standing, the degree to which he aspires. The tribunals of state, of war, and of the revenue, as well as of literature, are conducted by graduates in their different studies: but while learning is the great road to preferment, it terminates, in being able to read, and to write; and the great object of government consists in raising, and in consuming the fruits of the earth. With all theſe reſources, and this learned preparation, which is made to turn theſe reſources to uſe, the ſtate is in reality weak; has repeatedly given the example which we ſeek to explain; and among the doctors of war or of policy, among the millions who are ſet apart for the military profeſſion, can find none of its members who are fit to ſtand forth in the dangers of their country, or to form a defence againſt the repeated inroads of an enemy reputed to be artleſs and mean.

It is difficult to tell how long the decay of ſtates might be ſuſpended by the cultivation of arts on which their real felicity and ſtrength depend; by cultivating in the higher ranks thoſe talents for the council and the field, which cannot, without great diſadvantage, be ſeparated; and in the body of a people, that zeal for their country, and that military character, which enable them to take a ſhare in defending its rights.

Times may come, when every proprietor muſt defend his own poſſeſſions, and every free people maintain their own independence. We may imagine, that againſt ſuch an extremity, an army of hired troops is a ſufficient precaution; but their own troops are the very enemy againſt which a people is ſometimes obliged to fight. We may flatter ourſelves, that extremities of this ſort, in any particular caſe, are remote; but we cannot, in reaſoning on the general fortunes of mankind, avoid putting the caſe, and referring to the examples in which it has happened.

pened. It has happened in every instance where the polished have fallen a prey to the rude, and where the pacific inhabitant has been reduced to subjection by military force.

If the defence and government of a people be made to depend on a few, who make the conduct of state or of war their profession; whether these be foreigners or natives; whether they be called away of a sudden, like the Roman legion from Britain; whether they turn against their employers, like the army of Carthage, or be overpowered and dispersed by a stroke of fortune, the multitude of a cowardly and undisciplined people must, on such an emergence, receive a foreign or a domestic enemy, as they would a plague or an earthquake, with hopeless amazement and terror, and by their numbers, only swell the triumphs, and enrich the spoil of a conqueror.

Statesmen and leaders of armies, accustomed to the mere observance of forms, are disconcerted by a suspension of customary rules; and on slight grounds despair of their country. They were qualified only to go the rounds of a particular track; and when forced from their stations, are in reality unable to act with men. They only took part in formalities, of which they understood not the tendency; and together with the modes of procedure, even the very state itself, in their apprehension, has ceased to exist. The numbers, possessions, and resources of a great people, only serve, in their

view,

view, to conſtitute a ſcene of hopeleſs confuſion and terror.

In rude ages, under the appellations of *a community, a people*, or *a nation*, was underſtood a number of men; and the ſtate, while its members remained, was accounted entire. The Scythians, while they fled before Darius, mocked at his childiſh attempt; Athens ſurvived the devaſtations of Xerxes; and Rome, in its rude ſtate, thoſe of the Gauls. With poliſhed and mercantile ſtates, the caſe is ſometimes reverſed. The nation is a territory, cultivated and improved by its owners; deſtroy the poſſeſſion, even while the maſter remains, the ſtate is undone.

That weakneſs and effeminacy of which poliſhed nations are ſometimes accuſed, has its place probably in the mind alone. The ſtrength of animals, and that of man in particular, depends on his feeding, and the kind of labour to which he is uſed. Wholeſome food, and hard labour, the portion of many in every poliſhed and commercial nation, ſecure to the public a number of men endued with bodily ſtrength, and inured to hardſhip and toil.

Even delicate living, and good accommodation, are not found to enervate the body. The armies of Europe have been obliged to make the experiment; and the children of opulent families, bred in effeminacy, or nurſed with tender care, have been made to contend with the ſavage.

savage. By imitating his arts, they have learned, like him, to traverse the forest; and, in every season, to subsist in the desert. They have, perhaps, recovered a lesson, which it has cost civilized nations many ages to unlearn, That the fortune of a man is entire while he remains possessed of himself.

It may be thought, however, that few of the celebrated nations of antiquity, whose fate has given rise to so much reflection on the vicissitudes of human affairs, had made any great progress in those enervating arts we have mentioned; or made those arrangements from which the danger in question could be supposed to arise. The Greeks, in particular, at the time of their fall under the Macedonian yoke, had certainly not carried the commercial arts to so great a height as is common with the most flourishing and prosperous nations of Europe. They had still retained the form of independent republics; the people were generally admitted to a share in the government; and not being able to hire armies, they were obliged, by necessity, to bear a part in the defence of their country. By their frequent wars and domestic commotions, they were accustomed to danger, and were familiar with alarming situations: they were accordingly still accounted the best soldiers and the best statesmen of the known world. The younger Cyrus promised himself the empire of Asia by means of their aid; and after his fall, a body of ten thousand, although bereft of their leaders, baffled, in their retreat, all the military force of the Persian empire. The

victor

victor of Aſia did not think himſelf prepared for that conqueſt, till he had formed an army from the ſubdued republics of Greece.

It is, however, true, that in the age of Philip, the military and political ſpirit of thoſe nations appears to have been conſiderably impaired, and to have ſuffered, perhaps, from the variety of intereſts and purſuits, as well as of pleaſures, with which their members came to be occupied: they even made a kind of ſeparation between the civil and military character. Phocion, we are told by Plutarch, having obſerved that the leading men of his time followed different courſes, that ſome applied themſelves to civil, others to military affairs, determined rather to follow the examples of Themiſtocles, Ariſtides, and Pericles, the leaders of a former age, who were equally prepared for either.

We find in the orations of Demoſthenes, a perpetual reference to this ſtate of manners. We find him exhorting the Athenians, not only to declare war, but to arm themſelves for the execution of their own military plans. We find that there was an order of military men, who eaſily paſſed from the ſervice of one ſtate to that of another; and who, when they were neglected from home, turned away to enterpriſes on their own account. There were not, perhaps, better warriors in any former age; but thoſe warriors were not attached to any ſtate; and the ſettled inhabitants of every city thought themſelves diſqualified for military ſervice.

The

The discipline of armies was perhaps improved; but the vigour of nations was gone to decay. When Philip, or Alexander, defeated the Grecian armies, which were chiefly composed of soldiers of fortune, they found an easy conquest with the other inhabitants: and when the latter, afterwards supported by those soldiers, invaded the Persian empire, he seems to have left little martial spirit behind him; and by removing the military men, to have taken precaution enough, in his absence, to secure his dominion over this mutinous and refractory people.

THE subdivision of arts and professions, in certain examples, tends to improve the practice of them, and to promote their ends. By having separated the arts of the clothier and the tanner, we are the better supplied with shoes and with cloth. But to separate the arts which form the citizen and the statesman, the arts of policy and war, is an attempt to dismember the human character, and to destroy those very arts we mean to improve. By this separation, we in effect deprive a free people of what is necessary to their safety; or we prepare a defence against invasions from abroad, which gives a prospect of usurpation, and threatens the establishment of military government at home.

WE may be surprised to find the beginning of certain military instructions at Rome, referred to a time no earlier than that of the Cimbric war. It was then, we are told by Valerius Maximus, that Roman soldiers were made to learn from gladiators the use of a sword:

 and

and the antagonifts of Phyrrhus and of Hannibal were, by the account of this writer, ftill in need of inftruction in the firft rudiments of their trade. They had already, by the order and choice of their incampments, impreffed the Grecian invader with awe and refpect; they had already, not by their victories, but by their national vigour and firmnefs, under repeated defeats, induced him to fue for peace. But the haughty Roman, perhaps, knew the advantage of order and of union, without having been broke to the inferior arts of the mercenary foldier; and had the courage to face the enemies of his country, without having practifed the ufe of his weapon under the fear of being whipped. He could ill be perfuaded, that a time might come, when refined and intelligent nations would make the art of war to confift in a few technical forms; that citizens and foldiers might come to be diftinguifhed as much as women and men; that the citizen would become poffeffed of a property which he would not be able, or required, to defend; that the foldier would be appointed to keep for another what he would be taught to defire, and what he would be enabled to feize for himfelf; that, in fhort, one fet of men were to have an intereft in the prefervation of civil eftablifhments, without the power to defend them; that the other were to have this power, without either the inclination or the intereft.

This people, however, by degrees came to put their military force on the very footing to which this defcription alludes. Marius made a capital change in the manner of levying soldiers at Rome: He filled his legions with the mean and the indigent, who depended on military pay for subsistence; he created a force which rested on mere discipline alone, and the skill of the gladiator; he taught his troops to employ their swords against the constitution of their country, and set the example of a practice which was soon adopted and improved by his successors.

The Romans only meant by their armies to incroach on the freedom of other nations, while they preserved their own. They forgot, that in assembling soldiers of fortune, and in suffering any leader to be master of a disciplined army, they actually resigned their political rights, and suffered a master to arise for the state. This people, in short, whose ruling passion was depredation and conquest, perished by the recoil of an engine which they themselves had erected against mankind.

The boasted refinements, then, of the polished age, are not divested of danger. They open a door, perhaps, to disaster, as wide and accessible as any of those they have shut. If they build walls and ramparts, they enervate the minds of those who are placed to defend them; if they form disciplined armies, they reduce the military spirit of entire nations; and by placing the sword where they have given a distaste to civil establishments, they prepare for mankind the government of force.

It is happy for the nations of Europe, that the disparity between the ſoldier and the pacific citizen can never be ſo great as it became among the Greeks and the Romans. In the uſe of modern arms, the novice is made to learn, and to practiſe with eaſe, all that the veteran knows; and if to teach him were a matter of real difficulty, happy are they who are not deterred by ſuch difficulties, and who can diſcover the arts which tend to fortify and preſerve, not to enervate and ruin their country.

SECT. V.

Of National Waste.

THE strength of nations consists in the wealth, the numbers, and the character, of their people. The history of their progress from a state of rudeness, is, for the most part, a detail of the struggles they have maintained, and of the arts they have practised, to strengthen, or to secure themselves. Their conquests, their population, and their commerce, their civil and military arrangements, their skill in the construction of weapons, and in the methods of attack and defence; the very distribution of tasks, whether in private business or in public affairs, either tend to bestow, or promise to employ with advantage, the constituents of a national force, and the resources of war.

If we suppose, that together with these advantages, the military character of a people remains, or is improved, it must follow, that what is gained in civilization, is a real increase of strength; and that the ruin of nations could never take its rise from themselves. Where states have stopped short in their progress, or have

have actually gone to decay, we may ſuſpect, that however diſpoſed to advance, they have found a limit, beyond which they could not proceed; or from a remiſſion of the national ſpirit, and a weakneſs of character, were unable to make the moſt of their reſources, and natural advantages. On this ſuppoſition, from being ſtationary, they may begin to relapſe, and by a retrograde motion, in a ſucceſſion of ages, arrive at a ſtate of greater weakneſs, than that which they quitted in the beginning of their progreſs; and with the appearance of better arts, and ſuperior conduct, expoſe themſelves to become a prey to barbarians, whom, in the attainment, or the height of their glory, they had eaſily baffled or deſpiſed.

WHATEVER may be the natural wealth of a people, or whatever may be the limits beyond which they cannot improve on their ſtock, it is probable, that no nation has ever reached thoſe limits, or has been able to poſtpone its misfortunes, and the effects of miſconduct, until its fund of materials, and the fertility of its ſoil, were exhauſted, or the numbers of its people were greatly reduced. The ſame errors in policy, and weakneſs of manners, which prevent the proper uſe of reſources, likewiſe check their increaſe, or improvement.

THE wealth of the ſtate conſiſts in the fortune of its members. The actual revenue of the ſtate is that ſhare of every private fortune, which the public has been accuſtomed to demand for national purpoſes. This revenue cannot be always proportioned to what may be ſuppoſed redundant in the private eſtate, but to what is, in ſome meaſure, thought ſo by the owner; and to what he may be made to ſpare, without intrenching on his manner of living, and without ſuſpending his projects of expence, or of commerce. It ſhould appear, therefore, that any immoderate increaſe of private expence is a prelude to national weakneſs: government, even while each of its ſubjects conſumes a princely eſtate, may be ſtraitened in point of revenue, and the paradox be explained by example, That the public is poor, while its members are rich.

We are frequently led into error by miſtaking money for riches; we think that a people cannot be impoveriſhed by a waſte of money which is ſpent among themſelves. The fact is, that men are impoveriſhed, only in two ways; either by having their gains ſuſpended, or by having their ſubſtance conſumed; and money expended at home, being circulated, and not conſumed, cannot, any more than the exchange of a tally, or a counter, among a certain number of hands, tend to diminiſh the wealth of the company among whom it is handed about. But while money circulates at home, the neceſſaries of life, which are the real conſtituents of wealth, may be idly conſumed; the induſtry which might be employed to increaſe the ſtock of a people, may be ſuſpended, or turned to abuſe.

Great armies, maintained either at home or abroad, without any national object, are ſo many mouths unneceſſarily opened to waſte the ſtores of the public, and ſo

many

many hands with-held from the arts by which its profits are made. Unſucceſsful enterpriſes are ſo many ventures thrown away, and loſſes ſuſtained, proportioned to the capital employed in the ſervice. The Helvetii, in order to invade the Roman province of Gaul, burnt their habitations, dropt their inſtruments of huſbandry, and conſumed, in one year, the ſavings of many. The enterpriſe failed of ſucceſs, and the nation was undone.

STATES have endeavoured, in ſome inſtances, by pawning their credit, inſtead of employing their capital, to diſguiſe the hazards they ran. They have found, in the loans they raiſed, a caſual reſource, which encouraged their enterpriſes. They have ſeemed, by their manner of erecting transferable funds, to leave the capital for purpoſes of trade, in the hands of the ſubject, while it is actually expended by the government. They have, by theſe means, proceeded to the execution of great national projects, without ſuſpending private induſtry, and have left future ages to anſwer, in part, for debts contracted with a view to future emolument. So far the expedient is plauſible, and appears to be juſt. The growing burden too, is thus gradually laid; and if a nation be to ſink in ſome future age, every miniſter hopes it may ſtill keep afloat in his own. But the meaſure, for this very reaſon, is, with all its advantages, extremely dangerous, in the hands of a precipitant and ambitious adminiſtration, regarding only the preſent occaſion, and imagining a ſtate to be inexhauſtible, while a capital can be borrowed, and the intereſt be paid.

WE

We are told of a nation, who, during a certain period, rivalled the glories of the ancient world, threw off the dominion of a master armed against them with the powers of a great kingdom, broke the yoke with which they had been oppressed, and almost within the course of a century, raised, by their industry and national vigour, a new and formidable power, which struck the former potentates of Europe with awe and suspense, and turned the badges of poverty with which they set out, into the ensigns of war and dominion. This end was attained by the great efforts of a spirit awaked by oppression, by a successful pursuit of national wealth, and by a rapid anticipation of future revenue. But this illustrious state is supposed, not only in the language of a former section, to have preoccupied the business; they have sequestered the inheritance of many ages to come.

Great national expence, however, does not imply the necessity of any national suffering. While revenue is applied with success, to obtain some valuable end; the profits of every adventure, being more than sufficient to repay its costs, the public should gain, and its resources should continue to multiply. But an expence, whether sustained at home or abroad, whether a waste of the present, or an anticipation of future, revenue, if it bring no proper return, is to be reckoned among the causes of national ruin.

PART SIXTH.

Of Corruption and Political Slavery.

SECT. I.

Of Corruption in general.

IF the fortune of nations, and their tendency to aggrandifement, or to ruin, were to be eftimated by merely balancing, on the principles of laft fection, articles of profit and lofs, every argument in politics would reft on a comparifon of national expence with national gain; on a comparifon of the numbers who confume, with thofe who produce or amafs the neceffaries of life. The columns of the induftrious, and the idle, would include all orders of men; and the ftate itfelf, being allowed as many magiftrates, politicians, and warriors, as were barely fufficient for its defence and its government,

vernment, ſhould place, on the ſide of its loſs, every name that is ſupernumerary on the civil or the military liſt; all thoſe orders of men, who, by the poſſeſſion of fortune, ſubſiſt on the gains of others, and by the nicety of their choice, require a great expence of time and of labour, to ſupply their conſumption; all thoſe who are idly employed in the train of perſons of rank; all thoſe who are engaged in the profeſſions of law, phyſic, or divinity, together with all the learned, who do not, by their ſtudies, promote or improve the practice of ſome lucrative trade. The value of every perſon, in ſhort, ſhould be computed from his labour; and that of labour itſelf, from its tendency to procure and amaſs the means of ſubſiſtence. The arts employed on mere ſuperfluities ſhould be prohibited, except when their produce could be exchanged with foreign nations, for commodities that might be employed to maintain uſeful men for the public.

These appear to be the rules by which a miſer would examine the ſtate of his own affairs, or thoſe of his country; but ſchemes of perfect corruption are at leaſt as impracticable as ſchemes of perfect virtue. Men are not univerſally miſers; they will not be ſatisfied with the pleaſure of hoarding; they muſt be ſuffered to enjoy their wealth, in order that they may take the trouble of becoming rich. Property, in the common courſe of human affairs, is unequally divided: we are therefore obliged to ſuffer the wealthy to ſquander, that the poor may ſubſiſt; we are obliged to tolerate certain orders of men, who are above the neceſſity of labour, in order that, in their condition, there may be an object of ambition, and a rank to which the buſy aſpire. We are not only obliged to admit numbers, who, in ſtrict œconomy, may be reckoned ſuperfluous, on the civil, the military, and the political liſt; but becauſe we are men, and prefer the occupation, improvement, and felicity of our nature, to its mere exiſtence, we muſt even wiſh, that as many members as poſſible, of every community, may be admitted to a ſhare of its defence and its government.

MEN, in fact, while they purſue in ſociety different objects, or ſeparate views, procure a wide diſtribution of power, and by a ſpecies of chance, arrive at a poſture for civil engagements, more favourable to human nature than what human wiſdom could ever calmly deviſe.

IF the ſtrength of a nation, in the mean time, conſiſts in the men on whom it may rely, and who are fortunately or wiſely combined for its preſervation, it follows, that manners are as important as either numbers or wealth; and that corruption is to be accounted a principal cauſe of national declenſion and ruin.

WHOEVER perceives what are the qualities of man in his excellence, may eaſily, by that ſtandard, diſtinguiſh his defects or corruptions. If an intelligent, a courageous, and an affectionate mind, conſtitutes the perfection of his nature, remarkable failings in any of

thoſe

thoſe particulars, muſt proportionally ſink or debaſe his character.

WE have obſerved, that it is the happineſs of the individual to make a right choice of his conduct; that this choice will lead him to loſe in ſociety the ſenſe of a perſonal intereſt; and, in the conſideration of what is due to the whole, to ſtifle thoſe anxieties which relate to himſelf as a part.

THE natural diſpoſition of man to humanity, and the warmth of his temper, may raiſe his character to this fortunate pitch. His elevation, in a great meaſure, depends on the form of his ſociety; but he can, without incurring the charge of corruption, accommodate himſelf to great variations in the conſtitutions of government. The ſame integrity, and vigorous ſpirit, which, in democratical ſtates, renders him tenacious of his equality, may, under ariſtocracy or monarchy, lead him to maintain the ſubordinations eſtabliſhed. He may entertain, towards the different ranks of men with whom he is yoked in the ſtate, maxims of reſpect and of candour: he may, in the choice of his actions, follow a principle of juſtice, and of honour, which the conſiderations of ſafety, preferment, or profit, cannot efface.

FROM our complaints of national depravity, it ſhould, notwithſtanding, appear, that whole bodies of men are ſometimes infected with an epidemical weakneſs of the head, or corruption of heart, by which they become

unfit

unfit for the ſtations they occupy, and threaten the ſtates they compoſe, however flouriſhing, with a proſpect of decay, and of ruin.

A change of national manners for the worſe, may ariſe from a diſcontinuance of the ſcenes in which the talents of men were happily cultivated, and brought into exerciſe; or from a change in the prevailing opinions relating to the conſtituents of honour or of happineſs. When mere riches, or court-favour, are ſuppoſed to conſtitute rank; the mind is miſled from the conſideration of qualities on which it ought to rely. Magnanimity, courage, and the love of mankind, are ſacrificed to avarice and vanity, or ſuppreſſed under a ſenſe of dependence. The individual conſiders his community ſo far only as it can be rendered ſubſervient to his perſonal advancement or profit: he ſtates himſelf in competition with his fellow-creatures; and, urged by the paſſions of emulation, of fear and jealouſy, of envy and malice, he follows the maxims of an animal deſtined to preſerve his ſeparate exiſtence, and to indulge his caprice or his appetite, at the expence of his ſpecies.

On this corrupt foundation, men become either rapacious, deceitful, and violent, ready to treſpaſs on the rights of others; or ſervile, mercenary, and baſe, prepared to relinquiſh their own. Talents, capacity, and force of mind, poſſeſſed by a perſon of the firſt deſcription, ſerve to plunge him the deeper in miſery, and to ſharpen the agony of cruel paſſions; which lead him to wreak

wreak on his fellow-creatures the torments that prey on himſelf. To a perſon of the ſecond, imagination, and reaſon itſelf, only ſerve to point out falſe objects of fear, or deſire, and to multiply the ſubjects of diſappointment, and of momentary joy. In either caſe, and whether we ſuppoſe that corrupt men are urged by covetouſneſs, or betrayed by fear, and without ſpecifying the crimes which from either diſpoſition they are prepared to commit, we may ſafely affirm, with Socrates, "That every maſter ſhould pray he may not meet with "ſuch a ſlave; and every ſuch perſon, being unfit for "liberty, ſhould implore that he may meet with a mer-"ciful maſter."

MAN, under this meaſure of corruption, although he may be bought for a ſlave by thoſe who know how to turn his faculties and his labour to profit; and although, when kept under proper reſtraints, his neighbourhood may be convenient or uſeful; yet is certainly unfit to act on the footing of a liberal combination or concert with his fellow-creatures: his mind is not addicted to friendſhip or confidence; he is not willing to act for the preſervation of others, nor deſerves that any other ſhould hazard his own ſafety for his.

THE actual character of mankind, mean-time, in the worſt, as well as the beſt condition, is undoubtedly mixed: and nations of the beſt deſcription are greatly obliged for their preſervation, not only to the good diſpoſition of their members, but likewiſe to thoſe political inſtitutions, by which the violent are reſtrained from the commiſſion of crimes, and the cowardly, or the ſelfiſh, are made to contribute their part to the public defence or proſperity. By means of ſuch inſtitutions, and the wiſe precautions of government, nations are enabled to ſubſiſt, and even to proſper, under very different degrees of corruption, or of public integrity.

So long as the majority of a people is ſuppoſed to act on maxims of probity, the example of the good, and even the caution of the bad, give a general appearance of integrity, and of innocence. Where men are to one another objects of affection and of confidence, where they are generally diſpoſed not to offend, government may be remiſs; and every perſon may be treated as innocent, till he is found to be guilty. As the ſubject in this caſe does not hear of the crimes, ſo he need not be told of the puniſhments inflicted on perſons of a different character. But where the manners of a people are conſiderably changed for the worſe, every ſubject muſt ſtand on his guard, and government itſelf muſt act on ſuitable maxims of fear and diſtruſt. The individual, no longer fit to be indulged in his pretenſions to perſonal conſideration, independence, or freedom, each of which he would turn to abuſe, muſt be taught, by external force, and from motives of fear, to counterfeit thoſe effects of innocence, and of duty, to which he is not diſpoſed: he muſt be referred to the whip, or the gibbet, for arguments in ſupport of a caution, which the ſtate now requires him to aſſume, on a ſuppoſition that he is inſen-

ſible

ſible to the motives which recommend the practice of virtue.

THE rules of deſpotiſm are made for the government of corrupted men. They were indeed followed on ſome remarkable occaſions, even under the Roman commonwealth; and the bloody axe, to terrify the citizen from his crimes, and to repel the caſual and temporary irruptions of vice, was repeatedly committed to the arbitrary will of the dictator. They were finally eſtabliſhed on the ruins of the republic itſelf, when either the people became too corrupted for freedom, or when the magiſtrate became too corrupted to reſign his dictatorial power. This ſpecies of government comes naturally in the termination of a continued and growing corruption; but has no doubt, in ſome inſtances, come too ſoon, and has ſacrificed remains of virtue, that deſerved a better fate, to the jealouſy of tyrants, who were in haſte to augment their power. This method of government cannot, in ſuch caſes, fail to introduce that meaſure of corruption, againſt whoſe external effects it is deſired as a remedy. When fear is ſuggeſted as the only motive to duty, every heart becomes rapacious or baſe. And this medicine, if applied to a healthy body, is ſure to create the diſtemper it is deſtined to cure.

THIS is the manner of government into which the covetous, and the arrogant, to ſatiate their unhappy deſires, would hurry their fellow-creatures: it is a manner of government to which the timorous and the ſervile submit at discretion; and when these characters of the rapacious and the timid divide mankind, even the virtues of Antoninus or Trajan, can do no more than apply, with candour and with vigour, the whip and the sword; and endeavour, by the hopes of reward, or the fear of punishment, to find a speedy and a temporary cure for the crimes, or the imbecilities of men.

OTHER states may be more or less corrupted: this has corruption for its basis. Here justice may sometimes direct the arm of the despotical sovereign; but the name of justice is most commonly employed to signify the interest, or the caprice, of a reigning power. Human society, susceptible of such a variety of forms, here finds the simplest of all. The toils and possessions of many are destined to asswage the passions of one or a few; and the only parties that remain among mankind, are the oppressor who demands, and the oppressed who dare not refuse.

NATIONS, while they were intitled to a milder fate, as in the case of the Greeks, repeatedly conquered, have been reduced to this condition by military force. They have reached it too in the maturity of their own depravations; when, like the Romans, returned from the conquest, and loaded with the spoils, of the world, they gave loose to faction, and to crimes too bold and too frequent for the correction of ordinary government; and when the sword of justice, dropping with blood, and perpetually required to suppress accumulating disorders

orders on every ſide, could no longer await the delays and precautions of an adminiſtration fettered by laws.

It is, however, well known from the hiſtory of mankind, that corruption of this, or of any other degree, is not peculiar to nations in their decline, or in the reſult of ſignal proſperity, and great advances in the arts of commerce. The bands of ſociety, indeed, in ſmall and infant eſtabliſhments, are generally ſtrong; and their ſubjects, either by an ardent devotion to their own tribe, or a vehement animoſity againſt enemies, and by a vigorous courage founded on both, are well qualified to urge, or to ſuſtain, the fortune of a growing community. But the ſavage, and the barbarian, have given, notwithſtanding, in the caſe of entire nations, ſome examples of a weak and timorous character *. They have, in more inſtances, fallen into that ſpecies of corruption which we have already deſcribed in treating of barbarous nations; they have made rapine their trade, not merely as a ſpecies of warfare, or with a view to enrich their community, but to poſſeſs, in property, what they learned to prefer even to the ties of affection or of blood.

In the loweſt ſtate of commercial arts, the paſſions for wealth, and for dominion, have exhibited ſcenes of oppreſſion, or ſervility, which the moſt finiſhed corrup-

* The barbarous nations of Siberia, in general, are ſervile and timid.

tion of the arrogant, the cowardly, and the mercenary, founded on the desire of procuring, or the fear of losing, a fortune, could not exceed. In such cases, the vices of men, unrestrained by forms, and unawed by police, are suffered to riot at large, and to produce their entire effects. Parties accordingly unite, or separate, on the maxims of a gang of robbers; they sacrifice to interest the tenderest affections of human nature. The parent supplies the market for slaves, even by the sale of his own children; the cottage ceases to be a sanctuary for the weak and the defenceless stranger; and rites of hospitality, often so sacred among nations in their primitive state, come to be violated, like every other tie of humanity, without fear or remorse *.

Nations, which in later periods of their history became eminent for civil wisdom and justice, had, perhaps, in a former age, paroxysms of lawless disorder, to which this description might in part be applied. The very policy by which they arrived at their degree of national felicity, was devised as a remedy for outrageous abuse. The establishment of order was dated from the commission of rapes and murders; indignation, and private revenge, were the principles on which nations proceeded to the expulsion of tyrants, to the emancipation of mankind, and the full explanation of their political rights.

* Chardin's travels through Mingrelia into Persia.

Defects of government, and of law, may be in ſome caſes conſidered as a ſymptom of innocence and of virtue. But where power is already eſtabliſhed, where the ſtrong are unwilling to ſuffer reſtraint, or the weak unable to find a protection, the defects of law are marks of the moſt perfect corruption.

Among rude nations, government is often defective; both becauſe men are not yet acquainted with all the evils for which poliſhed nations have endeavoured to find a redreſs; and becauſe, even where evils of the moſt flagrant nature have long afflicted the peace of ſociety, they have not yet been able to apply the cure. In the progreſs of civilization, new diſtempers break forth, and new remedies are applied: but the remedy is not always applied the moment the diſtemper appears; and laws, though ſuggeſted by the commiſſion of crimes, are not the ſymptom of a recent corruption, but of a deſire to find a remedy that may cure, perhaps, ſome inveterate evil which has long afflicted the ſtate.

There are corruptions, however, under which men ſtill poſſeſs the vigour and the reſolution to correct themſelves. Such are the violence and the outrage which accompany the colliſion of fierce and daring ſpirits, occupied in the ſtruggles which ſometimes precede the dawn of civil and commercial improvements. In ſuch caſes, men have frequently diſcovered a remedy for evils, of which their own miſguided impetuoſity, and ſuperior

ſuperior force of mind, were the principal cauſes. But if to a depraved diſpoſition, we ſuppoſe to be joined a weakneſs of ſpirit; if to an admiration, and deſire of riches, be joined an averſion to danger or buſineſs; if thoſe orders of men whoſe valour is required by the public, ceaſe to be brave; if the members of ſociety, in general, have not thoſe perſonal qualities which are required to fill the ſtations of equality, or of honour, to which they are invited by the forms of the ſtate; they muſt ſink to a depth from which their imbecility, even more than their depraved inclinations, may prevent their riſe.

SECT. II.

Of Luxury.

WE are far from being agreed on the application of the term *luxury*, or on that degree of its meaning which is consistent with national prosperity, or with the moral rectitude of our nature. It is sometimes employed to signify a manner of life which we think necessary to civilization, and even to happiness. It is, in our panegyric of polished ages, the parent of arts, the support of commerce, and the minister of national greatness, and of opulence. It is, in our censure of degenerate manners, the source of corruption, and the presage of national declension and ruin. It is admired, and it is blamed; it is treated as ornamental and useful; and it is proscribed as a vice.

WITH all this diversity in our judgements, we are generally uniform in employing the term to signify that complicated apparatus which mankind devise for the ease and convenience of life. Their buildings, furniture, equipage, cloathing, train of domestics, refinement of the table, and, in general, all that assemblage which is rather intended to please the fancy, than to obviate real wants, and which is rather ornamental than useful.

WHEN

WHEN we are diſpoſed, therefore, under the appellation of *luxury*, to rank the enjoyment of theſe things among the vices, we either tacitly refer to the habits of ſenſuality, debauchery, prodigality, vanity, and arrogance, with which the poſſeſſion of high fortune is ſometimes attended; or we apprehend a certain meaſure of what is neceſſary to human life, beyond which all enjoyments are ſuppoſed to be exceſſive and vicious. When, on the contrary, luxury is made an article of national luſtre and felicity, we only think of it as an innocent conſequence of the unequal diſtribution of wealth, and as a method by which different ranks are rendered mutually dependent, and mutually uſeful. The poor are made to practiſe arts, and the rich to reward them. The public itſelf is made a gainer by what ſeems to waſte its ſtock, and it receives a perpetual increaſe of wealth, from the influence of thoſe growing appetites, and delicate taſtes, which ſeem to menace conſumption and ruin.

IT is certain, that we muſt either, together with the commercial arts, ſuffer their fruits to be enjoyed, and even, in ſome meaſure, admired; or, like the Spartans, prohibit the art itſelf, while we are afraid of its conſequences, or while we think that the conveniencies it brings exceed what nature requires.

WE may propoſe to ſtop the advancement of arts at any ſtage of their progreſs, and ſtill incur the cenſure of luxury from thoſe who have not advanced ſo far. The

houſe-

houſe-builder and the carpenter at Sparta were limited to the uſe of the axe and the ſaw; but a Spartan cottage might have paſſed for a palace in Thrace: and if the diſpute were to turn on the knowledge of what is phyſically neceſſary to the preſervation of human life, as the ſtandard of what is morally lawful, the faculties of phyſic, as well as of morality, would probably divide on the ſubject, and leave every individual, as at preſent, to find ſome rule for himſelf. The caſuiſt, for the moſt part, conſiders the practice of his own age and condition, as a ſtandard for mankind. If in one age or condition, he condemn the uſe of a coach, in another he would have no leſs cenſured the wearing of ſhoes; and the very perſon who exclaims againſt the firſt, would probably not have ſpared the ſecond, if it had not been already familiar in ages before his own. A cenſor born in a cottage, and accuſtomed to ſleep upon ſtraw, does not propoſe that men ſhould return to the woods and the caves for ſhelter; he admits the reaſonableneſs and the utility of what is already familiar; and apprehends an exceſs and corruption, only in the neweſt refinement of the riſing generation.

THE clergy of Europe have preached ſucceſſively againſt every new faſhion, and every innovation in dreſs. The modes of youth are the ſubject of cenſure to the old; and modes of the laſt age, in their turn, are matter of ridicule to the flippant, and the young. Of this there is not always a better account to be given, than that the old are diſpoſed to be ſevere, and the young to be merry.

THE argument againſt many of the conveniencies of life, drawn from the mere conſideration of their not being neceſſary, was equally proper in the mouth of the ſavage, who diſſuaded from the firſt applications of induſtry, as it is in that of the moraliſt, who inſiſts on the vanity of the laſt. " Our anceſtors," he might ſay, " found their dwelling under this rock ; they gathered " their food in the foreſt ; they allayed their thirſt from " the fountain ; and they were clothed in the ſpoils of " the beaſt they had ſlain. Why ſhould we indulge a " falſe delicacy, or require from the earth fruits which ſhe " is not accuſtomed to yield ? The bow of our fathers is " already too ſtrong for our arms ; and the wild beaſt " begins to lord it in the woods."

THUS the moraliſt may have found, in the proceedings of every age, thoſe topics of blame, from which he is ſo much diſpoſed to arraign the manners of his own ; and our imbarraſſment on the ſubject, is, perhaps, but a part of that general perplexity which we undergo, in trying to define moral characters by external circumſtances, which may, or may not, be attended with faults in the mind and the heart. One man finds a vice in the wearing of linen ; another does not, unleſs the fabric be fine : and if, mean-time, it be true, that a perſon may be dreſſed in manufacture, either coarſe or fine ; that he may ſleep in the fields, or lodge in a palace ; tread upon carpet, or plant his foot on the ground ; while the mind either retains, or has loſt, its penetration, and its vigour, and the heart its affection to mankind, it is vain, under any ſuch circumſtance, to ſeek for the diſtinctions

of

of virtue and vice, or to tax the poliſhed citizen with weakneſs for any part of his equipage, or for his wearing a fur, perhaps, in which ſome ſavage was dreſſed before him. Vanity is not diſtinguiſhed by any peculiar ſpecies of dreſs. It is betrayed by the Indian in the phantaſtic aſſortments of his plumes, his ſhells, his party-coloured furs, and in the time he beſtows at the glaſs and the toilet. Its projects in the woods and in the town are the ſame: in the one, it ſeeks, with the viſage bedaubed, and with teeth artificially ſtained, for that admiration, which it courts in the other with a gilded equipage, and liveries of ſtate.

Polished nations, in their progreſs, often come to ſurpaſs the rude in moderation, and ſeverity of manners. "The Greeks," ſays Thucydides, "not long ago, like barbarians, wore golden ſpangles in the hair, and went armed in times of peace." Simplicity of dreſs in this people, became a mark of politeneſs: and the mere materials with which the body is nouriſhed or clothed, are probably of little conſequence to any people. We muſt look for the characters of men in the qualities of the mind, not in the ſpecies of their food, or in the mode of their apparel. What are now the ornaments of the grave, and ſevere; what is owned to be a real conveniency, were once the fopperies of youth, or were deviſed to pleaſe the effeminate. The new faſhion, indeed, is often the mark of the coxcomb; but we frequently change our faſhions, without increaſing the meaſures of our vanity or folly.

ARE the apprehenſions of the ſevere, therefore, in every age, equally groundleſs and unreaſonable? Are we never to dread any error in the article of a refinement beſtowed on the means of ſubſiſtence, or the conveniencies of life? The fact is, that men are perpetually expoſed to the commiſſion of error in this article, not merely where they are accuſtomed to high meaſures of accommodation, or to any particular ſpecies of food, but where-ever theſe objects, in general, may come to be preferred to friends, to a country, or to mankind; they actually commit ſuch error, where-ever they admire paultry diſtinctions or frivolous advantages; where-ever they ſhrink from ſmall inconveniencies, and are incapable of diſcharging their duty with vigour. The uſe of morality on this ſubject, is not to limit men to any particular ſpecies of lodging, diet, or cloaths; but to prevent their conſidering theſe conveniencies as the principal objects of human life. And if we are aſked, Where the purſuit of trifling accommodations ſhould ſtop, in order that a man may devote himſelf entirely to the higher engagements of life? we may anſwer, That it ſhould ſtop where it is. This was the rule followed at Sparta: The object of the rule was, to preſerve the heart entire for the public, and to occupy men in cultivating their own nature, not in accumulating wealth, and external conveniencies. It was not expected otherwiſe, that the axe or the ſaw ſhould be attended with greater political advantage, than the plane and the chiſel. When Cato walked the ſtreets of Rome without his robe, and without ſhoes, he did ſo, moſt probably, in contempt of what his countrymen were ſo prone to admire; not in hopes of finding a virtue in one ſpecies of dreſs, or a vice in another.

Luxury, therefore, conſidered as a predilection in favour of the objects of vanity, and the coſtly materials of pleaſure, is ruinous to the human character; conſidered as the mere uſe of accommodations and conveniencies which the age has procured, rather depends on the progreſs which the mechanical arts have made, and on the degree in which the fortunes of men are unequally parcelled, than on the diſpoſitions of particular men either to vice or to virtue.

Different meaſures of luxury are, however, variouſly ſuited to different conſtitutions of government. The advancement of arts ſuppoſes an unequal diſtribution of fortune; and the means of diſtinction they bring, ſerve to render the ſeparation of ranks more ſenſible. Luxury is, upon this account, apart from all its moral effects, adverſe to the form of democratical government; and in any ſtate of ſociety, can be ſafely admitted in that degree only in which the members of the community are ſuppoſed of unequal rank, and conſtitute public order by means of a regular ſubordination. High degrees of it appear ſalutary, and even neceſſary, in monarchical and mixed governments; where, beſides the encouragement to arts and commerce, it ſerves to give luſtre to thoſe hereditary or conſtitutional dignities which have a place of importance in the political ſyſtem. Whether even here luxury leads to abuſe peculiar to ages of high refinement

refinement and opulence, we ſhall proceed to conſider in the following ſections.

SECT. III.

Of the Corruption incident to Poliſhed Nations.

LUXURY and corruption are frequently coupled together, and even paſs for ſynonymous terms. But in order to avoid any diſpute about words, by the firſt we may underſtand that accumulation of wealth, and that refinement on the ways of enjoying it, which are the objects of induſtry, or the fruits of mechanic and commercial arts: And by the ſecond a real weakneſs, or depravity of the human character, which may accompany any ſtate of thoſe arts, and be found under any external circumſtances or condition whatſoever. It remains to inquire, What are the corruptions incident to poliſhed nations, arrived at certain meaſures of luxury, and poſſeſſed of certain advantages, in which they are generally ſuppoſed to excel?

WE need not have recourſe to a parallel between the manners of entire nations, in the extremes of civilization and rudeneſs, in order to be ſatisfied, that the vices of men are not proportioned to their fortunes; or that the habits of avarice, or of ſenſuality, are not founded on any certain

certain measures of wealth, or determinate kind of enjoyment. Where the situations of particular men are varied as much by their personal stations, as they can be by the state of national refinements, the same passions for interest, or pleasure, prevail in every condition. They arise from temperament, or an acquired admiration of property; not from any particular manner of life in which the parties are engaged, nor from any particular species of property, which may have occupied their cares and their wishes.

TEMPERANCE and moderation are, at least, as frequent among those whom we call the superior, as they are among the lower classes of men; and however we may affix the character of sobriety to mere cheapness of diet, and other accommodations with which any particular age, or rank of men, appear to be contented, it is well known, that costly materials are not necessary to constitute a debauch, nor profligacy less frequent under the thatched roof, than under the lofty ceiling. Men grow equally familiar with different conditions, receive equal pleasure, and are equally allured to sensuality, in the palace, and in the cave. Their acquiring in either habits of intemperance or sloth, depends on the remission of other pursuits, and on the distaste of the mind to other engagements. If the affections of the heart be awake, and the passions of love, admiration, or anger, be kindled, the costly furniture of the palace, as well as the homely accommodations of the cottage, are neglected: and men, when roused, reject their repose; or, when

wearied,

wearied, embrace it alike on the ſilken bed, or on the couch of ſtraw.

We are not, however, from hence to conclude, that luxury, with all its concomitant circumſtances, which either ſerve to favour its increaſe, or which, in the arrangements of civil ſociety, follow it as conſequences, can have no effect to the diſadvantage of national manners. If that reſpite from public dangers and troubles which gives a leiſure for the practice of commercial arts, be continued, or increaſed, into a diſuſe of national efforts; if the individual, not called to unite with his country, be left to purſue his private advantage; we may find him become effeminate, mercenary, and ſenſual; not becauſe pleaſures and profits are become more alluring, but becauſe he has fewer calls to attend to other objects; and becauſe he has more encouragement to ſtudy his perſonal advantages, and purſue his ſeparate intereſts.

If the diſparities of rank and fortune which are neceſſary to the purſuit or enjoyment of luxury, introduce falſe grounds of precedency and eſtimation; if, on the mere conſiderations of being rich or poor, one order of men are, in their own apprehenſion, elevated, another debaſed; if one be criminally proud, another meanly dejected; and every rank in its place, like the tyrant, who thinks that nations are made for himſelf, be diſpoſed to aſſume on the rights of mankind: although, upon the compariſon, the higher order may be leaſt corrupted; or from education, and a ſenſe of perſonal dignity, have moſt good qualities remaining; yet the one becoming mercenary and ſervile; the other imperious and arrogant; both regardleſs of juſtice, and of merit; the whole maſs is corrupted, and the manners of a ſociety changed for the worſe, in proportion as its members ceaſe to act on principles of equality, independence, or freedom.

UPON this view, and conſidering the merits of men in the abſtract, a mere change from the habits of a republic to thoſe of a monarchy; from the love of equality, to the ſenſe of a ſubordination founded on birth, titles, and fortune, is a ſpecies of corruption to mankind. But this degree of corruption is ſtill conſiſtent with the ſafety and proſperity of ſome nations; it admits of a vigorous courage, by which the rights of individuals, and of kingdoms, may be long preſerved.

UNDER the form of monarchy, while yet in its vigour, ſuperior fortune is, indeed, one mark by which the different orders of men are diſtinguiſhed; but there are ſome other ingredients, without which wealth is not admitted as a foundation of precedency, and in favour of which it is often deſpiſed, and laviſhed away. Such are birth and titles, the reputation of courage, courtly manners, and a certain elevation of mind. If we ſuppoſe, that theſe diſtinctions are forgotten, and nobility itſelf only to be known by the ſumptuous retinue which money alone may procure; and by a laviſh expence, which the more recent fortunes can generally beſt ſuſtain; luxury muſt then be allowed to corrupt the monarchical as much as the republican ſtate, and to introduce a fatal diſſolution of manners, under which men of every condition, although they are eager to acquire, or to diſplay their wealth, have no remains of real ambition. They have neither the elevation of nobles, nor the fidelity of ſubjects; they have changed into effeminate vanity, that ſenſe of honour which gave rules to the perſonal courage; and into a ſervile baſeneſs, that loyalty, which bound each in his place, to his immediate ſuperior, and the whole to the throne.

NATIONS are moſt expoſed to corruption from this quarter, when the mechanical arts, being greatly advanced, furniſh numberleſs articles, to be applied in ornament to the perſon, in furniture, entertainment, or equipage; when ſuch articles as the rich alone can procure are admired; and when conſideration, precedence, and rank, are accordingly made to depend on fortune.

IN a more rude ſtate of the arts, although wealth be unequally divided, the opulent can amaſs only the ſimple means of ſubſiſtence: They can only fill the granary, and furniſh the ſtall; reap from more extended fields, and drive their herds over a larger paſture. To enjoy their magnificence, they muſt live in a croud; and to ſecure their poſſeſſions, they muſt be ſurrounded with friends that eſpouſe their quarrels. Their honours, as well as their ſafety, conſiſt in the numbers who attend them;

and

and their personal distinctions are taken from their liberality, and supposed elevation of mind. In this manner, the possession of riches serves only to make the owner assume a character of magnanimity, to become the guardian of numbers, or the public object of respect and affection. But when the bulky constituents of wealth, and of rustic magnificence, can be exchanged for refinements; and when the produce of the soil may be turned into equipage, and mere decoration; when the combination of many is no longer required for personal safety; the master may become the sole consumer of his own estate: he may refer the use of every subject to himself; he may employ the materials of generosity to feed a personal vanity, or to indulge a sickly and effeminate fancy, which has learned to enumerate the trappings of weakness or folly among the necessaries of life.

The Persian satrape, we are told, when he saw the King of Sparta at the place of their conference, stretched on the grass with his soldiers, blushed at the provision he had made for the accommodation of his own person: he ordered the furs and the carpets to be withdrawn; he felt his own inferiority; and recollected, that he was to treat with a man, not to vie with a pageant in costly attire and magnificence.

When, amidst circumstancs that make no trial of the virtues or talents of men, we have been accustomed to the air of superiority, which people of fortune derive from their retinue, we are apt to lose every sense of distinction arising from merit, or even from abilities. We rate our fellow-citizens by the *figure* they are able to make; by their buildings, their dreſs, their equipage, and the train of their followers. All theſe circumſtances make a part in our eſtimate of what is excellent; and if the maſter himſelf is known to be a pageant in the midſt of his fortune, we nevertheleſs pay our court to his ſtation, and look up with an envious, ſervile, or dejected mind, to what is, in itſelf, ſcarcely fit to amuſe children; though, when it is worn as a badge of diſtinction, it inflames the ambition of thoſe we call the great, and ſtrikes the multitude with awe and reſpect.

WE judge of entire nations by the productions of a few mechanical arts, and think we are talking of men, while we are boaſting of their eſtates, their dreſs, and their palaces. The ſenſe in which we apply the terms, *great*, and *noble*, *high rank*, and *high life*, ſhew, that we have, on ſuch occaſions, transferred the idea of perfection from the character to the equipage; and that excellence itſelf is, in our eſteem, a mere pageant, adorned at a great expence, by the labours of many workmen.

To thoſe who overlook the ſubtile tranſitions of the imagination, it might appear, ſince wealth can do no more than furniſh the means of ſubſiſtence, and purchaſe animal pleaſures, that covetouſneſs, and venality itſelf, ſhould keep pace with our fears of want, or with our appetite for ſenſual enjoyments; and that where the appetite is ſatiated, and the fear of want is removed, the mind

mind should be at ease on the subject of fortune. But they are not the mere pleasures that riches procure, nor the choice of viands which cover the board of the wealthy, that inflame the passions of the covetous and the mercenary. Nature is easily satisfied in all her enjoyments. It is an opinion of eminence, connected with fortune; it is a sense of debasement attending on poverty, which renders us blind to every advantage, but that of the rich; and insensible to every disgrace, but that of the poor. It is this unhappy apprehension, that occasionally prepares us for the desertion of every duty, for a submission to every indignity, and for the commission of every crime that can be accomplished in safety.

AURENGZEBE was not more renowned for sobriety in his private station, and in the conduct of a supposed dissimulation, by which he aspired to sovereign power, than he continued to be, even on the throne of Indostan. Simple, abstinent, and severe in his diet, and other pleasures, he still led the life of a hermit, and occupied his time with a seemingly painful application to the affairs of a great empire *. He quitted a station in which, if pleasure had been his object, he might have indulged his sensuality without reserve; he made his way to a scene of disquietude and care; he aimed at the summit of human greatness, in the possession of imperial fortune, not at the gratifications of animal appetite, or the enjoyment

* Gemelli Carceri.

of eaſe. Superior to ſenſual pleaſure, as well as to the feelings of nature, he dethroned his father, and he murdered his brothers, that he might roll on a carriage incruſted with diamond and pearl; that his elephants, his camels, and his horſes, on the march, might form a line extending many leagues; might preſent a glittering harneſs to the ſun; and loaded with treaſure, uſher to the view of an abject and admiring croud, that awful majeſty, in whoſe preſence they were to ſtrike the forehead on the ground, and be overwhelmed with the ſenſe of his greatneſs, and with that of their own debaſement.

As theſe are the objects which prompt the deſire of dominion, and excite the ambitious to aim at the maſtery of their fellow-creatures; ſo they inſpire the ordinary race of men with a ſenſe of infirmity and meanneſs, that prepares them to ſuffer indignities, and to become the property of perſons, whom they conſider as of a rank and a nature ſo much ſuperior to their own.

THE chains of perpetual ſlavery, accordingly, appear to be rivetted in the Eaſt, no leſs by the pageantry which is made to accompany the poſſeſſion of power, than they are by the fears of the ſword, and the terrors of a military execution. In the Weſt, as well as the Eaſt, we are willing to bow to the ſplendid equipage, and ſtand at an awful diſtance from the pomp of a princely eſtate. We too, may be terrified by the frowns, or won by the ſmiles, of thoſe whoſe favour is riches and honour,

and

and whose displeasure is poverty and neglect. We too may overlook the honours of the human soul, from an admiration of the pageantries that accompany fortune. The procession of elephants harnessed with gold might dazzle into slaves, the people who derive corruption and weakness from the effect of their own arts and contrivances, as well as those who inherit servility from their ancestors, and are enfeebled by their natural temperament, and the enervating charms of their soil, and their climate.

It appears, therefore, that although the mere use of materials which constitute luxury, may be distinguished from actual vice; yet nations under a high state of the commercial arts, are exposed to corruption, by their admitting wealth, unsupported by personal elevation and virtue, as the great foundation of distinction, and by having their attention turned on the side of interest, as the road to consideration and honour.

With this effect, luxury may serve to corrupt democratical states, by introducing a species of monarchical subordination, without that sense of high birth and hereditary honours which render the boundaries of rank fixed and determinate, and which teach men to act in their stations with force and propriety. It may prove the occasion of political corruption, even in monarchical governments, by drawing respect towards mere wealth; by casting a shade on the lustre of personal qualities, or family-

family-diſtinctions; and by infecting all orders of men, with equal venality, ſervility, and cowardice.

SECT. IV.

The ſame ſubject continued.

THE increaſing regard with which men appear, in the progreſs of commercial arts, to ſtudy their profit, or the delicacy with which they refine on their pleaſures; even induſtry itſelf, or the habit of application to a tedious employment, in which no honours are won, may, perhaps, be conſidered as indications of a growing attention to intereſt, or of effeminacy, contracted in the enjoyment of eaſe and conveniency. Every ſucceſſive art, by which the individual is taught to improve on his fortune, is, in reality, an addition to his private engagements, and a new avocation of his mind from the public.

CORRUPTION, however, does not ariſe from the abuſe of commercial arts alone; it requires the aid of political ſituation; and is not produced by the objects that occupy a ſordid and a mercenary ſpirit, without the aid of circumſtances that enable men to indulge in ſafety any mean diſpoſition they have acquired.

PROVIDENCE

PROVIDENCE has fitted mankind for the higher engagements which they are sometimes obliged to fulfil; and it is in the midst of such engagements that they are most likely to acquire or to preserve their virtues. The habits of a vigorous mind are formed in contending with difficulties, not in enjoying the repose of a pacific station; penetration and wisdom are the fruits of experience, not the lessons of retirement and leisure; ardour and generosity are the qualities of a mind roused and animated in the conduct of scenes that engage the heart, not the gifts of reflection or knowledge. The mere intermission of national and political efforts is, notwithstanding, sometimes mistaken for public good; and there is no mistake more likely to foster the vices, or to flatter the weakness, of feeble and interested men.

IF the ordinary arts of policy, or rather, if a growing indifference to objects of a public nature, should prevail, and, under any free constitution, put an end to those disputes of party, and silence that noise of dissension, which generally accompany the exercise of freedom, we may venture to prognosticate corruption to the national manners, as well as remissness to the national spirit. The period is come, when, no engagement remaining on the part of the public, private interest, and animal pleasure, become the sovereign objects of care. When men, being relieved from the pressure of great occasions, bestow their attention on trifles; and having carried what they are pleased to call *sensibility* and *delicacy*, on the subject of ease or molestation, as far as real weakneſs or folly can go, have recourſe to affectation, in order to enhance the pretended demands, and accumulate the anxieties, of a ſickly fancy, and enfeebled mind.

In this condition, mankind generally flatter their own imbecility under the name of *politeneſs*. They are perſuaded, that the celebrated ardour, generoſity, and fortitude, of former ages, bordered on frenzy, or were the mere effects of neceſſity, on men who had not the means of enjoying their eaſe, or their pleaſure. They congratulate themſelves on having eſcaped the ſtorm which required the exerciſe of ſuch arduous virtues; and with that vanity which accompanies the human race in their meaneſt condition, they boaſt of a ſcene of affectation, of languor, or of folly, as the ſtandard of human felicity, and as furniſhing the propereſt exerciſe of a rational nature.

It is none of the leaſt menacing ſymptoms of an age prone to degeneracy, that the minds of men become perplexed in the diſcernment of merit, as much as the ſpirit becomes enfeebled in conduct, and the heart miſled in the choice of its objects. The care of mere fortune is ſuppoſed to conſtitute wiſdom; retirement from public affairs, and real indifference to mankind, receive the applauſes of moderation and virtue.

Great fortitude, and elevation of mind, have not always, indeed, been employed in the attainment of valuable

valuable ends; but they are always respectable, and they are always necessary when we would act for the good of mankind, in any of the more arduous stations of life. While, therefore, we blame their misapplication, we should beware of depreciating their value. Men of a severe and sententious morality have not always sufficiently observed this caution; nor have they been duly aware of the corruptions they flattered, by the satire they employed against what is aspiring and prominent in the character of the human soul.

It might have been expected, that in an age of hopeless debasement *, the talents of Demosthenes and Tully, even the ill-governed magnanimity of a Macedonian, or the daring enterprise of a Carthaginian leader, might have escaped the acrimony of a satirist, who had so many objects of correction in his view, and who possessed the arts of declamation in so high a degree:

I, demens, et sævos curre per Alpes,
Ut pueris placeas, et declamatio fias,

is part of the illiberal censure which is thrown by this poet on the person and action of a leader, who, by his courage and conduct, in the very service to which the satire referred, had well nigh saved his country from the ruin with which it was at last overwhelmed.

* Juvenal's 10th satire.

Heroes are much the ſame, the point's agreed,
From Macedonia's madman to the Swede,

is a diſtich, in which another poet of beautiful talents, has attempted to depreciate a name, to which, probably, few of his readers are found to aſpire.

If men muſt go wrong, there is a choice of their very errors, as well as of their virtues. Ambition, the love of perſonal eminence, and the deſire of fame, although they ſometimes lead to the commiſſion of crimes, yet always engage men in purſuits that require to be ſupported by ſome of the greateſt qualities of the human ſoul; and if eminence is the principal object of purſuit, there is, at leaſt, a probability, that thoſe qualities may be ſtudied on which a real elevation of mind is raiſed. But when public alarms have ceaſed, and contempt of glory is recommended as an article of wiſdom, the ſordid habits, and mercenary diſpoſitions, to which, under a general indifference to national objects, the members of a poliſhed or commercial ſtate are expoſed, muſt prove at once the moſt effectual ſuppreſſion of every liberal ſentiment, and the moſt fatal reverſe of all thoſe principles from which communities derive their hopes of preſervation, and their ſtrength.

It is noble to poſſeſs happineſs and independence, either in retirement, or in public life. The characteriſtic of the happy, is to acquit themſelves well in every condition; in the court, or in the village; in the ſenate, or in the private retreat. But if they affect any particular ſta-

tion,

tion, it is surely that in which their actions may be rendered most extensively useful. Our considering mere retirement, therefore, as a symptom of moderation, and of virtue, is either a remnant of that system, under which monks and anchorets, in former ages, have been canonized; or proceeds from a habit of thinking, which appears equally fraught with moral corruption, from our considering public life as a scene for the gratification of mere vanity, avarice, and ambition; never as furnishing the best opportunity for a just and a happy engagement of the mind and the heart.

EMULATION, and the desire of power, are but sorry motives to public conduct; but if they have been, in any case, the principal inducements from which men have taken part in the service of their country, any diminution of their prevalence or force is a real corruption of national manners; and the pretended moderation assumed by the higher orders of men, has a fatal effect in the state. The disinterested love of the public, is a principle without which some constitutions of government cannot subsist: but when we consider how seldom this has appeared a reigning passion, we have little reason to impute the prosperity or preservation of nations, in every case, to its influence.

IT is sufficient, perhaps, under one form of government, that men should be fond of their independence; that they should be ready to oppose usurpation, and to repel personal indignities: under another, it is sufficient, that they

they ſhould be tenacious of their rank, and of their honours; and inſtead of a zeal for the public, entertain a vigilant jealouſy of the rights which pertain to themſelves. When numbers of men retain a certain degree of elevation and fortitude, they are qualified to give a mutual check to their ſeveral errors, and are able to act in that variety of ſituations which the different conſtitutions of government have prepared for their members: but, under the diſadvantages of a feeble ſpirit, however directed, and however informed, no national conſtitution is ſafe; nor can any degree of enlargement to which a ſtate has arrived, ſecure its political welfare.

In ſtates where property, diſtinction, and pleaſure, are thrown out as baits to the imagination, and incentives to paſſion, the public ſeems to rely for the preſervation of its political life, on the degree of emulation and jealouſy with which parties mutually oppoſe and reſtrain each other. The deſires of preferment and profit in the breaſt of the citizen, are the motives from which he is excited to enter on public affairs, and are the conſiderations which direct his political conduct. The ſuppreſſion, therefore, of ambition, of party-animoſity, and of public envy, is probably, in every ſuch caſe, not a reformation, but a ſymptom of weakneſs, and a prelude to more ſordid purſuits, and ruinous amuſements.

On the eve of ſuch a revolution in manners, the higher ranks, in every mixed or monarchical government, have

have need to take care of themſelves. Men of buſineſs, and of induſtry, in the inferior ſtations of life, retain their occupations, and are ſecured, by a kind of neceſſity, in the poſſeſſion of thoſe habits on which they rely for their quiet, and for the moderate enjoyments of life. But the higher orders of men, if they relinquiſh the ſtate, if they ceaſe to poſſeſs that courage and elevation of mind, and to exerciſe thoſe talents which are employed in its defence, and its government, are, in reality, by the ſeeming advantages of their ſtation, become the refuſe of that ſociety of which they once were the ornament; and from being the moſt reſpectable, and the moſt happy, of its members, are become the moſt wretched and corrupt. In their approach to this condition, and in the abſence of every manly occupation, they feel a diſſatisfaction and languor which they cannot explain: They pine in the midſt of apparent enjoyments; or, by the variety and caprice of their different purſuits and amuſements, exhibit a ſtate of agitation, which, like the diſquiet of ſickneſs, is not a proof of enjoyment or pleaſure, but of ſuffering and pain. The care of his buildings, his equipage, or his table, is choſen by one; literary amuſement, or ſome frivolous ſtudy, by another. The ſports of the country, and the diverſions of the town; the gaming-table *, dogs, horſes, and wine,

* Theſe different occupations differ from each other, in reſpect to their dignity, and their innocence; but none of them are the ſchools from which men are brought to ſuſtain the tottering fortune of nations; they are equally avocations from what ought to be the principal purſuit of man, the good of mankind.

are employed to fill up the blank of a liſtleſs and unprofitable life. They ſpeak of human purſuits, as if the whole difficulty were to find ſomething to do: They fix on ſome frivolous occupation, as if there was nothing that deſerved to be done: They conſider what tends to the good of their fellow-creatures, as a diſadvantage to themſelves: They fly from every ſcene, in which any efforts of vigour are required, or in which they might be allured to perform any ſervice to their country. We miſapply our compaſſion in pitying the poor; it were much more juſtly applied to the rich, who become the firſt victims of that wretched inſignificance, into which the members of every corrupted ſtate, by the tendency of their weakneſſes, and their vices, are in haſte to plunge themſelves.

It is in this condition, that the ſenſual invent all thoſe refinements on pleaſure, and deviſe thoſe incentives to a ſatiated appetite, which tend to foſter the corruptions of a diſſolute age. The effects of brutal appetite, and the mere debauch, are more flagrant, and more violent, perhaps, in rude ages, than they are in the later periods of commerce and luxury: but that perpetual habit of ſearching for animal pleaſure where it is not to be found, in the gratifications of an appetite that is cloyed, and among the ruins of an animal conſtitution, is not more fatal to the virtues of the ſoul, than it is even to the enjoyment of ſloth, or of pleaſure; it is not a more certain avocation from public affairs, or a ſurer prelude to national decay, than it is a diſappointment to our hopes of private felicity.

In these reflections, it has been the object, not to ascertain a precise measure to which corruption has risen in any of the nations that have attained to eminence, or that have gone to decay; but to describe that remissness of spirit, that weakness of soul, that state of national debility, which is likely to end in political slavery; an evil which remains to be considered as the last object of caution, and beyond which there is no subject of disquisition in the perishing fortunes of nations.

SECT. V.

Of Corruption, as it tends to Political Slavery.

Liberty, in one sense, appears to be the portion of polished nations alone. The savage is personally free, because he lives unrestrained, and acts with the members of his tribe on terms of equality. The barbarian is frequently independent from a continuance of the same circumstances, or because he has courage and a sword. But good policy alone can provide for the regular administration of justice, or constitute a force in the state, which is ready on every occasion to defend the rights of its members.

It has been found, that, except in a few singular cases, the commercial and political arts have advanced together.

gether. These arts have been in modern Europe so interwoven, that we cannot determine which were prior in the order of time, or derived most advantage from the mutual influences with which they act and re-act upon one another. It has been observed, that in some nations the spirit of commerce, intent on securing its profits, has led the way to political wisdom. A people, possessed of wealth, and become jealous of their properties, have formed the project of emancipation, and have proceeded, under favour of an importance recently gained, still farther to enlarge their pretensions, and to dispute the prerogatives which their sovereign had been in use to employ. But it is in vain that we expect in one age, from the possession of wealth, the fruit which it is said to have borne in a former. Great accessions of fortune, when recent, when accompanied with frugality, and a sense of independence, may render the owner confident in his strength, and ready to spurn at oppression. The purse which is open, not to personal expence, or to the indulgence of vanity, but to support the interests of a faction, to gratify the higher passions of party, render the wealthy citizen formidable to those who pretend to dominion; but it does not follow, that in a time of corruption, equal, or greater, measures of wealth should operate to the same effect.

On the contrary, when wealth is accumulated only in the hands of the miser, and runs to waste from those of the prodigal; when heirs of family find themselves straitened and poor, in the midst of affluence; when the cravings of luxury silence even the voice of party and faction;

faction; when the hopes of meriting the rewards of compliance, or the fear of losing what is held at discretion, keep men in a state of suspense and anxiety; when fortune, in short, instead of being considered as the instrument of a vigorous spirit, becomes the idol of a covetous or a profuse, of a rapacious or a timorous mind; the foundation on which freedom was built, may serve to support a tyranny; and what, in one age, raised the pretensions, and fostered the confidence of the subject, may, in another, incline him to servility, and furnish the price to be paid for his prostitutions. Even those, who, in a vigorous age, gave the example of wealth, in the hands of the people, becoming an occasion of freedom, may, in times of degeneracy, verify likewise the maxim of Tacitus, That the admiration of riches leads to despotical government *

MEN who have tasted of freedom, and who have felt their personal rights, are not easily taught to bear with incroachments on either, and cannot, without some preparation, come to submit to oppression. They may receive this unhappy preparation, under different forms of government, from different hands, and arrive at the same end by different ways. They follow one direction in republics, another in monarchies, and in mixed governments. But where-ever the state has, by means that do not preserve the virtue of the subject, effectually guarded his safety; remissness, and neglect of the public, are likely to follow; and polished nations of every

* Est apud illos et opibus honos; eoque unus imperitat, *&c. Tacitus de mor. Ger. c.* 44.

deſcription, appear to encounter a danger, on this quarter, proportioned to the degree in which they have, during any continuance, enjoyed the uninterrupted poſſeſſion of peace and proſperity.

LIBERTY reſults, we ſay, from the government of laws; and we are apt to conſider ſtatutes, not merely as the reſolutions and maxims of a people determined to be free, not as the writings by which their rights are kept on record; but as a power erected to guard them, and as a barrier which the caprice of man cannot tranſgreſs.

WHEN a baſha, in Aſia, pretends to decide every controverſy by the rules of natural equity, we allow that he is poſſeſſed of diſcretionary powers. When a judge in Europe is left to decide, according to his own interpretation of written laws, is he in any ſenſe more reſtrained than the former? Have the multiplied words of a ſtatute an influence over the conſcience, and the heart, more powerful than that of reaſon and nature? Does the party, in any judicial proceeding, enjoy a leſs degree of ſafety, when his rights are diſcuſſed, on the foundation of a rule that is open to the underſtandings of mankind, than when they are referred to an intricate ſyſtem, which it has become the object of a ſeparate profeſſion to ſtudy and to explain?

IF forms of proceeding, written ſtatutes, or other conſtituents of law, ceaſe to be enforced by the very ſpirit

rit from which they arofe; they ferve only to cover, not to reftrain, the iniquities of power: they are poffibly refpected even by the corrupt magiftrate, when they favour his purpofe; but they are contemned or evaded, when they ftand in his way: And the influence of laws, where they have any real effect in the prefervation of liberty, is not any magic power defcending from fhelves that are loaded with books, but is, in reality, the influence of men refolved to be free; of men, who, having adjufted in writing the terms on which they are to live with the ftate, and with their fellow-fubjects, are determined, by their vigilance and fpirit, to make thefe terms be obferved.

We are taught, under every form of government, to apprehend ufurpations, from the abufe, or from the extenfion of the executive power. In pure monarchies, this power is commonly hereditary, and made to defcend in a determinate line. In elective monarchies, it is held for life. In republics, it is exercifed during a limited time. Where men, or families, are called by election to the poffeffion of temporary dignities, it is more the object of ambition to perpetuate, than to extend their powers. In hereditary monarchies, the fovereignty is already perpetual; and the aim of every ambitious prince, is to enlarge his prerogative. Republics, and, in times of commotion, communities of every form, are expofed to hazard, not from thofe only who are formally raifed to places of truft, but from every perfon whatever,

ever, who is incited by ambition, and who is ſupported by faction.

IT is no advantage to a prince, or other magiſtrate, to enjoy more power than is conſiſtent with the good of mankind; nor is it of any benefit to a man to be unjuſt: but theſe maxims are a feeble ſecurity againſt the paſſions and follies of men. Thoſe who are intruſted with any meaſures of influence, are diſpoſed, from a mere averſion to conſtraint, to remove oppoſition. Not only the monarch who wears a hereditary crown, but the magiſtrate who holds his office for a limited time, grows fond of his dignity. The very miniſter, who depends for his place on the momentary will of his prince, and whoſe perſonal intereſts are, in every reſpect, thoſe of a ſubject, ſtill has the weakneſs to take an intereſt in the growth of prerogative, and to reckon as gain to himſelf the incroachments he has made on the rights of a people, with whom he himſelf and his family are ſoon to be numbered.

EVEN with the beſt intentions towards mankind, we are inclined to think, that their welfare depends, not on the felicity of their own inclinations, or the happy employment of their own talents, but on their ready compliance with what we have deviſed for their good. Accordingly, the greateſt virtue of which any ſovereign has hitherto ſhown an example, is not a deſire of cheriſhing in his people the ſpirit of freedom and independence; but what is in itſelf ſufficiently rare, and

highly

highly meritorious, a ſteady regard to the diſtribution of juſtice in matters of property, a diſpoſition to protect and to oblige, to redreſs the grievances, and to promote the intereſt of his ſubjects. It was from a reference to theſe objects, that Titus computed the value of his time, and judged of its application. But the ſword, which in this beneficent hand was drawn to protect the ſubject, and to procure a ſpeedy and effectual diſtribution of juſtice, was likewiſe ſufficient in the hands of a tyrant, to ſhed the blood of the innocent, and to cancel the rights of men. The temporary proceedings of humanity, though they ſuſpended the exerciſe of oppreſſion, did not break the national chains: the prince was even the better enabled to procure that ſpecies of good which he ſtudied; becauſe there was no freedom remaining, and becauſe there was no where a force to diſpute his decrees, or to interrupt their execution.

WAS it in vain, that Antoninus became acquainted with the characters of Thraſea, Helvidius, Cato, Dion, and Brutus? Was it in vain, that he learned to underſtand the form of a free community, raiſed on the baſis of equality and juſtice; or of a monarchy, under which the liberties of the ſubject were held the moſt ſacred object of adminiſtration *? Did he miſtake the means of procuring to mankind what he points out as a bleſſing? Or did the abſolute power with which he was

* M. Antoninus, lib. 1.

furniſhed,

furniſhed, in a mighty empire, only diſable him from executing what his mind had perceived as a national good? In ſuch a caſe, it were vain to flatter the monarch or his people. The firſt cannot beſtow liberty, without raiſing a ſpirit, which may, on occaſion, ſtand in oppoſition to his own deſigns; nor the latter receive this bleſſing, while they own that it is in the right of a maſter to give or to with-hold it. The claim of juſtice is firm and peremptory. We receive favours with a ſenſe of obligation and kindneſs; but we would inforce our rights, and the ſpirit of freedom in this exertion cannot take the tone of ſupplication, or of thankfulneſs, without betraying itſelf. "You have intreated Octavius," ſays Brutus to Cicero, "that he would ſpare thoſe who ſtand "foremoſt among the citizens of Rome. What if he will "not? Muſt we periſh? Yes; rather than owe our "ſafety to him."

Liberty is a right which every individual muſt be ready to vindicate for himſelf, and which he who pretends to beſtow as a favour, has by that very act in reality denied. Even political eſtabliſhments, though they appear to be independent of the will and arbitration of men, cannot be relied on for the preſervation of freedom; they may nouriſh, but ſhould not ſuperſede that firm and reſolute ſpirit, with which the liberal mind is always prepared to reſiſt indignities, and to refer its ſafety to itſelf.

Were a nation, therefore, given to be moulded by a ſovereign, as the clay is put into the hands of the potter,

ter, this project of bestowing liberty on a people who are actually servile, is, perhaps, of all others, the most difficult, and requires most to be executed in silence, and with the deepest reserve. Men are qualified to receive this blessing, only in proportion as they are made to apprehend their own rights; and are made to respect the just pretensions of mankind; in proportion as they are willing to sustain, in their own persons, the burden of government, and of national defence; and are willing to prefer the engagements of a liberal mind, to the enjoyments of sloth, or the delusive hopes of a safety purchased by submission and fear.

I speak with respect, and, if I may be allowed the expression, even with indulgence, to those who are intrusted with high prerogatives in the political system of nations. It is, indeed, seldom their fault that states are inslaved. What should be expected from them, but that being actuated by human desires, they should be averse to disappointment, or even to delay; and in the ardour with which they pursue their object, that they should break through the barriers that would stop their career? If millions recede before single men, and senates are passive, as if composed of members who had no opinion or sense of their own; on whose side have the defences of freedom given way, or to whom shall we impute their fall? to the subject, who has deserted his station; or to the sovereign, who has only remained in his own; and who, if the collateral or subordinate members of government shall ceaſe to queſtion his power, muſt continue to govern without any reſtraint?

It is well known, that conſtitutions framed for the preſervation of liberty, muſt conſiſt of many parts; and that ſenates, popular aſſemblies, courts of juſtice, magiſtrates of different orders, muſt combine to balance each other, while they exerciſe, ſuſtain, or check the executive power. If any part is ſtruck out, the fabric muſt totter, or fall; if any member is remiſs, the others muſt incroach. In aſſemblies conſtituted by men of different talents, habits, and apprehenſions, it were ſomething more than human that could make them agree in every point of importance; having different opinions and views, it were want of integrity to abſtain from diſputes: our very praiſe of unanimity, therefore, is to be conſidered as a danger to liberty. We wiſh for it, at the hazard of taking in its place, the remiſſneſs of men grown indifferent to the public; the venality of thoſe who have ſold the rights of their country; or the ſervility of others, who give implicit obedience to a leader by whom their minds are ſubdued. The love of the public, and reſpect to its laws, are the points in which mankind are bound to agree; but if, in matters of controverſy, the ſenſe of any individual or party is invariably purſued, the cauſe of freedom is already betrayed.

He whoſe office it is to govern a ſupine or an abject people, cannot, for a moment, ceaſe to extend his powers. Every execution of law, every movement of the ſtate, every civil and military operation, in which his power is exerted, muſt ſerve to confirm his authority, and preſent him to the view of the public, as the ſole object of conſideration, fear, and reſpect. Thoſe very eſtabliſhments which were deviſed, in one age, to limit, or to direct the exerciſe of an executive power, will ſerve, in another, to ſettle its foundations, and to give it ſtability; they will point out the channels in which it may run, without giving offence, or without exciting alarms, and the very councils which were inſtituted to check its incroachments, will, in a time of corruption, furniſh an aid to its uſurpations.

THE paſſion for independence, and the love of dominion, frequently ariſe from a common ſource: There is, in both, an averſion to controul; and he, who, in one ſituation, cannot bruik a ſuperior, muſt, in another, diſlike to be joined with an equal.

WHAT the prince, under a pure or limited monarchy, is, by the conſtitution of his country, the leader of a faction would willingly become in republican governments. If he attains to this envied condition, his own inclination, or the tendency of human affairs, ſeem to open before him the career of a royal ambition: but the circumſtances in which he is deſtined to act, are very different from thoſe of a king. He encounters with men who are unuſed to diſparity; he is obliged, for his own ſecurity, to hold the dagger continually unſheathed. When he hopes to be ſafe, he poſſibly means to be juſt; but is hurried, from the firſt moment of his uſurpation, into every exercise of deſpotical power. The heir of a crown has no ſuch quarrel to maintain with his ſubjects: his ſituation is flattering; and the heart muſt be uncommonly bad, that does not glow with affection to a people, who are, at once, his admirers, his ſupport, and the ornaments of his reign. In him, perhaps, there is no explicit deſign of treſpaſſing on the rights of his ſubjects; but the forms intended to preſerve their freedom, are not, on this account, always ſafe in his hands.

SLAVERY has been impoſed upon mankind in the wantonneſs of a depraved ambition, and tyrannical cruelties have been committed in the gloomy hours of jealouſy and terror: yet theſe demons are not neceſſary to the creation, or to the ſupport of an arbitrary power. Although no policy was ever more ſucceſsful than that of the Roman republic in maintaining a national fortune; yet ſubjects, as well as their princes, frequently imagine that freedom is a clog on the proceedings of government: they imagine, that deſpotical power is beſt fitted to procure diſpatch and ſecrecy in the execution of public councils; to maintain what they are pleaſed to call *political order* *, and

* Our notion of order in civil ſociety is frequently falſe: it is taken from the analogy of ſubjects inanimate and dead; we conſider commotion and action as contrary to its nature; we think it conſiſtent only with obedience, ſecrecy, and the ſilent paſſing of affairs through the hands of a few. The good order of ſtones in a wall, is their being properly fixed in the places for which they are hewn; were they to ſtir the building muſt fall: but the good order of men

and to give a ſpeedy redreſs of complaints. They even ſometimes acknowledge, that if a ſucceſſion of good princes could be found, deſpotical government is beſt calculated for the happineſs of mankind. While they reaſon thus, they cannot blame a ſovereign who, in the confidence that he is to employ his power for good purpoſes, endeavours to extend its limits; and, in his own apprehenſion, ſtrives only to ſhake off the reſtraints which ſtand in the way of reaſon, and which prevent the effect of his friendly intentions.

THUS prepared for uſurpation, let him, at the head of a free ſtate, employ the force with which he is armed, to cruſh the ſeeds of apparent diſorder in every corner of his dominions; let him effectually curb the ſpirit of diſſenſion and variance among his people; let him remove the interruptions to government, ariſing from the refractory humours and the private intereſts of his ſubjects; let him collect the force of the ſtate againſt its enemies, by availing himſelf of all it can furniſh in the way of taxation and perſonal ſervice: it is extremely probable, that, even under the direction of wiſhes for the good of mankind, he may break through every barrier of liberty, and eſtabliſh a deſpotiſm, while he flat-

men in ſociety, is their being placed where they are properly qualified to act. The firſt is a fabric made of dead and inanimate parts, the ſecond is made of living and active members. When we ſeek in ſociety for the order of mere inaction and tranquillity, we forget the nature of our ſubject, and find the order of ſlaves, not that of free men.

ters

ters himſelf, that he only follows the dictates of ſenſe and propriety.

When we ſuppoſe government to have beſtowed a degree of tranquillity which we ſometimes hope to reap from it, as the beſt of its fruits, and public affairs to proceed, in the ſeveral departments of legiſlation and execution, with the leaſt poſſible interruption to commerce and lucrative arts; ſuch a ſtate, like that of China, by throwing affairs into ſeparate offices, where conduct conſiſts in detail, and in the obſervance of forms, by ſuperſeding all the exertions of a great or a liberal mind, is more akin to deſpotiſm than we are apt to imagine.

Whether oppreſſion, injuſtice, and cruelty, are the only evils which attend on deſpotical government, may be conſidered apart. In the mean time it is ſufficient to obſerve, that liberty is never in greater danger than it is when we meaſure national felicity by the bleſſings which a prince may beſtow, or by the mere tranquillity which may attend on equitable adminiſtration. The ſovereign may dazzle with his heroic qualities; he may protect his ſubjects in the enjoyment of every animal advantage or pleaſure: but the benefits ariſing from liberty are of a different ſort; they are not the fruits of a virtue, and of a goodneſs, which operate in the breaſt of one man, but the communication of virtue itſelf to many; and ſuch a diſtribution of functions in civil ſociety, as gives to numbers the exerciſes and occupations which pertain to their nature.

The

THE best constitutions of government are attended with inconvenience; and the exercise of liberty may, on many occasions, give rise to complaints. When we are intent on reforming abuses, the abuses of freedom may lead us to incroach on the subject from which they are supposed to arise. Despotism itself has certain advantages, or at least, in times of civility and moderation, may proceed with so little offence, as to give no public alarm. These circumstances may lead mankind, in the very spirit of reformation, or by mere inattention, to apply or to admit of dangerous innovations in the state of their policy.

SLAVERY, however, is not always introduced by mere mistake; it is sometimes imposed in the spirit of violence and rapine. Princes become corrupt as well as their people; and whatever may have been the origin of despotical government, its pretensions, when fully explained, give rise to a contest between the sovereign and his subjects, which force alone can decide. These pretensions have a dangerous aspect to the person, the property, or the life of every subject; they alarm every passion in the human breast; they disturb the supine; they deprive the venal of his hire; they declare war on the corrupt as well as the virtuous; they are tamely admitted only by the coward; but even to him must be supported by a force that can work on his fears. This force the conqueror brings from abroad; and the domestic usurper endeavours to find in his faction at home.

WHEN

WHEN a people is accuſtomed to arms, it is difficult for a part to ſubdue the whole; or before the eſtabliſhment of diſciplined armies, it is difficult for any uſurper to govern the many by the help of a few. Theſe difficulties, however, the policy of civilized and commercial nations has ſometimes removed; and by forming a diſtinction between civil and military profeſſions, by committing the keeping and the enjoyment of liberty to different hands, has prepared the way for the dangerous alliance of faction with military power, in oppoſition to mere political forms, and the rights of mankind.

A people who are diſarmed in compliance with this fatal refinement, have reſted their ſafety on the pleadings of reaſon and juſtice at the tribunal of ambition and of force. In ſuch an extremity, laws are quoted, and ſenates are aſſembled, in vain. They who compoſe a legiſlature, or who occupy the civil departments of ſtate, may deliberate on the meſſages they receive from the camp or the court; but if the bearer, like the centurion who brought the petition of Octavius to the Roman ſenate, ſhew the hilt of his ſword *, they find that petitions are become commands, and that they themſelves are become the pageants, not the repoſitories of ſovereign power.

THE reflections of this ſection may be unequally ap-

* Sueton.

plied

plied to nations of unequal extent. Small communities, however corrupted, are not prepared for despotical government: their members, crouded together, and contiguous to the seats of power, never forget their relation to the public; they pry, with habits of familiarity and freedom, into the pretensions of those who would rule; and where the love of equality, and the sense of justice, have failed, they act on motives of faction, emulation, and envy. The exiled Tarquin had his adherents at Rome; but if by their means he had recovered his station, it is probable, that in the exercise of his royalty, he must have entered on a new scene of contention with the very party that restored him to power.

In proportion as territory is extended, its parts lose their relative importance to the whole. Its inhabitants cease to perceive their connection with the state, and are seldom united in the execution of any national, or even of any factious, designs. Distance from the seats of administration, and indifference to the persons who contend for preferment, teach the majority to consider themselves as the subjects of a sovereignty, not as the members of a political body. It is even remarkable, that enlargement of territory, by rendering the individual of less consequence to the public, and less able to intrude with his counsel, actually tends to reduce national affairs within a narrower compass, as well as to diminish the numbers who are consulted in legislation, or in other matters of government.

THE diſorders to which a great empire is expoſed, require ſpeedy prevention, vigilance, and quick execution. Diſtant provinces muſt be kept in ſubjection by military force; and the dictatorial powers, which, in free ſtates, are ſometimes raiſed to quell inſurrections, or to oppoſe other occaſional evils, appear, under a certain extent of dominion, at all times equally neceſſary to ſuſpend the diſſolution of a body, whoſe parts were aſſembled, and muſt be cemented, by meaſures forcible, deciſive, and ſecret. Among the circumſtances, therefore, which in the event of national proſperity, and in the reſult of commercial arts, lead to the eſtabliſhment of deſpotiſm, there is none, perhaps, that arrives at this termination, with ſo ſure an aim, as the perpetual enlargement of territory. In every ſtate, the freedom of its members depends on the balance and adjuſtment of its interior parts; and the exiſtence of any ſuch freedom among mankind, depends on the balance of nations. In the progreſs of conqueſt, thoſe who are ſubdued are ſaid to have loſt their liberties; but from the hiſtory of mankind, to conquer, or to be conquered, has appeared, in effect, the ſame.

SECT.

S E C T. VI.

Of the Progreſs and Termination of Deſpotiſm.

MANKIND, when they degenerate, and tend to their ruin, as well as when they improve, and gain real advantages, frequently proceed by ſlow, and almoſt inſenſible, ſteps. If, during ages of activity and vigour, they fill up the meaſure of national greatneſs to a height which no human wiſdom could at a diſtance foreſee; they actually incur, in ages of relaxation and weakneſs, many evils which their fears did not ſuggeſt, and which, perhaps, they had thought far removed by the tide of ſucceſs and proſperity.

WE have already obſerved, that where men are remiſs or corrupted, the virtue of their leaders, or the good intention of their magiſtrates, will not always ſecure them in the poſſeſſion of political freedom. Implicit ſubmiſſion to any leader, or the uncontrouled exerciſe of any power, even when it is intended to operate for the good of mankind, may frequently end in the ſubverſion of legal eſtabliſhments. This fatal revolution, by whatever means it is accompliſhed, terminates in military government; and this, though the ſimpleſt of all governments, is rendered complete by degrees. In the firſt period

riod of its exerciſe over men who have acted as members of a free community, it can have only laid the foundation, not completed the fabric, of a deſpotical policy. The uſurper, who has poſſeſſed, with an army, the centre of a great empire, ſees around him, perhaps, the ſhattered remains of a former conſtitution; he may hear the murmurs of a reluctant and unwilling ſubmiſſion; he may even ſee danger in the aſpect of many, from whoſe hands he may have wreſted the ſword, but whoſe minds he has not ſubdued, nor reconciled to his power.

The ſenſe of perſonal rights, or the pretenſion to privilege and honours, which remain among certain orders of men, are ſo many bars in the way of a recent uſurpation. If they are not ſuffered to decay with age, and to wear away in the progreſs of a growing corruption, they muſt be broken with violence, and the entrance to every new acceſſion of power muſt be ſtained with blood. The effect, even in this caſe, is frequently tardy. The Roman ſpirit, we know, was not entirely extinguiſhed under a ſucceſſion of maſters, and under a repeated application of bloodſhed and poiſon. The noble and reſpectable family ſtill aſpired to its original honours: The hiſtory of the republic, the writings of former times, the monuments of illuſtrious men, and the leſſons of a philoſophy fraught with heroic conceptions, continued to nouriſh the ſoul in retirement, and formed thoſe eminent characters, whoſe elevation, and whoſe fate, are, perhaps, the moſt affecting ſubjects of human ſtory. Though unable to oppoſe the general

bent

bent to servility, they became, on account of their supposed inclinations, objects of distrust and aversion ; and were made to pay with their blood, the price of a sentiment which they fostered in silence, and which glowed only in the heart.

WHILE despotism proceeds in its progress, by what principle is the sovereign conducted in the choice of measures that tend to establish his government ? By a mistaken apprehension of his own good, sometimes even of that of his people, and by the desire which he feels on every particular occasion, to remove the obstructions which impede the execution of his will. When he has fixed a resolution, whoever reasons or remonstrates against it is an enemy ; when his mind is elated, whoever pretends to eminence, and is disposed to act for himself, is a rival. He would leave no dignity in the state, but what is dependent on himself ; no active power, but what carries the expression of his momentary pleasure. Guided by a perception as unerring as that of instinct, he never fails to select the proper objects of his antipathy or of his favour. The aspect of independence repels him ; that of servility attracts. The tendency of his administration is to quiet every restless spirit, and to assume every function of government to himself* When

* It is ridiculous to hear men of a restless ambition, who would be the only actors in every scene, sometimes complain of a refractory spirit in mankind;

When the power is adequate to the end, it operates as much in the hands of those who do not perceive the termination, as it does in the hands of others by whom it is best understood: the mandates of either, when just, should not be disputed; when erroneous or wrong, they are supported by force.

You must die, was the answer of Octavius to every suit, from a people that implored his mercy. It was the sentence which some of his successors pronounced against every citizen that was eminent for his birth or his virtues. But are the evils of despotism confined to the cruel and sanguinary methods, by which a recent dominion over a refractory and a turbulent people is established or maintained? And is death the greatest calamity which can afflict mankind under an establishment by which they are divested of all their rights? They are, indeed, frequently suffered to live; but distrust, and jealousy, the sense of personal meanness, and the anxieties which arise from the care of a wretched interest, are made to possess the soul; every citizen is reduced to a slave; and every charm by which the community engaged its members, has ceased to exist. Obedience is the only duty that remains, and this is exacted by force. If under such an establishment, it be necessary to witness scenes of debasement and horror, at the hazard of catching the infection, death becomes a relief; and the libation which Thrasea was made to pour from his arteries, is to be

kind; as if the same disposition from which they desire to usurp every office, did not incline every other person to reason and to act at least for himself.

considered

considered as a proper sacrifice of gratitude to Jove the Deliverer *.

OPPRESSION and cruelty are not always necessary to despotical government; and even when present, are but a part of its evils. It is founded on corruption, and on the suppression of all the civil and the political virtues; it requires its subjects to act from motives of fear; it would asswage the passions of a few men at the expence of mankind; and would erect the peace of society itself on the ruins of that freedom and confidence from which alone the enjoyment, the force, and the elevation of the human mind, are found to arise.

DURING the existence of any free constitution, and whilst every individual possessed his rank and his privilege, or had his apprehension of personal rights, the members of every community were to one another objects of consideration and of respect; every point to be carried in civil society, required the exercise of talents, of wisdom, persuasion, and vigour, as well as of power. But it is the highest refinement of a despotical government, to rule by simple commands, and to exclude every art but that of compulsion. Under the influence of this policy, therefore, the occasions which employed

* Porrectisque utriusque brachii venis, postquam cruorem effudit, humum super spargens, proprius vocato Quæstore, *Libemus*, inquit, *Jovi Liberatori*. Specta juvenis; et omen quidem Dii prohibeant; ceterum in ea tempora natus es, quibus firmare animum deceat constantibus exemplis. *Tacit. Ann. lib.* 16.

and cultivated the underſtandings of men, which awakened their ſentiments, and kindled their imaginations, are gradually removed; and the progreſs by which mankind attained to the honours of their nature, in being engaged to act in ſociety upon a liberal footing, was not more uniform, or leſs interrupted, than that by which they degenerate in this unhappy condition.

When we hear of the ſilence which reigns in the ſeraglio, we are made to believe, that ſpeech itſelf is become unneceſſary; and that the ſigns of the mute are ſufficient to carry the moſt important mandates of government. No arts, indeed, are required to maintain an aſcendant where terror alone is oppoſed to force, where the powers of the ſovereign are delegated entire to every ſubordinate officer: nor can any ſtation beſtow a liberality of mind in a ſcene of ſilence and dejection, where every breaſt is poſſeſſed with jealouſy and caution, and where no object, but animal pleaſure, remains to balance the ſufferings of the ſovereign himſelf, or thoſe of his ſubjects.

In other ſtates, the talents of men are ſometimes improved by the exerciſes which belong to an eminent ſtation: but here the maſter himſelf is probably the rudeſt and leaſt cultivated animal of the herd; he is inferior to the ſlave whom he raiſes from a ſervile office to the firſt places of truſt or of dignity in his court. The primitive ſimplicity which formed ties of familiarity and affection betwixt the ſovereign and the keeper of his herds

herds *, appears, in the absence of all affections, to be restored, or to be counterfeited amidst the ignorance and brutality which equally characterise all orders of men, or rather which level the ranks, and destroy the distinction of persons in a despotical court.

Caprice and passion are the rules of government with the prince. Every delegate of power is left to act by the same direction; to strike when he is provoked; to favour when he is pleased. In what relates to revenue, jurisdiction, or police, every governor of a province acts like a leader in an enemy's country; comes armed with the terrors of fire and sword; and instead of a tax, levies a contribution by force: he ruins or spares as either may serve his purpose. When the clamours of the oppressed, or the reputation of a treasure amassed at the expence of a province, have reached the ears of the sovereign, the extortioner is indeed made to purchase impunity by imparting a share, or by forfeiting the whole of his spoil; but no reparation is made to the injured; nay, the crimes of the minister are first employed to plunder the people, and afterwards punished to fill the coffers of the sovereign.

In this total discontinuance of every art that relates to just government and national policy, it is remarkable, that even the trade of the soldier is itself greatly neglected. Distrust and jealousy on the part of the

* See Odyssey.

prince, come in aid of his ignorance and incapacity; and theſe cauſes operating together, ſerve to deſtroy the very foundation on which his power is eſtabliſhed. Any undiſciplined rout of armed men paſſes for an army, whilſt a weak, diſperſed, and unarmed people, are ſacrificed to military diſorder, or expoſed to depredation on the frontier from an enemy, whom the deſire of ſpoil, or the hopes of conqueſt, may have drawn to their neighbourhood.

The Romans extended their empire till they left no poliſhed nation to be ſubdued, and found a frontier which was every where ſurrounded by fierce and barbarous tribes; they even pierced through uncultivated deſerts, in order to remove to a greater diſtance the moleſtation of ſuch troubleſome neighbours, and in order to poſſeſs the avenues through which they feared their attacks. But this policy put the finiſhing hand to the internal corruption of the ſtate. A few years of tranquillity were ſufficient to make even the government forget its danger; and in the cultivated province, prepared for the enemy, a tempting prize and an eaſy victory.

When by the conqueſt and annexation of every rich and cultivated province, the meaſure of empire is full, two parties are ſufficient to comprehend mankind; that of the pacific and the wealthy, who dwell within the pale of empire; and that of the poor, the rapacious, and the fierce, who are inured to depredation and war.

The

The last bear to the first nearly the same relation which the wolf and the lion bear to the fold; and they are naturally engaged in a state of hostility.

WERE despotic empire, mean-time, to continue for ever unmolested from abroad, while it retains that corruption on which it was founded, it appears to have in itself no principle of new life, and presents no hope of restoration to freedom and political vigour. That which the despotical *master has sown, cannot quicken unless it die*; it must languish and expire by the effect of its own abuse, before the human spirit can spring up anew, or bear those fruits which constitute the honour and the felicity of human nature. In times of the greatest debasement, indeed, commotions are felt; but very unlike the agitations of a free people: they are either the agonies of nature, under the sufferings to which men are exposed; or mere tumults, confined to a few who stand in arms about the prince, and who, by their conspiracies, assassinations, and murders, serve only to plunge the pacific inhabitant still deeper in the horrors of fear or despair. Scattered in the provinces, unarmed, unacquainted with the sentiments of union and confederacy, restricted by habit to a wretched œconomy, and dragging a precarious life on those possessions which the extortions of government have left; the people can no where, under these circumstances, assume the spirit of a community, nor form any liberal combination for their own defence. The injured may complain; and while he cannot obtain the mercy of government, he may implore the commiſeration of his fellow-ſubject. But that fellow-ſubject is comforted, that the hand of oppreſſion has not ſeized on himſelf: he makes his intereſt, or ſnatches his pleaſure, under that shade of ſafety which obſcurity and concealment beſtow

THE commercial arts, which ſeem to require no foundation in the minds of men, but the regard to intereſt; no encouragement, but the hopes of gain, and the ſecure poſſeſſion of property, muſt periſh under the precarious tenure of ſlavery, and under the apprehenſion of danger ariſing from the reputation of wealth. National poverty, however, and the ſuppreſſion of commerce, are the means by which deſpotiſm comes to accompliſh its own deſtruction. Where there are no longer any profits to corrupt, or fears to deter, the charm of dominion is broken, and the naked ſlave, as awake from a dream, is aſtoniſhed to find he is free. When the fence is deſtroyed, the wilds are open, and the herd breaks looſe. The paſture of the cultivated field is no longer preferred to that of the deſert. The ſufferer willingly flies where the extortions of government cannot overtake him; where even the timid and the ſervile may recollect they are men; where the tyrant may threaten, but where he is known to be no more than a fellow-creature; where he can take nothing but life, and even this at the hazard of his own.

AGREEABLY to this deſcription, the vexations of tyranny have overcome, in many parts of the Eaſt, the deſire

ſire of ſettlement. The inhabitants of a village quit their habitations, and infeſt the public ways; thoſe of the valleys fly to the mountains, and, equipt for flight, or poſſeſſed of a ſtrong hold, ſubſiſt by depredation, and by the war they make on their former maſters.

These diſorders conſpire with the impoſitions of government to render the remaining ſettlements ſtill leſs ſecure: but while devaſtation and ruin appear on every ſide, mankind are forced anew upon thoſe confederacies, acquire again that perſonal confidence and vigour, that ſocial attachment, that uſe of arms, which, in former times, rendered a ſmall tribe the ſeed of a great nation; and which may again enable the emancipated ſlave to begin the career of civil and commercial arts. When human nature appears in the utmoſt ſtate of corruption, it has actually begun to reform.

In this manner, the ſcenes of human life have been frequently ſhifted. Security and preſumption forfeit the advantages of proſperity; reſolution and conduct retrieve the ills of adverſity; and mankind, while they have nothing on which to rely but their virtue, are prepared to gain every advantage; and when they confide moſt in their fortune, are moſt expoſed to feel its reverſe. We are apt to draw theſe obſervations into rule; and when we are no longer willing to act for our country, we plead in excuſe of our own weakneſs or folly, a ſuppoſed fatality in human affairs.

THE institutions of men are, indeed, likely to have their end as well as their beginning: but their duration is not fixed to any limited period; and no nation ever suffered internal decay but from the vice of its members. We are sometimes willing to acknowledge this vice in our countrymen; but who was ever willing to acknowledge it in himself? It may be suspected, however, that we do more than acknowledge it, when we cease to oppose its effects, and when we plead a fatality, which, at least, in the breast of every individual, is dependent on himself. Men of real fortitude, integrity, and ability, are well placed in every scene; they reap, in every condition, the principal enjoyments of their nature; they are the happy instruments of providence employed for the good of mankind; or, if we must change this language, they show, that while they are destined to live, the states they compose are likewise doomed by the fates to survive, and to prosper.

THE END.